Contents

Acknowledgements

In addition to the authors named in the **List of Contributors** to this manual, Scottish Cycling acknowledges the following individuals and organisations for their part in developing this resource and supporting the work of the SMBLA.

Richard Arrowsmith, Lagganlia Outdoor Centre
Bridget Dales and Eleanor MacGregor, Scottish Natural Heritage
Gavin Howat, Health & Safety Executive
Bob Telfer, Adventure Activities Licensing Authority
All SMBLA Tutors

Scottish Advisory Panel for Outdoor Education
British Cycling
sportscotland
The Hub in the Forest, Glentress
Glenmore Lodge National Training Centre
www.fine-adc.co.uk
Mountain Leader Training UK

Photography credits
Cyclewise Training
Stick Ballard
Jonathan Collins
George Farquharson
Emma Guy
Carl Haberl
Pete Hamilton
Graeme Herd
Lewis Jones
Ian Linton
Andy McCandlish
Drew Michie
Claire Nicol
Graham O'Hanlon
Ken Russell
Liam Scott
Cliff Smith
Ewan Thomson
Nancy Thomson
Neil Walker
Jack Wardell
Gary Willis

Editors' Note

The need for a revised edition of this Manual, just three years after its publication, reflects the rate of change within mountain biking and the development of the SMBLA Scheme to keep pace with these changes.

Each section has been updated to take account of new technologies and their application within mountain biking, new legislation which underpins many of the principles of leadership, and new directions which are shaping the use of leadership awards.

The introductory "SMBLA Scheme" section explains the structure of the Scheme and is essential pre-course reading for all candidates embarking on the leadership pathway. Learning outcomes are presented for each session within Trail Cycle Leader training. Assessment outcomes are provided for all SMBLA awards, stating the learning stage which each outcome is assessed at. This aims to give candidates greater clarity over what standards of competence they can be expected to reach to qualify as an SMBLA Leader.

Candidate feedback from SMBLA courses has been taken into account, prompting efforts to strengthen sections of the syllabus which are often found to be most challenging, including Navigation and Skills & Techniques.

In addition to the Trail Cycle Leader and Mountain Bike Leader awards, the revised Manual contains three additional SMBLA modules: Expedition, Night Riding, and Winter Conditions, each of which extends the scope of the original two awards and increases the repertoire of the dedicated mountain bike leader.

As in the first edition however, the theme of leadership remains primary throughout. The revised Manual is now an even more comprehensive training resource for leaders and a reference manual for any mountain biker, whether leading, being led, or operating alone.

Throughout the Manual some sections of text have been highlighted in blue; these represent information of particular importance for leaders to be aware of. The SMBLA logo has also been used to mark important points of information with respect to the Award Scheme, and to make the distinction between parts of the modules which apply specifically to either the Trail Cycle Leader or Mountain Bike Leader award.

Scottish Cycling is committed to maintaining and improving the high standards of the SMBLA Scheme and its resources. We welcome any comments on the Manual or on any aspect of the Scheme, which you can send to: smbla@scottishcycling.com

Cliff White, Jenny Wright & Claire Nicol

FOREWORD

The SMBLA Scheme celebrated its tenth anniversary in 2007. During this time the Scheme has continued to develop and is now widely recognised throughout the UK, and indeed further afield, as the market 'leader'. The increased uptake of SMBLA awards, with over 2500 people registering on the Scheme in the last 2 years, is reflective of an overall growth in popularity of mountain biking as an activity.

There are an estimated 5.5 million mountain bikers in the UK (Forestry Commission Scotland). Annual visitor numbers within the 7 Stanes network in Scotland, the majority of whom take are bikers, has reached 500,000 with an economic impact of £3 million, and this is only one part of the country! The market for mountain biking is very buoyant and subsequently the demand for leadership qualifications shows every sign of continuing. With the SMBLA Scheme, we aim to set the industry standard for the quality of leaders who are qualified to lead groups off-road cycling.

Scottish Cycling has invested heavily over this last year in mountain biking, including the sporting pathway, multi-agency consultation and, of course, in the organisation's continued support and endorsement of the SMBLA Scheme. With world class events, facilities and trails throughout Scotland, we plan to take a lead in the future development of mountain biking as a whole, across the UK.

I would like to take this opportunity to acknowledge the support of all those involved in the revision of this Manual. It has taken a huge amount of time and commitment of Tutors, external agencies, who we have tapped into for their particular expertise, and the staff team within Scottish Cycling. I thank everyone sincerely for their contribution.

As you embark on your journey to become an SMBLA Leader I wish you much enjoyment and reward as you facilitate the experience of mountain biking for others.

Enjoy!

Jackie Davidson
Director of Operations, Scottish Cycling

List of Contributors

The following contributors are from a variety of backgrounds. The majority are SMBLA Tutors, several of whom are among the original group of Tutors who established the Scheme in the early nineties. Others have qualified as Leaders and progressed to Tutor more recently. They bring together a vast range of knowledge and experience in the outdoors, the world of mountain biking, education, leisure management, health and sports science. Here they tell you in their own words a little about themselves.

John Cheesmond
John has a background in mountain instruction and was a key player in the development of ski leader qualifications during the eighties and early nineties. He enjoys mountain biking, though his main interest is now in cycle touring, both in Britain and Europe. He also participates in audax rides throughout Scotland, covering distances from 100km up to 600km.

Louisa Edmonstone
Louisa Edmonston has an MSc in Sports Medicine and has worked in the fields of exercise physiology, lifestyle and nutrition, with business professionals and club and elite-level athletes. More recently, she has been involved in coaching, testing and mentoring fellow athletes and addressing seminars on the physical and mental aspects of endurance training, and nutrition. Louisa is a Level 2 Triathlon Coach and Level 4 Strength and Conditioning Coach. She is also an ex-pro long distance triathlete with top placings in Ironman Lanzarote and European Long-course Champs.

John Fulton
John Fulton has been an SMBLA Tutor since 1998 and is Director of Wildcat Adventures. He has over 20 years leading mountain biking holidays in Europe, Asia, Middle East, and Morocco. John has competed in the Mountain Bike World Championships and British Championships. Formerly a Training Officer with the local Mountain Rescue Team, John has acquired a considerable amount of mountain experience both in Scotland and abroad, including 12 Alpine seasons.

Matt Healey
Matt is a Senior Instructor for YMCA Wales and holds professional qualifications in a variety of outdoor sports. He has been a committed mountain biker since 1987 and has been a Tutor for the SMBLA since 2001. He currently fulfills the role of Technical Advisor for the Outward Bound Trust under the terms of its Adventure Activities License and manages a wide range of adventurous personal development programs across the UK. He is also the Vice Chair for the Lake District Association of Mountain Bikers (LAMB) and represents the interests of the sport within the National Park in which he lives and works. He has competed in Trailquest and Polaris events and ridden recreationally all over the UK and Europe.

Lewis Jones
Lewis is the Senior Instructor at Ancrum Outdoor Education Centre in Dundee and has several outdoor leadership qualifications. A committed biker, he has been riding so long he remembers purple bar-ends and U-brakes! Lewis helped to implement the Night Biking Module, and has been leading groups since 1999.

Greg Knowles
Greg is the manager of Dumfries and Galloway Council Outdoor Activity Service. He was involved in setting up the SMBLA Award Scheme. A regular bike rider, Greg also races both on road and of-road and has been involved in many other outdoor activities at various levels.

Peter Leach
Peter has spent his teaching career in Outdoor Education. He now cycles, runs and mountaineers recreationally and works as an ecologist specialising in amphibians and reptiles. He is also a first aid trainer.

Rich Martin
Based in Cumbria , Rich has spent 15 years working in Outdoor Education. In the last seven years he has been a Director of Cyclewise Training, and guides and delivers courses throughout the UK and Europe. A dedicated and passionate biker, he races in all disciplines and as an SMBLA Tutor he is helping to develop the award to the highest industry standards.

Drew Michie
A former professional footballer, PE teacher and Outdoor Education Adviser with a Scottish local authority, Drew is one of the originators of the Scheme and is currently Chair of SMBLA. He has been involved in coach education since 1970, training and assessing kayak instructors. He also trains and assesses alpine ski leaders for Snowsport Scotland.

Claire Nicol
Claire Nicol joined Scottish Cycling in 2004. She became closely involved with the SMBLA and brings her own experience of mountain biking and working in outdoor and bike retail trades to the team. She now works in the Coach Education and Development team as Education and Training Officer.

Irene Riach
Irene qualified as an accredited sports dietitian in 1999 and has worked in sports nutrition ever since. Though she works full time for a premier league football team Irene has provided a sports nutrition service to a variety of sports during this time, including curling, athletics, badminton, swimming, triathlon, rugby and cycling. Irene attended the Commonwealth Games as a consultant Dietitian and she has traveled with both football and cycling nationally and internationally. She is an ISAK level 2 anthropometrist and is accredited with RESCU and the BOA. Irene is a keen mountain biker, cycle tourist, adventure racer and, more recently, a mum.

Jim Riach
Jim Riach is Education Officer for Cycling Scotland where he is responsible for a range of education and training courses. Formerly with Scottish Cyclists' Union, he is one of the founder members of the SMBLA

and was instrumental in setting up the scheme and developing the course material. Jim is a British Cycling Coach Educator, an ABCC Senior Coach, a BC MTB A-Grade Commissaire, and has coached and officiated at club and international level. He is a member of the SRSC Safe Cycle Working Group and the Scottish Mountain Safety Forum. Jim was a competitive mountain biker, having raced in both domestic and international MTB cross-country races and has ridden recreationally in Europe and America.

Brian Salvona
Brian works as a freelance cycle trainer. He has a lifelong passion for cycling and has raced on road and track. He commuted by bike through most of his former career, and has toured extensively as well as mountain biked since 1983. He now delivers training as part of the SMBLA candidate tutor pathway, as well as tutoring both on and off- road cycle courses.

Craig Scott
Following a career in sports and leisure management, Craig has for the past seven years been a Director of Cyclewise Training. He professionally guides around the UK and across the world and has been instrumental in the development of the SMBLA skills chapter. A dedicated passionate biker who races in all disciplines, he is gaining a reputation for being one of the UK's leading MTB coaches / guides.

Cliff Smith
Cliff Smith is Outdoor Education Development Officer for the City of Edinburgh Council. He holds a number of high level outdoor qualifications in mountaineering, kayaking, canoeing and mountain biking. He has a keen interest in long, self sufficient off-road mountain bike trips and got involved with the SMBLA to develop this part of the scheme. When not working in the great outdoors, his main passions are running marathons and paragliding. An unfulfilled ambition is to combine a mountain bike expedition with some paragliding...one day!

Cliff White
Cliff White is an SMBLA tutor with many years experience teaching outdoor education in secondary schools. He is active in Edinburgh RC, one of the foremost cycling clubs in the UK, is a Director of Scottish Cycling, and organises the Glentress Trailquest.

Nigel Williams
Nigel Williams is Head of Training at Glenmore Lodge. He has been a strong supporter of the SMBLA awards and has contributed his knowledge of the Mountain Training schemes through his involvement with the Scottish and UK Mountain Leader Training Boards.

Jenny Wright
Jenny Wright is Education and Training Officer with Scottish Cycling. She has a PhD in Botany and maintains a keen interest in the Scottish countryside. An active club cyclist, she formerly competed on the road, but came into the sport through mountain biking. Jenny is also a British Cycling Club Coach.

SMBLA Scheme

ORIGINS OF THE SMBLA SCHEME

The Scottish Mountain Bike Leader Scheme was developed by **Scottish Cycling** (SC) in conjunction with the **Scottish Advisory Panel for Outdoor Education** (SAPOE) in order to provide a framework and qualification for Leaders to deliver mountain biking as a safe and enjoyable sport and activity which would satisfy the needs of Local Authorities and The Activity Centres (Young Persons' Safety) Act 1995.

While the governing bodies of cycle sport in Britain had an established coaching structure aimed at improving competitive performance, there was no comparable leadership qualification scheme. However, it was recognised that there was a need for personnel with leadership competence who could facilitate non-competitive experience of the sport for groups of people of wide ranging abilities and aspirations. It was with this dual aim in mind - to develop a leadership qualification, and to encourage participation in mountain biking through group-led activities, that Scottish Cycling and SAPOE brought together their expertise across recreational and competitive mountain biking to found the SMBLA Scheme.

In summer 1997 the first SMBLA Tutors were trained and a pilot Trail Cycle Leader course took place at Gartmorn Country Park, Clackmannanshire. Now, ten years on from the birth of the scheme, over 2700 people have qualified as Trail Cycle Leaders, and the SMBLA Scheme has become known as the industry standard for mountain bike leadership qualifications in the UK.

Gartmorn Country Park, Clackmannanshire - where it all began!

Scottish Cycling, the governing body for cycle-sport in Scotland and an integral part of British Cycling, is the administrative and awarding body for all SMBLA qualifications.

SMBLA ENDORSEMENTS

The SMBLA scheme is recognised by the **Adventure Activities Licensing Service** (AALS) and **Mountain Leader Training Scotland** (MLTS), and by **British Cycling** (BC), the governing body for cycle-sport in Great Britain. Her Majesty's Forces is also endorsing the Scheme, with all potential Adventurous Training Instructors in the RAF undertaking the Trail Cycle Leader award at the Joint School for Adventurous Training Instructors in Llanrwst, Conway.

There are several other off-road cycle training organisations in the UK which operate as commercial training providers. However, the SMBLA Scheme is the only award scheme where the national governing body is responsible for both the administration and awarding functions.

SMBLA TUTORS

All SMBLA Tutors are registered with Scottish Cycling and provide SMBLA courses on behalf of Scottish Cycling. Tutors may be employed by a local authority or by an outdoor education provider, or they may work independently, but they all operate to the same guidelines course structure and syllabus agreed by the awarding body.

During their qualification, SMBLA Tutors undertake the Coach Educator Tutor Training course provided by **sport**scotland approved Trainers, and become competent to Tutor status through an apprenticeship period lasting approximately 12-18 months during which they are supported by an SMBLA Mentor Tutor. Most SMBLA Tutors hold equivalent qualifications in other outdoor activities such as canoeing, mountaineering, skiing and climbing.

Some of the SMBLA Tutors at a Tutor gathering

A full list of SMBLA Tutors is available from the Scottish Cycling website www.scottishcycling.com or by contacting Scottish Cycling.

STRUCTURE OF THE SMBLA AWARDS

The SMBLA scheme provides **training** and **assessment** in mountain bike leadership and offers two awards in progression:

1. **The Trail Cycle Leader Award (TCL)** consists of a minimum 16 hour training course followed by a 1-day assessment. A minimum period of 30 days consolidation and preparation is required between training and assessment during which an additional 10 appropriate mountain bike rides must be logged.

The Trail Cycle Leader is qualified to operate under the following conditions:

TCL

- √ **public highways, way marked routes, rights of way on which cycles are permitted, identifiable routes, tracks and trails with obvious navigational features**
- √ **routes which are at least 90-95% rideable over their total length**
- √ **terrain *no more than* 30 minutes walk from either**
  - **the nearest accessible (by ambulance) road or**
  - **a shelter from where it is possible to summon help**
- √ **normal summer conditions, during daylight**
- √ **multi-day trips where the group does not require to be self sufficient**

2: The Mountain Bike Leader Award (MBL) consists of an additional minimum 16 hours training plus a 1-day assessment for use under the following conditions:

MBL

- √ **public highways, way marked routes rights of way on which cycles are permitted, identifiable routes, tracks and trails with obvious navigational features**
- √ **routes which are at least 90-95% rideable over their total length**
- √ **terrain *more than* 30 minutes walk from the nearest accessible road or shelter from where it is possible to summon help (i.e. within AALS licensable terrain)**
- √ **any height above sea level**
- √ **normal summer conditions, during daylight**
- √ **multi-day trips where the group does not require to be self sufficient**

Note: the Adventure Activities Licensing Service (AALS) defines licensable terrain for trekking activities, including mountain biking, as:

> *'"any place which is moorland (open uncultivated land at any height above sea level) or on a mountain above 600m* ***and*** *from which it would take more than 30 minutes to walk back to an accessible (by ambulance) road or refuge from where it is possible to summon help"*

See also **Legal Issues & Liability** for more guidance on Adventure Activities Licensing and leader operating conditions.

LEADERSHIP

The ability of the SMBLA leader to take appropriate leadership decisions and use good judgement is crucial. For example, this judgement is called on when assessing a route or part of a route to be used. The leader's employer, or employing agency is likely to have in place a Risk Assessment and Standard Operational Procedures which may further specify the routes on which a leader can or cannot operate.

The question is frequently asked "what standard or grade of trail can a Trail Cycle Leader or Mountain Bike Leader lead on?" In the absence of a nationally agreed trail grading scheme, it is considered appropriate that a qualified "Leader" should be able to risk assess the level of challenge a route provides and the **standard of the group** being led. It should be noted that part of leadership is deciding whether, in the prevailing conditions, a particular trail is suitable for the group, irrespective of whatever technical grading that trail might have been given. A guidebook description or colour coding of a trail can **inform** a Leader but should not be used as a substitute for decision making based on personal experience and operational procedures. That is a decision for a competent leader to take.

A group operating in more remote MBL terrain is potentially exposed to higher risks, than a group in TCL terrain. These risks must be controlled by **matching the experience, abilities, motivation and equipment of your group to the terrain and routes you choose**. This is a critical part of controlling the risks when planning any ride.

SMBLA MODULES

There are three modules available to TCL or MBL award holders. These additional endorsements enable Leaders to increase the scope of their operation beyond the original remit of their award.

Expedition Module

This module consists of a 2-day training course followed by a 2-night/3-day assessment. Expedition Leaders can lead **expeditions** within the terrain covered by the remit of their SMBLA leader award.

Night Riding Module

This module consists of a 7 hour Training Course, with at least 50% of the practical element to be undertaken in darkness. Candidates must then pass a 3 hour assessment which will be undertaken entirely during darkness. Night Riding Leaders can operate in conditions outside the **'daytime only'** remit of their award.

Winter Conditions Module

This module consists of a 2 day training course and a 1-day assessment. Day 1 of training is classroom based and can take place at any time of the year. Day 2 of training is practical and will take place in 'winter' conditions, as they occur. Winter Conditions Leaders can operate in defined "**intermediate**" and "**winter**" conditions **but only in TCL terrain, regardless of the level of award that they hold.**

Refer to the individual module chapters for more detailed information.

SMBLA CANDIDATE PATHWAY

The Candidate Pathway provides a step by step guide for anyone wishing to undertake an SMBLA award. Candidates must be over 18 in order to comply with legislation and insurance for leading groups in the outdoors.

Anyone wishing to qualify as a **Trail Cycle Leader** must progress through the following stages 1-8 of the Candidate Pathway:

1. Register for the SMBLA Scheme at www.scottishcycling.com, or by sending a completed SMBLA Registration Form and cheque (payable to) Scottish Cycling (group bookings can be invoiced). Registered candidates are given a registration number, the SMBLA Training Manual and all course documentation

2. Complete the **SMBLA Logbook** (see guidance which follows) as evidence of mountain biking experience which is a pre-entry requirement for TCL training

3. Book and attend a **TCL training course.** Scottish Cycling's website has a list of courses and details of SMBLA Tutors who may be contacted to arrange a course to suit

4. Consolidate learning, using the **Action Plan** — feedback given by your Tutor after Training. At this stage you should log an **additional 10 rides over a minimum of 30 days before progressing to** assessment

5. Gain a valid **first aid qualification** (see below) which is a pre-requirement for TCL assessment

6. Apply for **membership of British Cycling** (see below)

7. Book and attend a **TCL assessment** where you will be expected to be competent in all theoretical and practical aspects of the TCL syllabus (see **TCL Assessment Outcomes** later in this chapter)

8. Successful candidates with **BC membership** and **a valid first aid qualification** will receive a **TCL certificate** awarded by Scottish Cycling

Please note, SMBLA Certificates will be **only** be issued by Scottish Cycling to candidates who have successfully passed an assessment, have current membership of British Cycling **and** a valid and appropriate first aid qualification.

A valid TCL certificate is a pre-entry requirement for all additional SMBLA awards, including **Mountain Bike Leader** for which the additional Pathway stages 1 – 6 on the following page apply.

Sample Trail Cycle Leader certificate

1. Book and attend an **MBL training course.** Scottish Cycling's website has a list of courses and details of SMBLA Tutors who may be contacted to arrange a course to suit

2. Consolidate learning, using the **Action Plan** - feedback given by your Tutor after MBL Training. At this stage you should log an **additional 10 rides over a minimum of 30 days before progressing to assessment**

3. Ensure that your **first aid qualification** (see below) is current

4. Book and attend an **MBL assessment course** where you will be expected to be competent in all theoretical and practical aspects of the MBL syllabus (see **MBL Assessment Outcomes** later in this chapter)

5. Successful candidates with current **BC membership** and a **valid first aid qualification** will receive an **MBL certificate** awarded by Scottish Cycling.

LOGBOOK COMPLETION

A logbook detailing previous mountain bike experience and providing a referee is a **pre-entry requirement** for TCL and MBL training. Blank Logbooks (see **Appendix**) are provided on registration.

For **TCL training** the Logbook evidence presented at training should consist of:

√ at least 20 mountain bike rides, on **separate days**, in appropriate terrain and in a variety of weather and conditions, of at least 1.5 h duration, of which;
- 8 rides of at least 2-3 hrs
- at least one ride of 6 hrs

(Note: an additional 10 rides must be logged between TCL training and assessment - see Candidate Pathway above)

For **MBL training** the Logbook evidence presented at training (gained **after** the TCL Assessment) should consist of:

√ at least 20 mountain bike trips, on **separate days**, in a variety of weather and conditions, of which;
- at least 10 rides covering routes of extended length (6 hrs riding)
- 10 rides on routes with a high degree of technical difficulty
- at least 3 rides in remote terrain.
- at least 12 rides acting as leader or assistant group leader

Note : all logbook rides may be undertaken in the UK or abroad at any time **within the last 12 months**.

FIRST AID QUALIFICATION
Prior to TCL assessment and for any SMBLA award to become and remain valid, Leaders must hold an appropriate first aid qualification. Candidates not presenting evidence of valid first aid training at the time of assessment will be automatically "deferred"; and must submit a copy of their first aid qualification to Scottish Cycling before a TCL certificate can be awarded.

Accepted first aid training courses should be provided by organisations approved by HSE (Health & Safety Executive) for the purpose of first aid training, and delivered by staff who are registered with that organisation as first aid trainers or assessors. Courses must be a minimum of **12 hours**, with no sessions shorter than 2 hours, and should contain material relevant to the outdoor environment.

First aid training courses must include:

- action at an incident
- management of an unconscious casualty
- resuscitation
- treatment and control of bleeding
- treatment of injuries to bones, muscles and joints.
- recognition and treatment of shock
- treatment of choking
- recognition and treatment of common illnesses
- contents of first aid kits

A list of approved first aid providers can be found in the downloads section of the Scottish Cycling website.

BRITISH CYCLING MEMBERSHIP
All Leaders must be members of British Cycling *before* their certificate will be issued and for their award to remain valid. Membership applications should be sent to **British Cycling** or made on-line at www.britishcycling.org.uk. Members will receive a membership card which has a 6-digit membership number, and is valid for 12 months from the date of issue. Your card will show "**Scottish MTB Leaders**" as your membership group and you will be given the endorsement "Leader" by British Cycling at this stage. (Existing BC members of a club or race team affiliated to SC/BC should complete the relevant box in section 1 of the membership form to have "SMBLA" added as their second claim club).

There are three categories of BC membership: Bronze, Silver and Gold. **Bronze** membership provides basic membership benefits but no insurance cover to operate as a Leader. **Silver** and **Gold** membership provide **Third Party (Public Liability)** insurance and legal advice and assistance (to UK residents). **Gold** members are additionally entitled to Personal Accident insurance. If you work **freelance** or are not covered by your **employer's insurance**, then **Silver or Gold membership is strongly recommended**.

Professional Indemnity insurance is available to all TCL and MBL holders who can present evidence of appropriate training in **Good Practice & Child Protection** at the time of membership application. Details of the insurance offered through membership are available from British Cycling.

SMBLA TRAINING COURSES

There is a **maximum of 8** candidate places on any SMBLA **training** course. Training courses normally take place over two full days and will last a minimum of 16 hours. The majority of courses are non-residential. A programme of courses for TCL, MBL and all SMBLA modules is available on the Scottish Cycling website. Courses may also be arranged on demand by contacting an SMBLA Tutor.

Tutors will provide individual feedback to candidates after a training course in the form of an "**Action Plan**". Candidates should use this to address areas where they need to improve their knowledge and experience in the 30 day consolidation period between training and assessment.

All candidates must take the following to their training course:

- **Proof of SMBLA registration – a Registration letter issued by Scottish Cycling with a unique SMBLA Registration number**
- **A completed Logbook**
- **TCL certificate if doing MBL training**
- **The SMBLA Training Manual which contains all the necessary course material**

Model Training Courses & Learning Outcomes

To ensure consistency in the delivery of training, two model courses for TCL Training have been designed. Both model courses are built around learning sessions, each one with clear **learning outcomes**. All tutors are required to use these model training courses unless the tutor has obtained exemption to run a modified TCL Training Course which will still deliver the **standard learning outcomes**.

The tables on the pages which follow show the two 16 hour TCL Model training courses:

Model 1 is a 2-Day course, with 2 full (8h) days of training
Model 2 is a 3-Day course, running from evening on day 1 to afternoon on Day 3.

Exact timings will be set by the course tutor and may vary slightly depending on the group.

MODEL 1 TCL Training Day 1	
SESSION TITLE AND LEARNING OUTCOMES	**TIMINGS + LOCATIONS**
Welcome and Introduction By the end of this session you will be able to state: o The origins and outline of the SMBLA Scheme o Requirements for assessment o Structure of your course	08.45 – 9.30 Classroom
Bikes and Equipment By the end of this session you will be able to: o Name the parts of your bike o Conduct a detailed safety check o Conduct a check of the most obvious faults o Make simple adjustments to the bike o Describe the use and need for specialised clothing	9.30 – 11.00 Classroom 11.00 – 11.15 break
Getting Started By the end of this session you should be able to explain: o Gear changing o The concept of "balance and control" o Effective braking	11.15 – 12.15 Grassy area with banking/ slopes
Cycling Skills By the end of this session you will have practiced the following basic skills: o Balance & control o Front wheel lift o Limbo o Wide and tight turns o Bumps o Ratcheting o Have set up a mini mountain bike cross country race course o Be aware of the risk assessment for the activity	12.15 – 13.15 Flat grass or tarmac area 13.15 – 14.00 Lunch
Bike Set Up By the end of this session you will be able to set up a bike for optimum performance, knowing why and how to adjust: o Saddle height and angle o Saddle fore and aft position o Stem height o Reach	14.00 – 15.00 Classroom

MODEL 1 TCL Training Day 1	
SESSION TITLE AND LEARNING OUTCOMES	**TIMINGS + LOCATIONS**
Riding as a Group on and Off Road By the end of this session you will be able to: o Effectively manage a group on a road o Effectively manage a group off road o Demonstrate the significance of cadence o Demonstrate ways of equalising group ability o Relate the session 4 skills to trail riding experience	15.00 – 17.30 Ride approx 15km
Day 1 Review and Close By the end of this session you will be able to: o Reflect on the days learning o Describe the preparation for day 2 o outline the principles of late back procedures	17.30 – 18.30

MODEL 1 TCL Training Day 2	
SESSION TITLE AND LEARNING OUTCOMES	**TIMINGS + LOCATIONS**
Welcome Again By the end of this session you will be able to: o Recall learning from day 1 o Describe the structure of the day	08.45 – 9.15 Classroom
Re-Focus Ride By the end of this session you will be able to: o Reflect on the reasons why people mountain bike o Describe the sights and sounds that a mountain biker is likely to experience o Describe the core skills a mountain biker will use	9.15 – 10.00 Skills Course or Technical Singletrack
Trailside Repairs By the end of this session you should be able to perform the following trailside repairs: o Puncture repair o Mend a broken chain o Gear adjustment o Brake adjustment	10.00 – 11.00 Classroom or outdoors 11.00 – 11.15 Break

MODEL 1 TCL Training Day 2	
SESSION TITLE AND LEARNING OUTCOMES	**TIMINGS + LOCATIONS**
Leadership By the end of this session you will be able to discuss: o The role of the leader o One leadership model o Responsibilities of the leader o What a leader must carry o How to manage a group o The principles of risk assessment	11.15 – 12.15 Classroom
Navigation By the end of this session you should be able to: o Orientate a map o Interpret a map o Use 6 figure grid references o Estimate time and distance (including use of cycle computer) o Plan a route o Relocate	12.15 – 13.00 Classroom 1300 - 1330 Lunch
Practical Ride and Teaching By the end of this session you should be able to: o Set up a mini downhill course and/or dual descender o Practice and apply prior learning in navigation, leadership and group management o Identify a range of teaching styles and their application o Discuss, describe and demonstrate what to do in a range of "scenarios" o Describe and demonstrate the skills of climbing and descending o Plan and prepare for a group ride including risk assessment and outline late back procedures	13.30 – 16.30 Ride on varied terrain, approx 20km
Review and What Next By the end of this session you will have: o Evaluated your performance on the course o Received personal feedback o Asked any outstanding questions o Completed an evaluation of the course	16-30 – 17.30 Classroom

MODEL 2 TCL Training Day 1 (Evening)	
SESSION TITLE AND LEARNING OUTCOMES	**TIMINGS + LOCATIONS**
SMBLA Scheme and Clothing By the end of this session you will be able to state: ○ The origins and outline of the scheme ○ The requirements for assessment ○ The structure of your course ○ What to bring (including food), and what to wear ○ Relevant access issues	30 mins Classroom
Safe Cycle By the end of this session you will be able to: ○ Name the parts of your bike ○ State how to conduct a detailed safety check and identify remedial action ○ Explain how to quickly check the most obvious faults ○ Make simple adjustments to the bike to make it safe	90 mins Classroom and/or outdoors

MODEL 2 TCL Training Day 2	
SESSION TITLE AND LEARNING OUTCOMES	**TIMINGS + LOCATIONS**
Introductory Skills By the end of this session you will be able to demonstrate: ○ Setting off ○ Gear changing ○ The concept of " balance and control" ○ Effective braking ○ Hand position ○ Covering brakes	60 mins Flat Grassy area with short slopes of varying angles
Skills Test By the end of this session you will have practiced the following basic skills: ○ Balance & control ○ Front wheel lift ○ Limbo ○ Wide turns & tight turns ○ Bumps and double cranking	90 mins Flat surface, grass preferable Lunch 30 mins
Working in a Team By the end of this session you will be able to state: ○ Effective group management on and off road ○ The significance of cadence ○ Ways of "equalising" the ability of the group ○ The content of a "games" session	3 hours Flat closed road or cycle track Quiet road with incline Open flat area

MODEL 2 TCL Training Day 2	
SESSION TITLE AND LEARNING OUTCOMES	**TIMINGS + LOCATIONS**
Trailside Repairs By the end of this session you should be able to perform the following trailside repairs and state what tools are required: o Puncture repair o Mend a broken chain o Gear adjustment o Brake adjustment	60 mins Classroom or outdoors

MODEL 2 TCL Training Day 3	
SESSION TITLE AND LEARNING OUTCOMES	**TIMINGS + LOCATIONS**
Bike Set Up By the end of this session you will be able to state how to set up a bike for optimum performance and know why and how to adjust: ○ Saddle height and angle ○ Handlebar height ○ Reach to handlebars	60 mins Outdoor flat area
Techniques By the end of this session you will have practiced the following basic skills: ○ Track stand ○ Front wheel lift ○ Un-weighting	45 mins Outdoor flat area
Teaching By the end of this session you will be able to identify a range of teaching styles and state how they might be used including: ○ Command ○ Practice ○ Reciprocal ○ Self-check ○ Inclusion ○ Convergent (guided discovery)	15 mins Classroom
Leadership By the end of this session you will be able to explain: ○ The role of the leader ○ One leadership model ○ The responsibilities of a leader ○ What a leader needs to carry ○ How to manage a group	45 mins Classroom

MODEL 2 TCL Training Day 3	
SESSION TITLE AND LEARNING OUTCOMES	**TIMINGS + LOCATIONS**
Navigation By the end of this session you will be able to describe how to: ○ Orientate a map ○ Interpret a map ○ Use 6 figure grid references ○ Estimate distance and time (including use of a cycle computer) ○ Plan a route ○ Make up and follow a route card ○ Relocate ○ Follow relevant access legislation and guidance	45 mins Classroom Lunch (30 mins)

MODEL 2 TCL Training Day 3	
SESSION TITLE AND LEARNING OUTCOMES	**TIMINGS + LOCATIONS**
Ride Out By the end of this session you will have practiced the following basic skills : ○ Following a route using a route card ○ Making the trip flow ○ Relocating in the countryside ○ Calculating the length and time for a trip ○ Effective group management using the Action Centred Leadership Model ○ Climbing and descending ○ Review of your own performance	3 hours Forest area with plenty of navigational challenges. (Non-linear route)
Planning By the end of this session you will understand the need for: ○ Safety bike checks ○ Group medical details ○ Weather forecasts ○ Appropriate clothing ○ Fuel and hydration ○ Individual and group equipment ○ Risk assessment ○ Dealing with emergencies ○ Child protection ○ Emergency arrangements ○ Late back procedures	30 mins Classroom

MODEL 2 TCL Training Day 3	
SESSION TITLE AND LEARNING OUTCOMES	**TIMINGS + LOCATIONS**
Review By the end of this session you will have: ○ One to one feedback and discussion on personal action plans in preparation for assessment ○ An opportunity to ask any outstanding questions about the course and give your impression of it	30 mins Classroom

SMBLA ASSESSMENT

There is a **maximum of 4** candidate places on an SMBLA **assessment**. Assessment lasts one full day.

All candidates must take the following to their assessment:

- A "Training Completed" form issued by the Tutor after a training course
- A completed Logbook, including the additional 10 rides undertaken during the TCL or MBL Consolidation period (see Candidate Pathway above)
- A copy of their First Aid certificate
- Their SMBLA Training Manual

Learning outcomes

It is recognised that there are stages of learning which people progress through (see **Teaching & Learning**). Using the Fitts and Posner Stages of Learning model the Assessment Outcomes listed below have been graded either 1, 2 or 3. These three levels refer to the three stages of learning:

"**awareness**" (Level 1)
"**practice**" (Level 2)
"**acquired**" (Level 3)

Each level corresponds to the **stage you require to be performing at** to be successful at assessment.

Accreditation of Prior Learning

There is no automatic entry to TCL or MBL assessment through Accreditation of Prior Learning (APL), even if candidates have considerable mountain bike experience and/or relevant teaching or leadership qualifications in other activities. Training with other off-road award schemes has proven not to meet the required standards of the SMBLA award and does not guarantee candidates will meet the SMBLA assessment criteria.

VALIDITY OUTSIDE THE UK

The SMBLA awards are currently valid anywhere in the UK and Europe. Insurance to work as a Leader provided through Scottish Cycling / British Cycling membership extends to all European countries. It currently excludes USA and Canada.

THE SMBLA AWARDS - Standards for Assessment

The following tables show the **Assessment Outcomes** for all SMBLA awards and modules. Candidates will be assessed on each of the Assessment Outcomes.

ASSESSMENT OUTCOMES FOR TCL *the standards expected at assessment*	**LEARNING STAGE**
Log Book Experience / Evidence	
• Provide written evidence of having completed at least 30 mountain bike rides, in appropriate terrain and in a variety of weather conditions, of at least 1.5 h duration including:	3
o 8 longer rides of at least 2-3 hours	3
o At least one ride of 6 hours	3
The Safe Cycle	
• Demonstrate a check on the bike and identify remedial action	3
• Demonstrate adjustments to brakes, gears, headsets and other components to make the bike safe	3
• State how to set up an optimum riding position for the candidate	2
Clothing and Equipment	
• Attend with a bike, helmet and equipment suitable for the task (including a bike computer)	3
• Wear appropriate clothing for a leader as a role model	3
• Describe bikes and accessories suitable for the task	2
• Describe appropriate clothing and safety equipment (gloves, glasses, helmets, footwear etc) for trail cycling	2
Fitness, Fuel and Hydration	
• Demonstrate a suitable level of physical fitness to lead trail cycling activities for a range of groups	2
• Describe what is meant by adequately fuelled and hydrated for a trip	3
• Select sufficient food/fluids to contend with a day's outing in TCL terrain and have energy in reserve	2
• Explain why cycling is principally an endurance activity	2
• Identify the major food groups and the refuelling requirements / limiting factors in endurance activity	2
Fundamental Techniques	
• Demonstrate the following basic techniques of mountain biking:	
1. the attack (or neutral) position	3
2. braking	3
3. gear changing	3
4. steering or cornering	3
5. weight shifting	3
6. line choice	3
7. climbing	3
8. descending	3

ASSESSMENT OUTCOMES FOR TCL ***the standards expected at assessment***	**LEARNING STAGE**
Core Skills • Demonstrate the following skills of mountain biking: 1. track stand or 5 second balance 2. manual front wheel lift 3. power assisted front wheel lifts 4. rear wheel lift	 2 2 2 2
Managing a group • Demonstrate responsible, effective and safe management of a group, both On-Road and Off-Road • Give verbal information on child protection and good practice issues	 3 2
Trailside Repairs • Demonstrate the following trailside repairs to enable a bike to be ridden back to base: o puncture repair o broken chain o setting gear-stop screws • Display a tool kit with appropriate tools • Describe potential wear and tear on equipment and state how to minimise this	 3 2 2 3 2
Leadership • Demonstrate a range of techniques involved in leading a trail cycle group • Demonstrate the use of appropriate tone, manner, pace and style • Demonstrate good use of the Action Centred Leadership model – ' team, task and individual '	 3 3 3
Teaching • Identify a range of teaching styles including Command, Practice, Reciprocal, Self-check, Inclusion, and Convergent (guided discovery) • State how they might be used to greatest effect	 1 1
Navigation • Identify correct location at all times to within 100 metres using a map, compass and cycle computer • Demonstrate the use of the above navigational aids, along with guidebooks and route cards, to plan and execute a flowing journey • Accurately state the length and time for a route or leg	 3 3 3

ASSESSMENT OUTCOMES FOR TCL ***the standards expected at assessment***	**LEARNING STAGE**
Planning and Preparation - the perfect trail cycling day	
• Identify where to obtain an up to date weather forecast for the area	3
• Recognise the effect of different weather conditions on both the group and the planned route	3
• Explain a suitable "Late Back Procedure"	2
• List relevant information of group qualities and competences, including medical history, parental consent and emergency contact number	3
Dealing with Emergencies	
• Describe how to carry out a risk assessment of the planned activity	3
• Explain techniques used to deal with an emergency	3
Countryside Awareness	
• State the current access legislation in Scotland and where to get information both locally and nationally	2
• Identify some routes suitable for trail cycling, and states where to source this information	2
• Describe various land use / management practices and how these affect mountain bikers	1
• Recognise the impact that mountain biking can have on the environment and what to do to minimise this	2
• **Cycle-Sport**	
• Identify where to source information on cycling clubs and events	1
• Describe the differences between downhill and cross-country mountain bike events	1
• Explain how to run a simple cross-country event for novices	1

ASSESSMENT OUTCOMES FOR MBL ***the standards expected at assessment***	**LEARNING STAGE**
Log Book Experience/Evidence (gained ***after*** TCL Assessment)	
• Provide written evidence of having completed at least 30 mountain bike trips, in a variety of weather and conditions, of which :	
o at least 10 rides must cover routes of extended length (6 hrs riding)	3
o another 10 must cover routes with a high degree of technical difficulty	3
o at least 3 of the 20 rides must be in remote terrain	3
o at least 12 of these rides should have been as leader or assistant group leader	3

ASSESSMENT OUTCOMES FOR MBL *the standards expected at assessment*	LEARNING STAGE
Fitness, Fuel & Hydration	
• Demonstrate a suitable level of physical fitness to lead mountain bike activities for a range of groups in MBL terrain	3
• State what is meant by adequately fuelled and hydrated and demonstrate with own selection of food/fluids how to maintain energy levels	3
• Explain the fitness demands made by a variety of MBL terrain	3
• Discuss fuelling and hydration with respect to their effects on health and performance	3
Core Skills	
• Demonstrate the ability to climb and descend steep tracks and ride routes of a high degree of technical difficulty in comfort and style	3
• In particular demonstrate the following skills of mountain biking:	
o drop offs	3
o step ups	3
o bunny hops	3
o lateral bunny hops	3
o cornering at speed	3
Teaching	
• Design a basic lesson plan and teach one or more of mountain bike skills from the above list.	3
• Employ a coaching technique and produce an improvement in the skill level of a novice and an intermediate cyclist.	3
• Analyse a performance and give constructive feedback	3
• Use at least three of Mosston's teaching styles and explain when these would be most appropriate	3
Clothing and Equipment	
• Explain availability and use of technical clothing and safety equipment relevant to MBL terrain (gloves, glasses, shoes, helmets, body armour)	3
• Explain the current range of mountain bikes and accessories suitable for MBL terrain.	3
• Use a bike and equipment suitable for the task and wear appropriate clothing and footwear for a leader as a role model	3
Multi Day Trips	
• Prioritise additional equipment and planning required to undertake multi-day trips in MBL terrain (that do not fall within the scope of Expedition endorsement)	3
• Explain the variety of accommodation available to support such a trip	3

ASSESSMENT OUTCOMES FOR MBL ***the standards expected at assessment***	**LEARNING STAGE**
Trailside Repairs	
• Demonstrate or describe the following trailside repairs so that a bike can be ridden back to base:	
o broken pedal	3
o bent rear derailleur	3
o buckled wheel	3
o rip in tyre sidewall	3
o broken spoke	3
o broken seat pin	3
o faults with disc brakes including replacing pads	3
o broken freewheel	3
• Explain how the Leader's expertise in trailside repairs can affect the choice of route in more remote environments.	3
• Discuss more advanced trailside repairs	3
Leadership & Style	
• Demonstrate responsible, effective and safe management of a group both :	
o On-road	3
o Off-Road in a remote environment	3
• Demonstrate use of the Hersey Blanchard Situational Leadership Model when leading a mountain bike group	3
• Describe other, more sophisticated, theoretical models of leadership	3
Navigation	
• Demonstrate the navigational techniques of :	
o Aiming off and attack points	3
o Using transits	3
o Using aspect of slope	3
o Back bearings	3
o Identifying a position using resection	3
o Timing and pacing on foot	3
o Following a given route using only a route card and cycle computer	3
• Demonstrate Naismith's rule or equivalent	3
• List and describe other navigational aids that can be used in mountain biking	3

ASSESSMENT OUTCOMES FOR MBL *the standards expected at assessment*	LEARNING STAGE
Planning and Preparation - The perfect mountain bike day	
• Demonstrate a good knowledge of weather and describes its effect on a group in a remote environment	3
• Interpret a variety of weather charts	3
• Have in place "Late Back Procedures	3
• List relevant knowledge of group qualities and competencies including: medical history, previous mtb experience and fitness	3
Dealing with Emergencies	
• Carry out and record a risk assessment of the planned activity	3
• Employ the techniques used to deal with an emergency in a remote environment	3
• Carry out a risk assessment of a stream crossing	3
• Demonstrate techniques used to deal with a variety of water hazards including using a bike to cross a stream	3
Countryside and Terrain Knowledge	
• State the current access legislation and where to get information both locally and nationally and explain the Scottish Outdoor Access Code and Local Access Forums	3
• State where to source information on mtb routes	3
• Explain how to decide whether a route on a map is likely to be rideable	3
• Describe a particular land use/management practice that can affect mountain biking	3
• Select and describe 2 examples when mountain biking can adversely affect the environment	3
Cycle-Sport	
• Describe the various off-road mtb disciplines	3
• Describe downhill, cross-country, trailquest (cycle-orienteering) and 4-cross competitions	3
• Organise an mtb competition for the group	3
• State where to source up to date information on these disciplines	3

Skills & Techniques

By the end of this section Leaders should be able to:-

- Describe the senses used by the mountain biker
- Explain the difference between techniques and skills
- Describe the fundamental skills and techniques of mountain biking
- List and demonstrate the main components of these skills and techniques

INTRODUCTION
The most challenging part of mountain biking is developing the necessary skills to deal with the huge variety of features encountered out on the trails. Overcoming most of these requires linking only a few basic moves. It might seem complex negotiating a series of obstacles, but after breaking down and practising the basic techniques, then putting it all together, it becomes instinctive.

The terms technique and skill are often used interchangeably but for the purpose of this section we will use the following meanings:

- **Technique is the way in which actions or patterns of movement are performed**
- **Skill is the ability to select and effectively apply the techniques in the right place at the right time**

Skill also has a relationship to the development level of the participant. Techniques can be taught and whilst the development of skill can be facilitated, it is more rider centred and intuitive.

It makes sense to start out on simple terrain, learning the basic techniques, before moving onto more complex techniques. This helps avoid frustration and the creation of physical and mental barriers to progress. Many of the techniques can be developed at slow speed on artificial skill courses and translated into "real live" or high speed skills out on the trail. Having competence and confidence at low speed often makes the skill happen naturally at higher speeds.

Before looking at techniques we will look at the senses that control them.

THE SENSES
Mountain biking relies heavily on the senses, particularly vision, touch and hearing, providing vital feedback to help develop riding skills.

Vision

Vision is the most important sense to the mountain biker; the position of the head and direction of vision will affect the direction of travel. In other words, you go where you look! This means that the best way to avoid the big rock in the middle of the trail is to look past it. Keep your head up and continually scan the trail in front to see what's ahead. In non-technical sections your eyes should be focused between 3 and 15 metres ahead of you. Don't stare at the front wheel or the ground as it passes beneath you.

Touch

On a mountain bike touch or "tactile feedback" comes through the hands, backside and feet. It is this sensory feedback that helps a rider to keep control of the bike. Beginners and out of control riders experience this feedback as if they were on top of a bucking stallion. More experienced riders become smooth and "light" on the bike, because they are moving with the bike rather than hanging on. Moving with the bike translates into making frequent adjustments (fore and aft, side to side, and up and down). When your timing is off, tactile feedback in the form of bumps and jolts will soon let you know it is time to take corrective action. If you momentarily lose your rhythm your elbows and knees can absorb some pretty big hits, *however your rear end cannot.* Big jolts through the saddle transmit too much shock to the spine. The best way to avoid this is to stand up when the going gets rough.

Hearing

While not the most important of the senses used in mountain biking, hearing is none the less important. The sound of your tyres provides feedback on the type of surface you are riding, from a low hum on tarmac to the warning sounds that loose gravel makes, or how well you are riding that berm.

You also need to know how to respond to your bike when it starts making unusual noises. The noises could just be annoying, like a misaligned derailleur, or small twigs caught in your wheel, but they could indicate something seriously wrong like the hiss of a puncture. Combining this sense with our other senses gives great feedback to riders.

THE BASIC RIDING TECHNIQUES

The basic techniques have been broken down into eight groups or headings and are the techniques that will be used on even the easiest of trails. Proficiency in these basic techniques is common to both the Trail Cycle Leader and Mountain Bike Leader awards.

THE BASIC TECHNIQUES

1. the attack (or neutral) position
2. braking
3. gear changing
4. steering and cornering
5. weight shifting
6. line choice
7. climbing
8. descending

TCL

MBL

1. The Attack Position

The Attack Position (also known as the **Ready** or **Neutral** position) is one of the most basic, but equally one of the most important riding positions to establish. It is the *ready-for-anything* position, and the starting and finishing point of most mountain bike techniques. The pedals are level, the body is relaxed and centered over the bike. From this stable platform the rider can move around the bike as the terrain changes. The rider should be tall but relaxed on the bike, allowing the body to act as a giant shock absorber.

The Attack Position

2. Braking

This is a technique that is often overlooked or assumed knowledge. Anticipation and looking ahead to see what obstacles are coming up are the key to a smooth and enjoyable ride. Effective braking and the anticipation required for braking and speed control are similar. Disc brakes are becoming increasingly common on many mountain bikes and are more powerful than rim brakes, so it's very important to use this braking power appropriately. Braking should be practised on a gentle slope until a "sensitive touch" is developed.

Braking requires good anticipation to keep the bike under control. Much of the skill in effective braking is developing a "feel" for the bike and tuning in to the feedback coming through the feet and hands, and the other senses. The braking force should be enough to slow the bike, but not enough to make it skid. Once the wheels are skidding, the effectiveness of braking is reduced. If the wheels start to lock the brakes can be modulated, i.e. pressure is released and then reapplied.

Skidding is not only less efficient but causes trail damage, wears out tyres and should be discouraged.

The front brake is more efficient when it comes to slowing down and stopping. It gives roughly 70% of braking power compared with just 30% from the rear brake.

A common fear is that pulling on the front brake too violently will launch a rider over the handlebars. This rarely happens; if it does it is more likely to be because the weight / body position is in the wrong place at the wrong time, not because the brakes were pulled too hard.

When it comes to sudden hard braking, if the weight is already over the rear of the bike the only way the body can go once the brakes are applied is forward, usually with a fair bit of momentum which results in the rider being catapulted forward. The forward thrust can be cancelled out by shifting the weight backwards as the brakes are applied, keeping rider on bike and allowing a controlled stop.

Trail conditions also influence the effectiveness of braking, and practice is required under different conditions. When using V-brakes wet rims increase the stopping distance, so a light pre-brake squeeze on the lever is advised to remove some of this excess water. Grimy rims also reduce braking capacity and will add to the repair bill! Keep an eye on how mucky the rims are getting, and whenever the opportunity arises wipe them clean with some moss which is a handy means of trailside maintenance for rims.

3. Gear Changing

Maintaining an efficient pedalling rate (or cadence) over varied terrain will help reduce fatigue. Maintaining optimal cadence requires frequent gear changes on variable/undulating terrain to stay within an optimum cadence range. Don't be afraid to use the full range of gears on a bike.

The majority of gear shifters on mountain bikes are either trigger shifters or twist grips. The left hand shifter operates the front derailleur (or front "mech") and the right hand shifter operates the rear derailleur (or rear "mech"). They usually operate index gear systems where one click / shift means changing up or down one gear.

The concept of *"spinning"* is encouraged. This means pedalling at a reasonably high rate of 75-100 rpm (revolutions or pedal strokes per minute) which requires a low pedal force and reduces local muscle fatigue, allowing the rider to stay fresh for longer.

Going uphill requires a lower gear to maintain this cadence. This does not always require a shift from the front derailleur, but will require a downshift at the rear (note that a downshift at the rear actually sends the chain 'up' to a larger sprocket which provides a lower gear that is easier to pedal).

Going downhill or riding with a tailwind may require an upshift at the rear (down to a smaller sprocket) and may mean an upshift at the front onto a larger chain ring.

After some practise, gear changing requires little thought, with leg speed the deciding factor. Gear changing can be made smoother and quicker by easing back on the power and soft pedalling whilst shifting. Though the gears will change under full power, easing back can make for faster and smoother changes and is kinder on components.

Although mountain bikes may have up to 30 gears there are some gear combinations that should be avoided to prevent damage to chain and derailleurs or unshipping the chain:

X small chain ring at the front + small sprocket at the rear

X large chain ring at the front + large sprocket at the rear

These combinations place the chain under maximum lateral stress and may even snap it; it is sometimes referred to as *cross gearing*. There are no cross gears in the middle ring, so novice riders may find operating in the middle ring gives them a sufficient choice of gears for introductory rides.

4. Steering and Cornering

These are two closely linked techniques which are performed differently at slow and medium-fast speeds. At low speeds, steering by turning the handlebars makes the bike go in the desired direction and in effect makes it turn a corner. When travelling at speed, cornering is effected by leaning the bike and the body; the lean allows the resultant force to stay within the base of support as the wheel is turned. Cornering can be made easier by putting weight on the inside handlebar and outside pedal.

Leaning forward puts more weight on the front wheel helping to improve traction. Lowering the centre of gravity and dropping the elbow into the turn is also important at high speeds. To demonstrate this concept try wheeling a bike along holding only the saddle. Upright, the bike travels in a straight line. Lean it toward you, and the front wheel turns followed by the rear, lean it away and the same thing happens in the opposite direction.

Good steering technique can make the bike corner like it is on rails; by steering into medium and high speed corners more speed can be maintained whilst still turning tightly. Steering at speed originates from the knees and hips. The knees and hips move and point into the turn, with most of the weight on the outside pedal. The position is very similar to that of a skier carving a turn. In most situations it isn't just the front wheel which turns a bike, but also the rider leaning the bike into the turn. The upper body remains square and the arms can be used to counter-steer, i.e. pull up with the outside arm and push down with the inside arm, to increase the steering effect.

5. Weight Shifting

Getting this technique right will improve riding skills. Control on a mountain bike requires constant shifts of the body to keep the weight centered over the bike. These moves help the bike flow over the terrain making the ride smoother, less tiring and more energy efficient. An experienced rider will do this almost subconsciously; less experienced riders are often less willing to move around as much and need to be encouraged to do so. **The more a rider can move around a bike the more control they will have**.

The following sequence of pictures illustrates weight shifting for moving over a small rise and down a slope. The same moves, starting from the Attack Position, will be performed countless times when encountering any trail undulations or technical features, adjusting the pattern and degree of weight shifting for each obstacle encountered.

Approach the bump in the attack position.

1. Move your weight forward as your bike climbs

2. As you crest the rise and start to drop over it, move your weight back and adopt the attack position

3. Continue to move your weight backwards as bike rolls over and off the bump

Cone of movement

The ability to move around the bike as the trail dictates relies on weight shift and a thorough understanding of the **cone of movement**. This concept is illustrated on the following pages. The amount of lean a rider can exert on his/her bike is determined by the focus of his/her stance, i.e. where their weight is fixed. In a seated position, the cone of movement is focused on the saddle and is relatively small. From a standing position the cone of movement is much greater than when seated. This gives the rider a vastly increased scope in terms of leans, weight shifts and control.

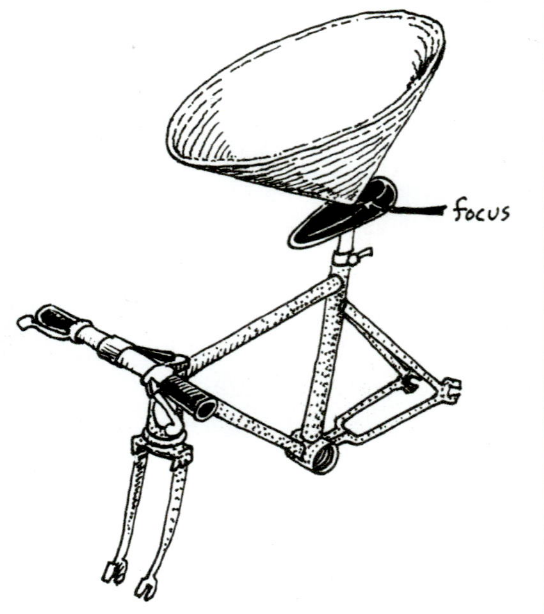

a

b

Cone of movement: 1. Seated Weight focused on saddle

In the seated position a rider has limited scope for shifting weight around the bike and using weight shift to control the bike.

Compare the amount of body lean whilst seated (b) with that possible whilst standing (e)

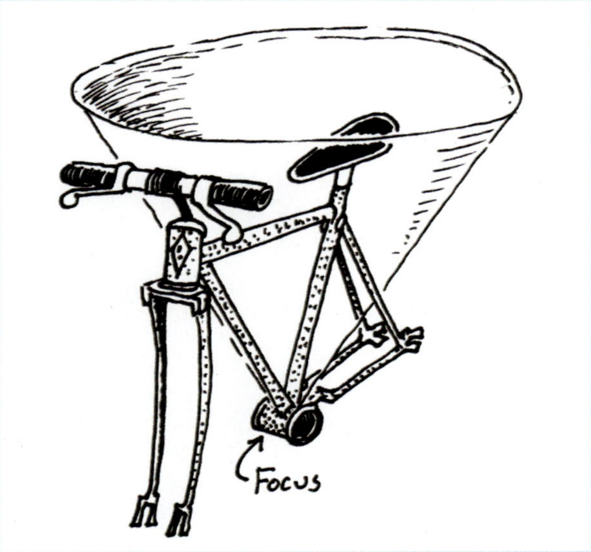

c

d

e

Cone of movement: 2. Standing Weight focused on pedals

In the standing position a rider has far greater scope for shifting weight around the bike and using weight shift to control the bike.

The pictures show how leaning the body can be used to assist with a steep climb (c), a descent (d) and to counteract bike lean to maintain balance

6. Choosing a line

Depending on where you ride, the terrain can vary greatly. For example, opposite sides of a hill or valley can have different ground conditions due to the type of soil, vegetation, slope and drainage. Trails can vary in an instant from smooth fire road, to rocks and roots, mud and water, and even sand. Knowing what happens to the bike on these surfaces is important to stay in control and react to the conditions.

Begin by linking the terrain and hazards in an area you know well and finding out the best lines. This experience can then be used on new trails allowing you to anticipate the hazards in different types of terrain.

According to experienced mountain bikers, "**the line is everything**". The challenge is to find the best line to get through each section. It will vary according to the surface and whether it climbs or descends. Anticipating the effect that natural hazards will have on the handling of the bike is the key to an enjoyable and flowing mountain bike ride. The following tips will help:

Rocks and roots

For rock strewn trails it is best to adopt the attack position and let the bike move underneath you. Tree roots can be similar to rocks and should be approached as close to 90° as possible; both can be extremely slippery when wet and should be treated with care.

Mud

Muddy patches are common, even in summer. Move your weight back to counteract the braking effect of the mud. Try and stay light on the bike and keep pedalling. If you do come to a standstill try heaving the bike into motion by throwing your weight backwards.

Water
Water should be tackled at low speed; underlying rocks can be slippery, and muddy water can conceal big holes and rocks. Dark, murky pools should be avoided.

Sand
Sand, which is often associated with water, has the ability to sap energy and usually needs speed to negotiate. Be careful however, as sand can throw steering out very quickly.

Picking a line and sticking to it can be difficult, especially on single track. Good riders and racers "visualize" their way down the trail. Try this technique by stopping at the start of a section, picking out the line you want to take, and building a mental picture or map of the section. Then ride it looking at that line, the one in your mental map. Let the bike follow your eyes, look where you want to go. Where you look is where you will end up.

7. Climbing
Before approaching a climb select the right gear; it is much more difficult to change gear when already climbing, especially if the bike is over-geared.

On long climbs stay seated and move your weight back on the saddle to maintain traction. Counter-balance any front wheel lift by shifting the weight of your upper body forward and leaning low onto the handlebars. Develop a rhythm by counting 1 - 2 - 3, pushing a little harder every third stroke. Use good pedalling technique by pedalling in a circle; with toe straps or clipless pedals, this allows you to pull up as well as push down.

On short "power climbs", getting up out of the saddle and powering over them should allow you to maintain momentum. Once up out of the saddle you must adjust your weight to maintain traction on the rear wheel. In all climbing positions your grip on the handlebars should remain light to allow for small steering adjustments.

8. Descending

The hard work is over, it is time for the exhilarating bit, the downhill. As you approach the descent make sure that you control your speed and get ready to move your weight back over the rear wheel. You should also put your bike into a gear that reduces chain-slap (i.e. middle or large chain ring at the front and middle to large sprocket at the rear).

Remember particularly when descending at speed that where you look is where you go; look at the rock and you will hit it. At slow speeds you will have more time to react, but when descending fast you have to process information about the trail well in advance and make decisions about line choice and braking that will get you down safely. Descending well is more about seeing and thinking ahead than it is about reacting to the trail as it passes beneath you.

On the descent keep two fingers over each brake lever so that you remain in control of your speed. Legs and arms act as suspension, with the pedals level and a wide hand grip, giving more control and feel for a good line choice. Most of the weight is on the feet, with the pedals horizontal or at the "quarter to three" position, ready to pedal when necessary. A firm but relaxed grip is used on the handlebars. A standing position is adopted, allowing easy changes of position and reducing the amount of shock transferred to your spine.

FUNDAMENTAL TECHNIQUES

The fundamental techniques combine many of the eight basic techniques into common "moves" that are repeated again and again when out biking. (Refer to the Assessment Outcomes for TCL and MBL in the SMBLA Scheme chapter for a list of the skills included in each level of the award. For the MBL award many of these techniques may be combined to form a skills test in the assessment.)

TCL

The Track Stand
Slow or zero speed skills help develop poise and balance on the bike and ultimately improve other skills that are done with some speed. Perhaps the most important mountain bike technique you can learn is the track stand. Biking is all about balance and track stands not only have real trail use but also teach true balance. This technique is best learnt on a gentle slope with flat pedals and the bike facing up the slope.

Practising balance skills will reduce the panic zone before unclipping from the pedals, and allows the necessary amount of time to make a good choice of route or technique for particular obstacles. The track stand (so called because it is a skill employed by sprint cyclists on the track) is also a cool technique to use while stopped at traffic lights. Rock strewn, gnarly sections are generally ridden at low speeds, and anyone without good balance skills will likely need to walk such sections. Practising track stands on steep ascents or descents helps define the most effective body position for riding these sections.

To successfully execute a track stand:

- **Position pedals level with favoured foot (lead foot) forward**
- **Keep legs and body straight but leaning forward**
- **Turn handlebars to favoured side, arms straight, shoulders parallel with bars**
- **Apply pressure on lead foot (which stops bike rolling back) maintain balance by shifting weight from one side of the body to the other whilst applying pressure on the bars**
- **DO NOT BRAKE. Using the brakes means pushing against a false force. No braking helps to find the perfect balance spot**

Ratcheting
At some point you are sure to encounter a trail so festooned with rocks, roots and deep ruts that normal pedalling is impossible because your pedals and cranks hit off these obstacles. You can keep your pedals and cranks clear of the obstacles by keeping the cranks more or less horizontal and pumping the pedals up and down. Combined with feathering of the brakes you should be able to ride over rocky/rooted sections without putting your feet down.

Canting

On uphill sections, where ratcheting is impossible as you reach stalling point, you can "cant" the bike on the downstroke of the pedal by leaning the bike to the side and gain a few extra inches of clearance for the pedals, chain ring and rear mech. In extreme situations it may allow you to limbo under low hanging branches. Combining these two techniques should allow you to deal with the gnarliest of terrain.

TCL

Manual Front Wheel Lift

An efficient skill used at speed to clear trail obstacles such as logs and rocks. This skill, like most, requires lots of weight shift, thus giving control.

To successfully execute a manual front wheel lift:-

- **Start from the attack position**
- **Move bodyweight forward**
- **Whilst moving bodyweight to the back of the bike, pull back with arms and push with feet**
- **Keep arms relatively straight and look where you want to land. The front wheel should land softly and quietly**
- **Don't push down on the forks; this does not give the required control**

TCL

Powered assisted front wheel lift

In contrast to the manual front wheel lift this is a slow speed skill normally used whilst climbing to clear trail obstacles such as rock steps and bumps.

To successfully execute a power-assisted front wheel lift:-

- **In a climbing gear, once the lead foot arrives at the top of the stroke power down (1 to 6 o'clock position). No more than one full pedal rotation.**
- **At the same time pull back with shoulders and lower back pivoting from the hips**
- **Keep arms straight and bodyweight back. Lift head as you pull**
- **Front wheel should land softly**

Rear wheel lift

MBL

Being able to clear the front wheel over an obstacle still leaves the back wheel to follow. A rear wheel lift will take care of this and, combined with a manual front wheel lift, is the beginnings of a bunny hop. This skill is best learnt on flat pedals.

To successfully execute a rear wheel lift:-

- **Rolling forward, transfer bodyweight from the back of the bike to the front in a lunging forward and upward motion (as body goes forward toes will point down)**
- **Now push feet into the back of the pedals and scoop with non-lead foot clearing the obstacle**
- **As the body moves twist wrists and push bars forward**
- **Finish in the attack position**

MBL

Drop-offs

Depending on speed there are three possible drop off techniques. A kerb height drop (about 15cm) requires no more than weight shift. For a drop more than wheel hub height (over 30cm) at slow speed, the correct technique will be an enhanced power assisted lift, only standing as you land. With speed, then simply use a manual front wheel lift with a twist.

To successfully execute a drop-off:-

- **Maximise landing distance by lifting the front wheel just before the drop.**
- **Try to match your air-borne bike position to the ground**
- **Landing in the attack position helps to absorb the impact**
- **Look for the landing - where you look is where you go**
- **You need to land at least one bike length from where you took off**
- **Keep your speed up**

MBL

Step-ups

The trail will always be full of surprises. The ability to ride along and step the bike up onto a section of trail like a rock step / ledge is just one of these occasions. The step-up provides a skill that allows a fluid passage up a step and on with the trail. Again, combinations of fundamental techniques are fused together.

To successfully execute a step-up:-

- **Approach step with eyes tracking beyond it**
- **Pull either a powered assisted (pictured) or front wheel lift to land the front wheel on top of the step**
- **Now transfer bodyweight (lunge) to the front of the bike**
- **Once bodyweight is forward perform a rear wheel lift up and onto the step**
- **Finish in the attack position ready for the next challenge.**

Bunny Hop

This skill gives the ability to hop the bike over an obstacle in a controlled manner. Again, it's a combination of several of the fundamental techniques used in sequence.

MBL

To successfully execute a bunny-hop:-

- **Start with a manual front wheel lift that is big enough to clear the obstacle**
- **As the front wheel clears the obstacle throw bodyweight forward and upward, lifting the rear wheel up and over**
- **Now push the bike through with the body pushing forward and down on the bars**
- **As the front wheel lands shift bodyweight back to the centre of the bike and allow the rear wheel to land nice and smoothly**
- **Relax the body to absorb the landing, ensuring pedals are level**
- **The bike should travel through the air in a nice smooth arc (it should be level at the point of crossing the obstacle)**

MBL

Lateral Bunny Hop

This skill is about the ability to hop the bike from one line on to another out on the trail.

To successfully execute a lateral bunny hop:

- **Prepare to set up as for bunny hops**
- **Just before hopping, gently steer and lean (by dropping a shoulder) to the desired direction then initiate the lift in that direction**
- **Once the front wheel is up, lift the rear then bring hips and heels across to bring the back of the bike on to the same line as the front**
- **Straighten up the front wheel as it lands, thus can be aided this by leaning slightly to the inside**
- **As the bike lands relax the body to absorb the impact**

MBL

Cornering at speed / riding a berm

Cornering at speed or riding a berm in a trail centre fundamentally uses the same techniques. The transition should look smooth, fluid and sound great as the tyres bite into the track.

To successfully execute a berm / corner at speed

- **Brake before entering the corner: slow in, fast out**
- **Look where you want to go**
- **Lean the bike (shift bodyweight) and using arms and feet, push down through the berm**
- **Keep speed up for the exit: slow in, fast out**

WAYS TO IMPROVE YOUR OFF-ROAD SKILLS
Practice, practice and more practice! However, there are various additional aids which may help you learn or master a technique.

Riding with others who can demonstrate good technique is a great way to "look and learn". However, unless they are willing to be patient and encourage you, they may not make the best riding partners.

Some mountain bike centres have "skills loops" with man-made sections specifically designed to require the execution of more advanced moves. Some may even run skills sessions.

Joining a club which offers regular mountain bike activities can be a good way to improve both riding skills and fitness, as stronger and more skilful riders in a group can motivate others to improve. Details of Scottish Cycling clubs, some of which are dedicated to mountain biking and many of which have an active mountain bike component, can be found on the Scottish Cycling website: (www.scottishcycling.com).

Some riders find they can benefit from the advice of an expert to help them think their way through a move. There are various books written by experienced riders, some of which are listed in the **Bibliography**. There are also a number of DVD's available, providing instruction and inspiration.

Finally, there is a growing number of magazines and websites offering advice, photos and video clips of mountain bike skills demos such as www.trials-online.com.

However, a leader should be discerning with respect to any information or advice they come across before trying to put any of it into practice or passing it on.

RIDING IN A GROUP ON THE ROAD
Often mountain bike trails are linked by sections of road, so an understanding of group riding techniques on the road will make these sections easier, more fun and, most importantly, safer.

Legally cyclists are entitled to the same space as a car but are not allowed to ride more than two-abreast or to cause an obstruction to traffic. The Highway Code also states that cyclists should ride in single file on narrow or busy roads.

Riding in a group formation gives the riders behind the leaders some shelter from the usual head wind and so makes it easier for the following riders. If the lead riders change regularly, then everyone can share the work and so make the group more efficient. You may have seen this technique demonstrated by road racers in big events like the Tour de France; where there are cross winds an "echelon" forms right across the road. Even with just two riders in a line, the rider drafting at the back can save 30% of the energy expended by the rider at the front.

The diagram below illustrates the positions of riders in a formation which gives riders in the group maximum shelter from the wind. If the road is wide enough and traffic is light, riders can pair up to ride two a breast; if the road is narrow or twisty it is safer to ride single file.
Riding in a group requires some practise, good communication and an

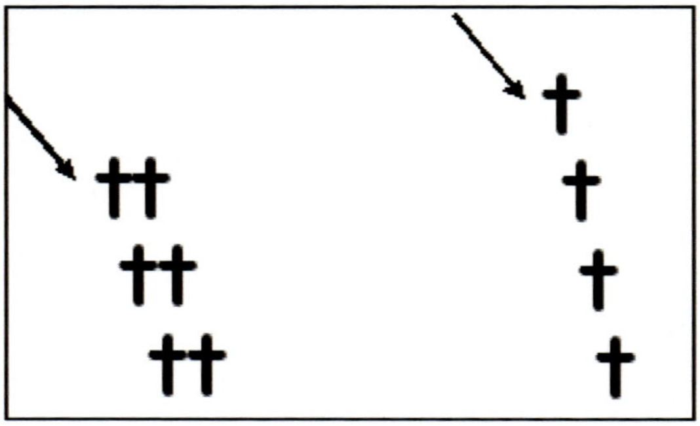

Riders in "echelon" formation
The arrows indicate the direction of the wind

understanding of what is happening. The group should ride in two lines with the inside line an appropriate distance from the edge of the road. If there are odd numbers in the group, the tail rider can ride in the middle or behind the outside line. Riders should be about 30cm behind the rider in front to allow them to benefit from the shelter created.

You should not focus on the wheel in front but look ahead around the rider in front. Stay off the brakes; if you need to reduce your speed momentarily, either stop pedalling or move out and let the wind slow you a bit. If you do have to brake, feather the brakes gently, and be aware of those behind you - warn them of your actions.

The group should have agreed signals and should verbalise or signal movements in advance. This means pointing out potholes, cars parked on the inside, glass etc. Point out hazards and shout, "hole", "rock" etc. The front and rear can advise of traffic, "Car Up", "Car Behind" etc. At predetermined times or distances the leading riders should change. This is accomplished by the outside rider moving across to the front of the inside line, while at the same time the inside line slows down marginally. This is achieved by the inside line soft-pedalling or freewheeling. The overall speed of the group should remain constant. Riders at the rear of the group move to the outside line so completing the chain. The rate of changes can be controlled by the leader by shouting out the changes at set intervals, for example, every minute or kilometre.

The speed should be adjusted to make it comfortable for the weaker riders. A call of "***easy***" from riders feeling the pace, should allow the speed of the group to be adjusted accordingly.

Rules for transitioning also need to be established. To transition from double to single file the inside lead rider slows to allow the outside rider to move in front. This happens all the way down the line from front to back. To move from single to double, the riders scan behind and often the "Clear" command is given from the rear. The lead rider moves to the front outside position, the second rider catches up and the other riders follow moving out and up as appropriate into neat symmetrical pairs.

With practice the above techniques are invaluable for headwind road sections, encouraging a tired group back after a long day's biking and keeping an eye on everyone. Weaker or tired riders can "rest" at the back of the group while the stronger riders work at the front. With good discipline the group shape changes little and allows other road users to be aware of the group and to take appropriate action.

Navigation

By the end of this section Leaders should be able to:-

- Describe the navigational aids available to a mountain biker
- Plan a route using these aids
- Use these aids while on the bike in charge of a group

INTRODUCTION

It is essential that mountain bike leaders and off-road bikers acquire an appreciation of the value of good map reading and the ability to use navigational aids and tools to ensure the safety and efficiency of their rides. Don't always leave the navigation to others, and most of all, pay attention to the route that you are following.

Observation is one of the key skills in navigation. In general it should be possible to avoid becoming completely lost by regularly checking your position against a map and route card. By paying attention to distinctive features which you can identify on your map, you can limit the need to use a compass and other navigational aids whilst riding.

It is worth remembering however, that maps aren't always up to date and some of the information may be missing. Most mountain bike rides involve following a track or trail of some kind which can make navigation easier, but not fool proof. With a suitable map, or better still, a pre-prepared route card, you can monitor your progress against features such as dry stone walls, streams, track junctions etc.

PLANNING A ROUTE

It is good practice to plan your route beforehand, even if you intend to follow signed trails within a mountain bike forest centre. Planning can be done in the comfort of your home or base camp, with the map spread out on the living room floor or kitchen table. Here you can plan where to start and end a day's ride, and design a circular route to avoid constant headwinds which can often spoil a good mountain bike day. Your chosen route must be within the abilities of you and/or your group, and it is important to include options for cutting the route short if necessary, and making a quicker return to base (see **Planning & Group Management** and **Terrain & Route Selection** for more on planning routes).

The mountain biker leader needs to be familiar with the navigational aids available, be capable of using these tools to plan the route and be able to use these aids while out on the bike.

NAVIGATIONAL TOOLS AND AIDS

The main and essential navigational tools and aids that a mountain biker should be familiar with and competent using are:

- √ **maps**
- √ **compass**
- √ **route card**
- √ **bicycle computer**

Other aids recently introduced and worth considering once you are competent with these basic aids are the altimeter, global positioning system (GPS) and mapping software. These have now reached an affordable price for many, but they should only be considered if your budget and needs extend to it, and should not be considered as a replacement for the basic techniques.

MAPS

Maps have always had a utilitarian purpose and many of the better maps are considered works of art. Experienced bikers are likely to have an extensive collection of well used maps, often preserved with pride and affection, providing memories of past journeys and dreams of future adventures.

Modern maps provide a comprehensive source of very useful information about the areas they cover, presented in a graphical manner. Though extremely useful, they are not always correct, because apart from errors they simply become out of date quite quickly. In forested areas in particular, new trails are constantly being developed and old trails lost or re-routed as part of forestry operations. In Britain a few organisations have developed a reputation for producing maps of consistent quality and detail to suit the needs of most mountain bikers. The two most commonly used are Ordnance Survey and Harvey.

The sensible leader will not venture out on a journey without a map of the area unless that area is very familiar to them. Using a map can add to the pleasure of cycling and provide a wealth of information about the route to be covered.

Planning the proposed route using a map can be a pleasurable experience in itself, and is the most important exercise to guarantee that the route is of a suitable length and has an appropriate degree of difficulty. This is particularly important if some or most of the route is to be off-road.

Which Map and Which Scale?

There are many different map scales. However, the most popular and convenient maps for cycling in Britain are sheets from the Ordnance Survey range using the scale 1:50,000 (O.S. Landranger Series). This means that 1 centimetre on the map is equal to 0.5 kilometres (500 metres) on the ground. Maps of 1:50,000 scale are divided into 2cm:1km squares and the dividing lines are numbered along both sides, plus top and bottom edges of the map using numbers between 1 and 1001 thus forming a grid. Each 100 x 100 km square is allocated a 2-letter reference as part of the National Grid and these letters are clearly marked on each map sheet and used in map reference numbers. Some map sheets contain the boundaries of two 100 km squares and will therefore have two sets of 2-letter references.

The area covered by each 1:50,000 scale map is 40 x 40km, but in many instances adjoining maps overlap to some extent. O.S. sheet maps are numbered beginning with No. 1 (North Shetlands) through to Nos. 203 and 204 which cover South Cornwall. The grid numbering on the edges of the maps goes from west to east along the top and bottom and from north to south down each side.

Though the O.S. Landranger maps are probably best for most cycling and easier mountain biking, the more detailed 1:25,000 O.S. Explorer Series is more appropriate for upland, moorland and remote areas, the greater detail helping with route selection and planning for mountain biking. These maps are also divided into 1km squares. About 300 Explorer maps and up to 50 Outdoor Leisure maps have replaced more than 1200 Pathfinders. Both of these series are also 1:25,000, but each map covers a greater area than the old Pathfinders. All Outdoor Leisure maps are in a 30km x 20km double sided format to give extra value for money, and the Explorer maps come in two formats, 30km x 20km single-sided or 20km x 20km double-sided. The area to be covered will decide the format to ensure that popular local features are fully covered on each map.

Mapping Software
An increasingly popular and valuable tool for route planning, digital maps have the advantage of being seamless, i.e. having no edges, and offering the viewer the chance to see a virtual landscape in 3D. Anquet (www.anquet.co.uk), Memory-map (www.memory-map.co.uk) and Tracklogs (www.tracklogs.co.uk) are based on 1:50,000 and 1:25,000 OS maps and feature a gazetteer, 3D viewing, route planning tools and compatibility with GPS.

Knowing the Legend
Familiarisation with the legend or key of an Ordnance Survey sheet will provide foreknowledge of the types of road or track and other terrain to be covered. Main 'A' roads are coloured red and identified by the smaller classification numbers, with A1 and A11 more major than, say, A123 or A1234. Routes can be planned using mostly tracks and bridleways which are marked with either double or single dotted lines, 'B' roads coloured orange, plus lanes and unclassified roads coloured yellow. See **Access Rights & Responsibilities** for a table of route/trail types and their representation on O.S. maps.

All over the country new roads and trails are being built and existing ones modified, so it is important to purchase maps that are as up-to-date as possible. In the more remote areas fewer changes take place with time and maps several years old may remain adequate.

Map Symbols
Knowledge of the map legend where all the symbols are listed is essential. This legend however, also needs a degree of interpretation. On 1:50,000 and 1:25,000 maps every solid black line indicates a boundary which is either fenced, walled, or hedged and that is all the map says about the

indicated boundary. When there is an unfenced boundary to a road or wood then you have a dotted line. Hence you can have a dotted line running parallel to a solid line indicating a track fenced on one side but not the other. Twin dotted lines indicates an unfenced track. A dotted line sometimes seen around the edge of a forest is not a footpath as many people think, rather it indicates a boundary which is unfenced. On a 1:25,000 map every fence / hedge / wall is marked so you can use the relocation skills outlined below quite easily when in rural areas. There are a couple of exceptions to the rule above; pylon lines, a railway line (both are marked differently on the different scales of map) and high water mark on a coastal area, are all quite distinct from a boundary line.

The map can also indicate hazards, such as a very sharp bend at the bottom of a hill, or a difficult junction with a main road. A leader who takes note of these features is prepared when they get there.

Measuring Distance

Once you know the scale of a map it is a relatively simple matter to measure the length between any two points in centimetres and convert this into distance along the ground; 1cm is equivalent to 500 metres on the 1:50,000 maps and to 250 metres on the 1:25,000 maps. Nearly all compasses are marked with a centimetre scale. The grid lines on Ordnance Survey maps are spaced at 1km apart, irrespective of the scale, so it is possible to estimate distance quite easily by counting the number of grid squares separating the points. It is useful to know that the diagonal from corner to corner of a grid square is approximately 1.5km apart. A map measurer (opisometer), many of which have a choice of scale and are calibrated in kilometres and miles, will enable the approximate length of a journey to be read off, by wheeling the instrument over the intended route on the map, though a check on their accuracy is required. Corrections for slope can be added as indicated later in this section.

Understanding Map References

A map reference number is used to locate a specific place on an Ordnance Survey Map. The full reference number is made up from the following letters/numbers in the order as listed:

1. The **two letter** reference of the particular 100 km square. Note that a single map sheet may contain portions of two 100 km squares
2. The particular **map sheet number** from No. 1 to No. 204
3. The **three numbers** from the map grid on the **bottom** or **top** edges called 'Easting'. For any particular place, read the two digit number from the West side of the one km grid square in which the place lies, estimating the extra tenths towards the East to form a three digit figure
4. The **three numbers** from the map grid on the **side edges** called 'Northing'. For any particular place, read the two digit number from the South edge of the one km grid square in which the place lies, estimating the extra tenths towards the North to form a three digit figure

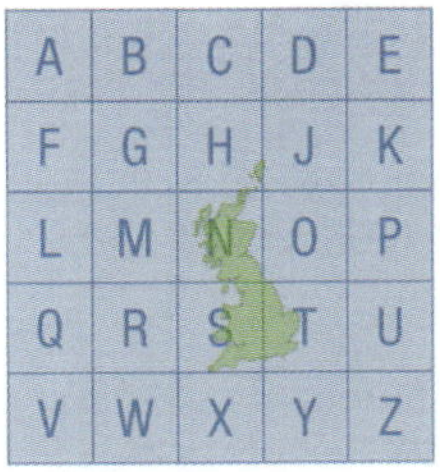

i. 500 kilometre squares of the National Grid

ii. Each 500 kilometres is divided into twenty-five 100 kilometre squares

iii. 100 kilometre squares that cover Great Britain with their reference letters

iv. 4-figure grid reference (1km square). Grid references must always be read in the following order:
Eastings – "Along the corridor..." (63, 64, 65 etc.)
Northings – "... and up the stairs" (49, 50, 51 etc.)

v. We can divide each grid square into 10 further Eastings and Northings to enable us to mark a feature to an accuracy of 100 metres. If we take this diagram as grid square 6450 we can plot a specific location within the one square kilometre.

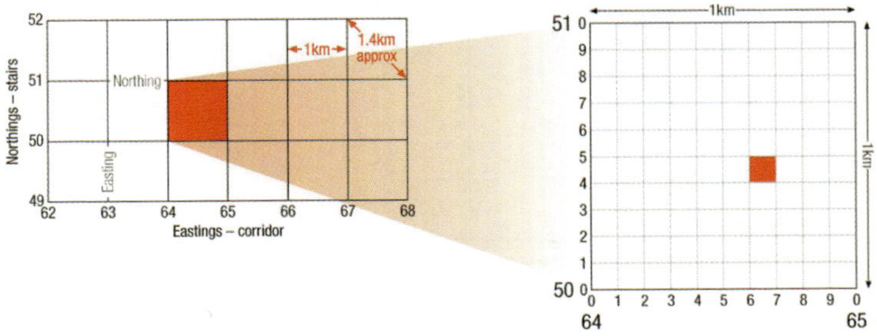

Using this system it is possible to reference any location on any map. For example, take the Scottish Centre, Dounans at Aberfoyle, the Map Reference for which is NS 527012. This map reference is made up as follows:

> The Centre lies inside the 100 km square 'NS'. It is situated between grid lines 52 and 53 reading along the bottom edge of the map, approximately seven tenths towards the East, so the location is given 'Easting 527'. Looking up the left or right hand edge of the map the Centre lies less than quarter way between grid lines 00 and 01 and is therefore given 'Northing 012'.

A simple phrase 'along the passage and up the stairs' should help to remind that the **top/bottom numbers are always given before the side numbers**.

Easting 527

Northing 012

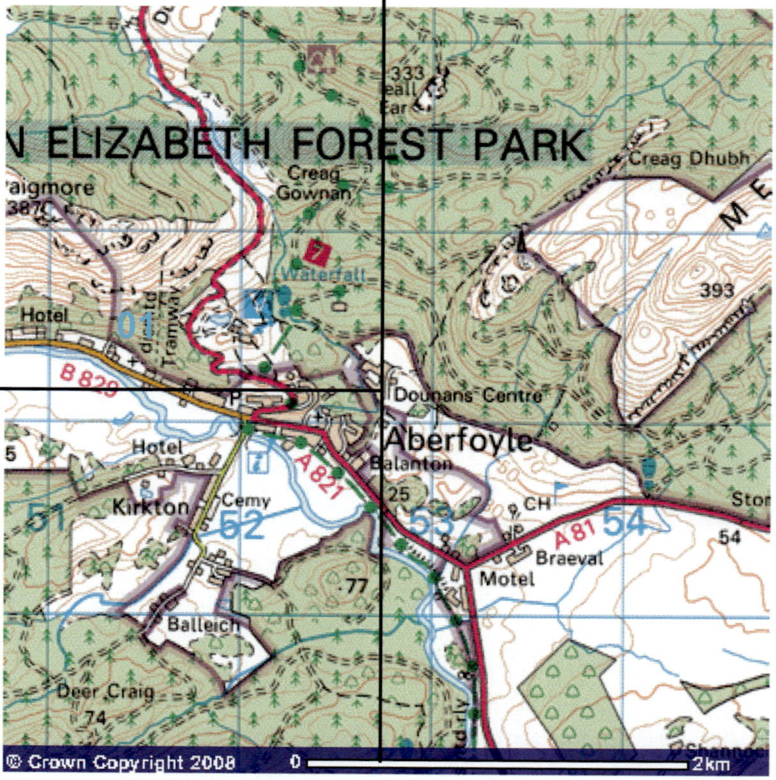

O.S. Grid ref. for Dounans Centre NN 527012

Understanding Relief and Contours

The contour lines on a map are the most important features to both road cyclist and mountain biker. Valley roads often make for a flat, fast route. Hilly routes can be tiring at first, but as cycling fitness develops, climbing hills becomes a challenge that can be enjoyed, and descending is always great fun. Hill tops provide wonderful views on a clear day and roads along a ridge are worth identifying so that the you can stay on high ground longer. Contour lines are a very reliable map feature, even when the ground is covered in snow.

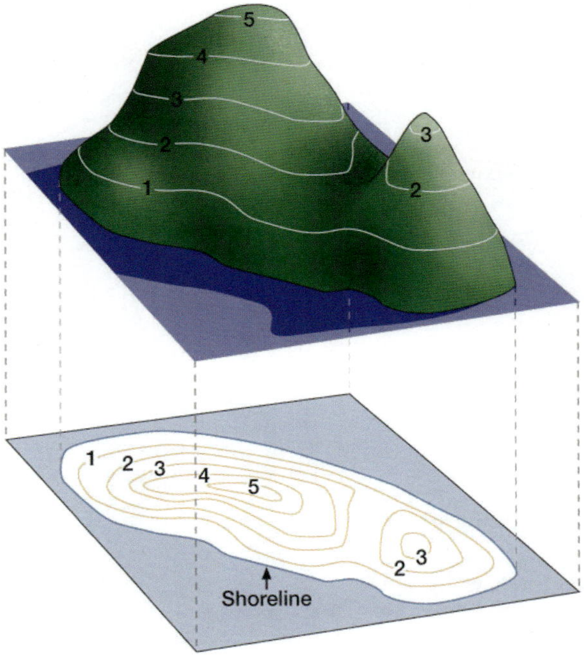

Illustration from 'Hill Walking' © MLTUK/ VG 2003

Contour lines on Ordnance Survey maps are brown lines which join points of equal height above sea level. These lines have their respective height indicated at intervals. The 1:50,000 and 1:25,000 O.S. maps show the heights in metres with 10m contour spacing, whilst Harvey maps use 15m intervals.

If the contour lines are close together this indicates a steep slope, whereas widely spread contour lines show the area to be much flatter. By studying the contours the severity of climbing and descending on a planned route can be easily determined. Interpreting the contours on a map involves relating the spacing and shape of the contours to the visible terrain. Some of the common contour features are shown in the diagram on the following page.

It takes some practice to interpret contours. It is good to get into the habit of trying to interpret contour features when you are on a ride, even if it's not really necessary for navigation at the time. By matching up ground features with the contours on a map you can build up a repertoire of images in your mind which you will store away for use on future occasions.

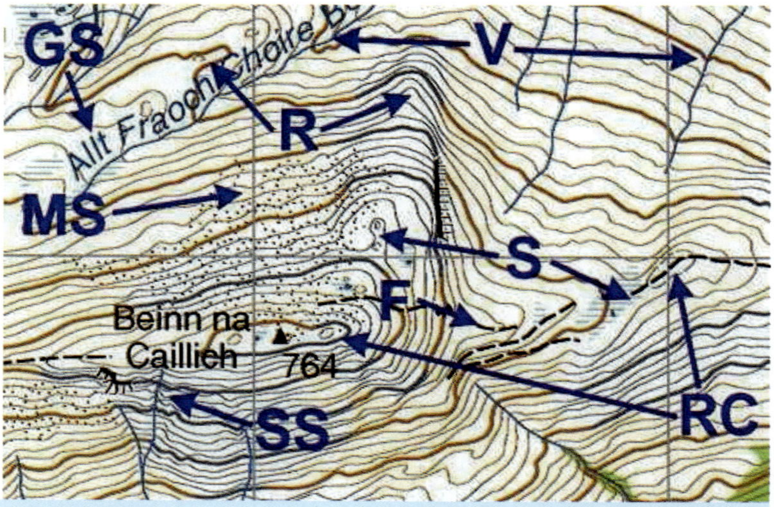

GS gentle slope

MS medium slope

SS steep slope

V valley or glen (many shapes)

S saddle or col (dip between two hills)

F flat area

RC ring contours (portray knolls and hill tops)

R ridge

Slope gradients
If a road shows ===>=== this symbol indicates a descent or climb of between 1 in 7 and 1 in 5. The symbol for steeper than 1 in 5 is ===>>=== with the arrowheads always pointing downhill.

Gradients can also be expressed in percentage terms with 1 in 5 being 20%, whereas 1 in 7 is 14% and 1 in 10 is 10%. Modern road signs now use this method of gradient marking. An understanding of this system is useful to the mountain biker.

Off-road gradients can be worked out by counting thick contours within 1cm of the map. The table below shows the relationship between slope angle and the spacing of thick (10m height interval) contour lines.

Slope Angle	Number of thick contour lines in 1cm of map	
	1:50000 map	1:25000 map
10°	2.0	1.0
15°	2.6	1.3
20°	3.5	1.8
25°	4.3	2.2
30°	6.0	3.0
35°	7.0	3.5
40°	8.0	4.0

The distance added by the terrain is not great but once it exceeds a slope angle of 20° it will become significant. The table below explains.

Slope Angle	Additional Distance
10°	1.5%
20°	6%
30°	15%

Off-road slopes of greater than 30° are usually unrideable, at least uphill, and only rideable downhill for those with the required level of skill.

THE COMPASS

The Chinese discovered the principles of the compass some 5000 years ago and these principles remain unchanged today. The compass is little more than a magnet suspended in the earth's magnetic field. It has been and remains the mainstay of the explorer and adventurer and is an essential tool of the mountain biker. Modern compasses are light, robust and generally easy to handle in adverse conditions. Specialist compasses are available for most requirements.

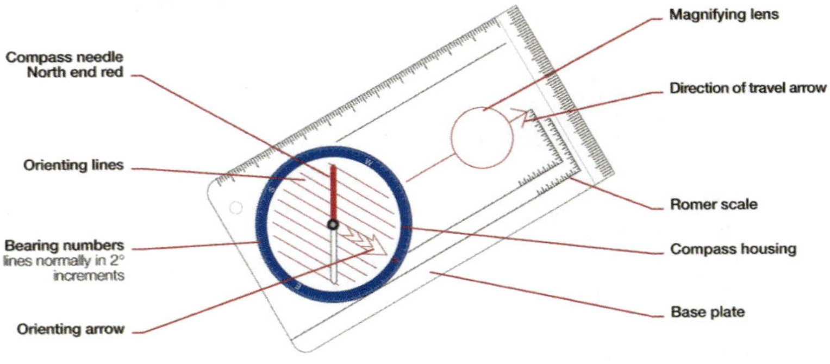

A recommended compass is one with a base plate with a **romer** (measurement scale) on it as well as a magnifying glass. Silva produce a wide range, the Type 4 preferred by hill walkers would also be suitable for mountain biking. Suunto is another company that makes a similar model, usually a little cheaper.

To use a Romer to measure the grid reference, place the corner of the relevant Romer on the point as shown below. Then read off the figures as indicated by the arrows – in this case the reading is 414 512.

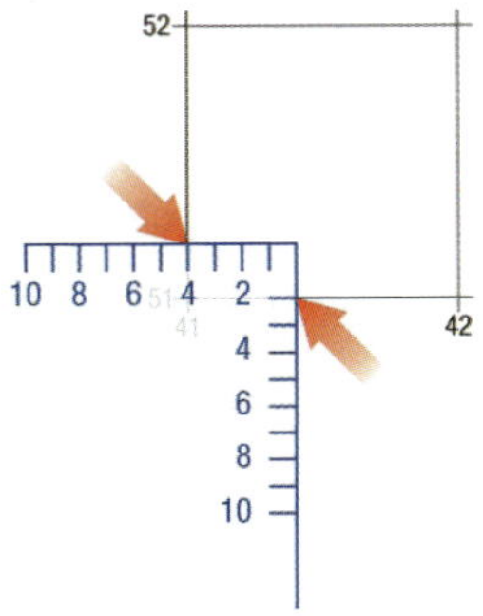

The terminology of the compass needs clarification before describing the skills using a compass you might employ on a ride. The **Base plate** is the oblong plastic plate with scales on it. **Housing** is the circular capsule in the base plate with lines on the bottom, points of the compass and degrees marked around the dial. Inside floats the **needle**. There are various arrows; **Marching** or **Direction of Travel arrow** down the centre of the base plate, **Housing or Orienting arrow** on the bottom of the housing with additional parallel lines (it points to the N on the housing dial). The ***Needle*** **is not an arrow,** it is magnetic and floats in the housing. It always point to the earth's magnetic pole (unless there is interference from another magnetic field)

Warning: your bike might have an affect on the needle if you use it too close to your bike such as resting the map on your handle bars whilst taking a bearing. The compass responds to the earth's magnetic fields but will also respond to other magnetic fields. Any object containing ferrous metal will distort the earth's magnetic field and this can cause erroneous readings on the compass.

THE CYCLE COMPUTER

Most, if not all cycle computers operate by receiving signals from a sensor (mounted on the forks or rear chain stay) that detects the number of wheel revolutions, sensed via a spoke-mounted wheel magnet. The computer unit (receiver) receives signals from the sensor and translates these into readings of speed, distance etc.

Setting up the computer

To obtain accurate values of speed, distance etc from your computer, you must calibrate it. To calibrate the computer it is necessary to measure the circumference of the wheel accurately. This is a relatively simple task and gives a more accurate reading than relying on pre-set values (usually supplied in a table in the bike computer's manual). Mark a starting point on the ground, and using the valve as a reference point, roll one full wheel revolution. Mark the ground at the end of the revolution and measure the distance between the two marks. For accuracy do this a couple of times and take the average value.

The value for circumference is usually entered into the computer in millimetres; make sure you use the right units, otherwise the calibration will be incorrect and readings of speed, distance etc could be very far out! For example, a bike with 26 x 1.9 tyres will have a wheel circumference of 206 cm (or 2060 mm). An error of (plus or minus) 1cm when setting up the computer will give an error of (plus or minus) 4.85 metres over 1km.

THE ROUTE CARD

One of the important rules of group leadership is that you must leave details of your intended route with someone who can raise the alarm should you not return before your expected deadline. Whilst this can be seen as the principle reason for producing a route card, there are other extremely useful benefits in so doing.

Why prepare a Route Card?

- It forces the detailed consideration of the demands that the particular route is going to make on the party
- To make estimates of distance, time, ascent/descent and compass bearings in the comfort of home or base
- To focus attention on ways of cutting the journey short should it become necessary
- It ensures a flowing journey without frequent stops to check the map
- It acts as an aide memoir to help monitor progress without reference to the map
- If checked against a computer average speeds can be calculated for subsequent use of the route

It is probably best to work in kilometres on both Route Card and cycle computer; this avoids the need for any conversions.

Most, if not all of our navigation will be using handrails. A handrail is a linear feature along which we travel, such as a track or trail. Somewhere along this handrail we will arrive at a decision making place. We need to know three things:

1. How far from my previous point do I need to travel to this next decision making place?

2. What is this next decision making place, i.e. is it a junction or a crossroads etc?

3. What do I do at this decision making place (i.e. turn left or right or go straight ahead etc.)?

The leader can avoid stopping too often to read a map by having an easily accessible route card with information about each leg or stage of the route. It should be brief and clear enough to read in snapshots, without losing concentration on bike handling.

It is advisable to make a point of checking your map or route card before descending. First check that your map is orientated correctly.

ROUTE DETAILS

The length of this sample route from Gartmorn Visitor Centre to Helensfield, is 2.0 km. There are three main decision making places (points 1, 2 and 4) plus one check point (point 3) to ensure the right route is being followed before arriving at the destination.

The map section on the next page shows the route marked and check points 1-4. This route is the one used on the three corresponding route cards which are shown on the following page. Each of the route cards could be used to navigate the route instead of carrying the map in a visible place. Versions 1 and 2 are text based whilst Version 3 is diagrammatic, using a system adapted from Audax riding.

A full version of the route card can be found in the Appendix.

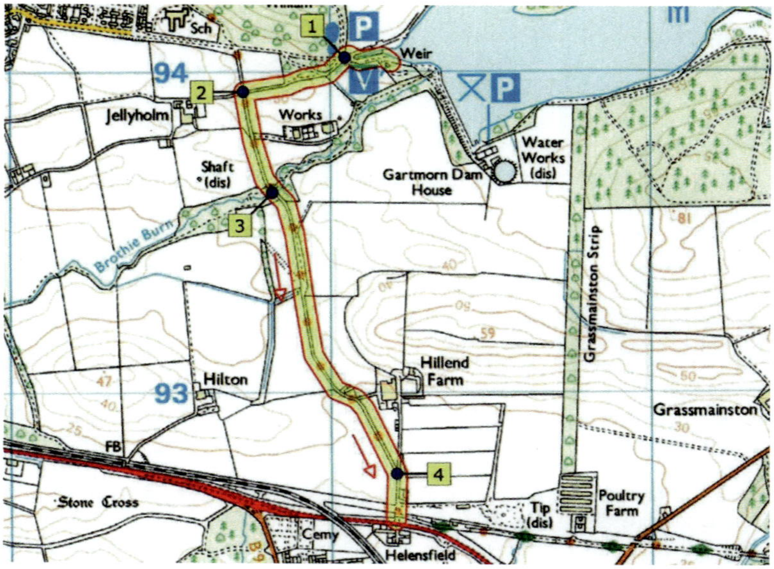

Map section for sample route from Gartmorn Visitor Centre to Helensfield, 2.0 km

	Route Card (v. 1 - unabbreviated)		
Cumulative Distance (km)	**O.S. Map(s): Explorer 366**		**Intermediate Distance (metres/km)**
	Grid ref.	**Decision to be taken**	
150 m	910940	**DECISION** Turn Left at the first Junction	150 m
500 m	907939	**DECISION** Turn L at the Crossroads	350 m
850 m	908936	**CHECK** Cross burn + pass through small strip of trees	300 m
1.8 km	912927	**DECISION** Turn R at inverted Y junction	1 km
2.0 km	912925	**DESTINATION** Stop at the main road	100 m

	Route Card (v. 2 same route but text abbreviated to ease reading)		
Cumulative Distance (metres/km)	**O.S. Map(s): Explorer 366**		**Intermediate Distance (metres/km)**
	Grid ref.	**Decision to be taken**	
150 m	910940	Turn L at Junction	150 m
500 m	907939	Left at X	350 m
850 m	908936	Cross burn	300 m
1.8 km	912927	R at Y	1 km
2.0 km	912925	Stop—main road	100 m

	Route Card (v. 3 text replaced by arrows. The route always starts at the circle and follows the directions shown by the arrow)		
Cumulative Distance (metres/km)	**O.S. Map(s): Explorer 366**		**Intermediate Distance (metres/km)**
	Grid ref.	**Decision to be taken**	
150 m	910940	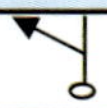	150 m
500 m	907939	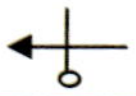	350 m
850 m	908936	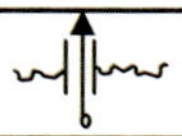	300 m
1.8 km	912927		1 km
2.0 km	912925	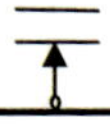	100 m

Using a route card and a bike computer has many advantages.

- It is probably the fastest way to navigate a pre-planned route
- It reduces the number of stops
- It convinces your group you know what you are doing
- Writing a route card forces you to look at a chosen route in detail during the planning stage

A well prepared concise route card can easily be slipped in and out of pockets or clipped to the handlebars for quick reference.

The technique of traffic lighting (used in orienteering) can be effectively used here. When a long way off a decision making place the speed can be high (green). On checking the computer, say around 250m from the decision making place, the pace should slow (orange). In the final 100m or so to the decision making place a leader should concentrate, looking for the exact spot so that you do not overshoot (red).

A group can be involved by breaking a route down into short legs and a different member of the group could be asked to be in front for their leg. They would require to go at a suitable speed, check no-one is being left behind, measure the distance using a computer to the end of their leg and identify it by successfully getting there. That person then goes to the rear of the group and the next person leads their section. This assists the "building and maintaining a team" part of the Action Centred Leadership model as well as developing the individual.

THE ALTIMETER

Atmospheric pressure reduces with altitude at a rate of approximately 10 millibars for every 100 metres of altitude above sea level. So if we measure the atmospheric pressure at any particular point, it should give us a reading for our altitude at that point. Altimeters measure air pressure and are calibrated to read height above sea level. Today they are relatively inexpensive and available in wrist watch or bicycle computer format and cost little more than a good quality compass.

It is possible to navigate without an altimeter but there are situations when a knowledge of height may help you pinpoint your position, perhaps in the absence of other features or in situations of poor visibility. The altimeter however has some drawbacks, the main one being its inability to distinguish between pressure changes brought about by altitude and those brought about by changes in weather. It is important therefore to reset the altimeter before the journey starts and throughout the day at places such as spot heights, trig points etc where the height is known. This keeps the altimeter up to date with pressure changes caused by the weather.

GLOBAL POSITIONING SYSTEM (GPS)

Satellite technology has now become affordable to many exponents of outdoor activities. GPS models are becoming cheaper, better and more readily available.

GPS uses a number of orbiting satellites each of which transmits a timed signal which is picked up by the receiver on the ground. Signals from several satellites (minimum of 4) are necessary to fix the receiver's position. The greater the number of signals, the greater the accuracy of the fix. Accuracy is now within plus or minus 15m horizontally, but up until quite recently they were only accurate up to plus or minus 100m to prevent their use as guidance for more sinister reasons. GPS should be viewed as an aid to other navigational techniques and not as a replacement for conventional map and compass skills. The need for batteries and the effect of temperature on battery life makes GPS less reliable than conventional methods in extreme situations.

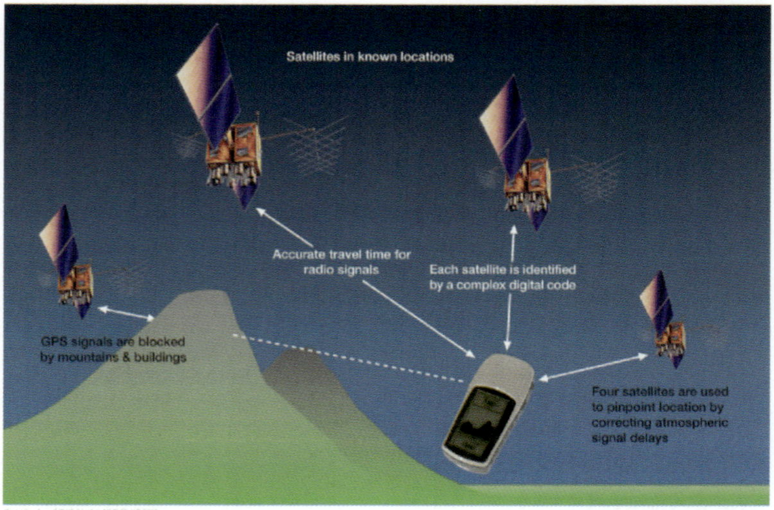

Illustration from 'Hill Walking' © MLTUK/ WG 2003

The GPS is possibly best used in mountain biking for re-location or confirmation of your position. This requires switching the machine on to get a fix, then off again once you have confirmed your position. This helps preserve battery life but may minimise your ability to use some of the other features of your GPS. However, map skills remain essential.

NAVIGATING OUT ON THE TRAIL

Orientating (Setting) the Map

An important aspect of map reading during a journey is positioning the map so that the visible features correspond with your location and the direction you are facing. This technique is called 'setting or orientating the map'.

Instead of reading the map as printed, the map sheet must be turned so that real life visible features are aligned with the map. Roads, waterways, farms and hilltops are all ideal major features to assist in setting the map to the same direction as the landscape. Once the map is correctly orientated it becomes much easier to accurately decide on the most appropriate route to take or to assist relocating if you become temporarily misplaced. When riding off-road, setting the map is even more important, but may be more difficult. Without man made features to work with it may be necessary to locate and closely study hill contour lines, valleys, natural high spots, wooded areas, streams and lakes. In good visibility you can set the map by eye. If identifiable features are not visible, for example obscured by mist, you can set the map by using a compass. Use the needle to find north and line up the north on the map with north on the ground.

Monitoring Progress

Using your cycle computer and route card you can monitor progress and in most cases avoid the need to refer to other navigational aids.

Using the compass when unsure of your location

Much map work should be straight forward and, by simply orientating or setting the map based on the features around, it should be easy to identify the current position. When faced with a choice of tracks in a forest not all of which appear to be marked on your map, it is necessary to first set the map accurately using a compass. The map should be held in one hand and the compass dropped on to it. The whole map should then be rotated until the compass needle points accurately to the top of your map. It is now set, and the compass can be put away. It is now time to see if any of the tracks on the map appear to line up with the tracks on the ground.

Map to Ground Bearing

If the above is not convincing a more accurate way is to take a bearing on the map along the track you wish to follow.

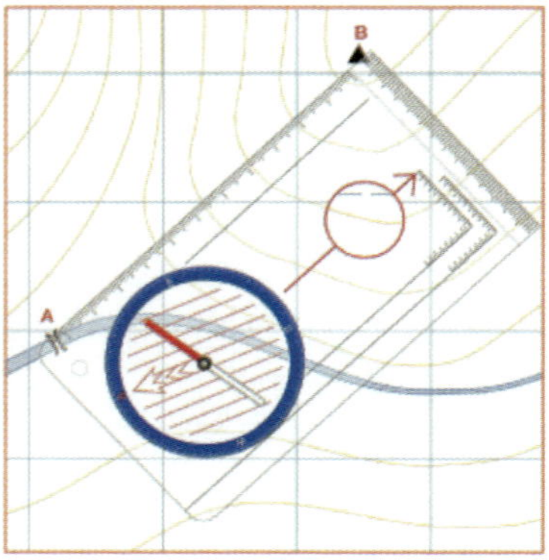

A Align the compass along the required route on map

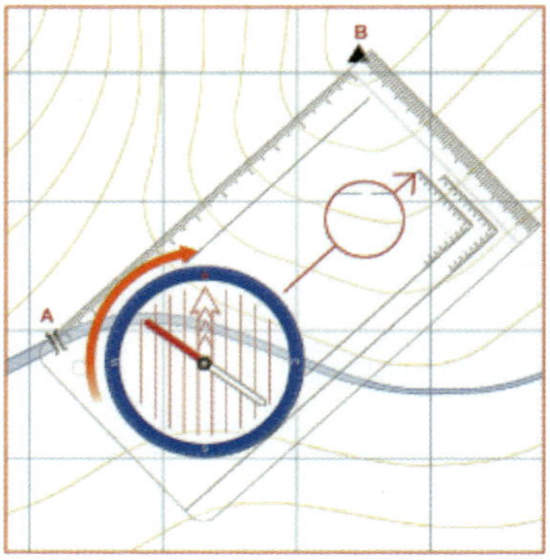

B Rotate the compass housing to align the orienting lines with the north-south grid lines on the map

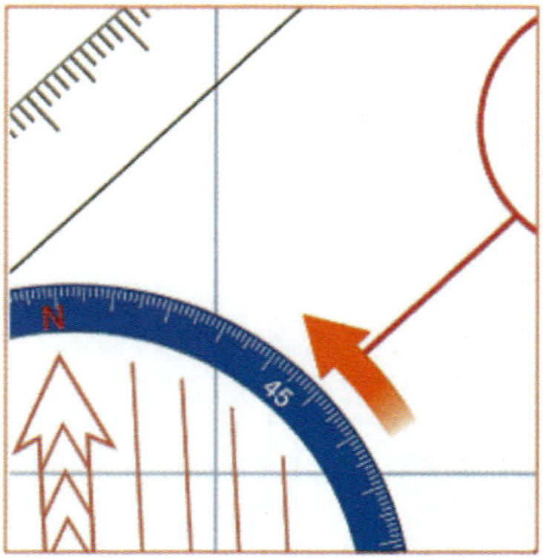

C Rotate the compass housing to compensate for magnetic variation

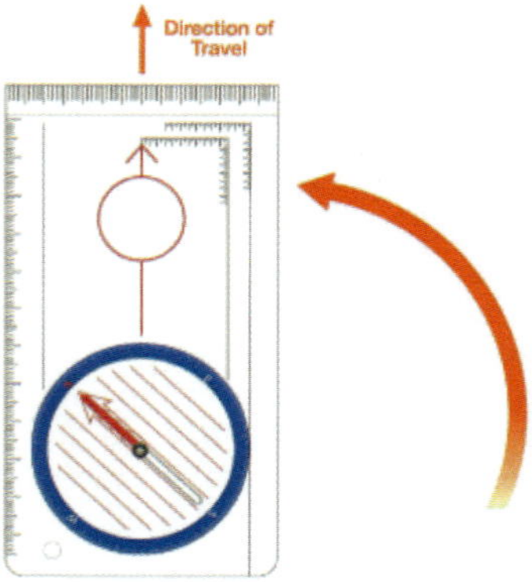

D Remove the compass from the map, rotate the compass so that north end of the needle and the orienting arrow are aligned and then proceed following the direction of travel arrow

- Align the compass along the required route on the map, make sure compass is the correct way around (diagram A)
- Rotate the compass housing to align the orienting lines with the north-south grid lines on the map (diagram B)
- Now take the compass off the map and add the magnetic variation (diagram C)
- Holding the compass in front of your body rotate the compass so that the north end of the needle and the orienting arrow are aligned and then follow the direction of travel arrow.

That should be the track you wish to take, but be vigilant and check the contours, bends in the track and streams you cross until you can verify you have the right one.

Ground to Map Bearing

What should you do when you feel very lost? You will have an idea within a couple of kilometres as to where you might be. Going back to your last known point is one way of relocating yourself. If you have passed some streams, track junctions or the edge of a forest, gone under a pylon line etc. go back to that point and take a bearing along that linear feature. Line up your compass by eye with the marching arrow pointing along the line the feature takes. This must be very accurate; get yourself exactly in line with the feature you are looking along and hold the compass up towards your eye level.

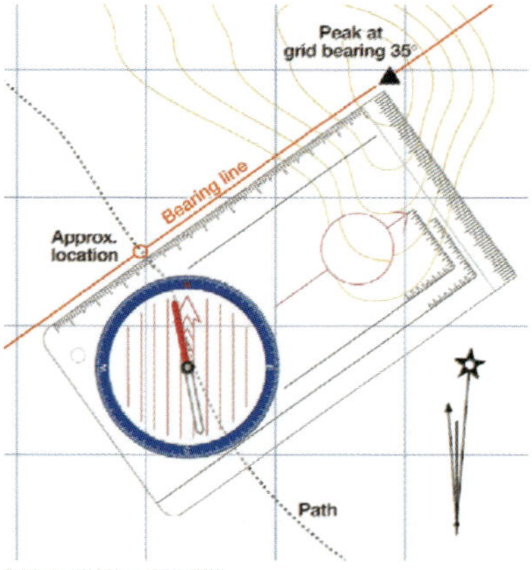

Keep the compass in this position as you turn the housing until the needle points to the N and is resting above the housing arrow. This is the bearing that the feature runs along. Subtract the magnetic variation, put the compass back onto the map with the N pointing to the top of the map and the housing arrow and lines lining up with the N/S Grid lines in roughly the area of map you think you are (Ignore the needle it will now only tell you if your map is orientated and at this point it is not relevant).

Keeping all the lines lined up, slide the whole compass around on your map until the edge of it aligns with a feature the same as you took a bearing along (a stream or track etc.) Does this have a junction with a track that you might be on? If so, that is where you are, orientate your map and try to confirm your location by observing other features around you. If this does not convince you move on and try another feature. When you think you have relocated yourself, you need to confirm this by looking for other features you pass along your route that you should be able to identify on the map and on the ground.

The above sequences ('map to ground' and 'ground to map') are the exact opposite of each other. Both methods can be used in relocation situations. Taking a bearing along a feature on the ground and putting it onto the map is usually less accurate than taking the bearing from the map. If seriously lost, the map to ground system may have to be done a number of times while you work out which stream you might be on. The ground to map system may solve the problem with only one bearing.

Slope Aspect

If utterly lost you may need to do the same as above but using contours only by measuring a slope aspect (the direction it faces). In the same way that you took a bearing along a track for instance, you take one looking down or possibly up a large slope near you. It is important that the direction of travel arrow is pointing directly down the "**fall line**" of the slope as accurately as possible, such that if contour lines were marked on the ground you would be aiming to cross them at 90 degrees.

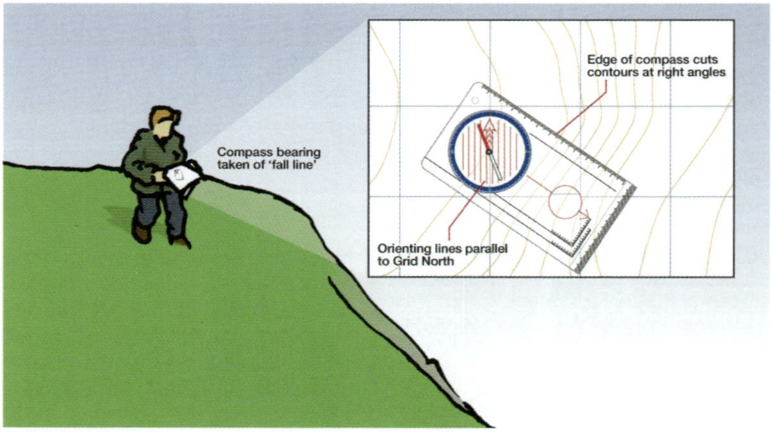

Illustration from 'Hill Walking' © MLTUK/ VG 2003

Once you have your bearing subtract the magnetic variation and place your compass on the map as before with all the orienting lines lining up and the N pointing to the top of the map. Now slide the compass around in the area you think you might be until the compass edge crosses some contours at 90 degrees. You are likely to be somewhere along that line. If there is more than one place that you could be you have to work out a way of eliminating it down to one place. It might be a case of heading along your track for 1 km and if you come to a stream you are in one place if not you are in another, and carry on from there.

Re-section
If you are travelling along a track and wish to get an idea of whether or not you might have missed a turning you can do a re-section. This skill is useful when you are not really lost but need to accurately confirm your location.

First identify an object up to 1-2 km away, a farm or hill top for example which you can recognise on the map and the ground, and which is approximately at right angles to the line of your track. Now use the ground to map bearing (re-section). Point the marching arrow at the object, rotate the housing until the needle points to N, subtract the magnetic variation, place the compass on the map. The edge of the compass (or one of the inner lines) must pass through the centre of the stream junction on the map, align the base plate so that the housing lines line up with the N/S grid lines with N towards the top of the map. Where the same edge of the base plate crosses the track is your location. Double check the plate is still passing through the stream junction on the map.

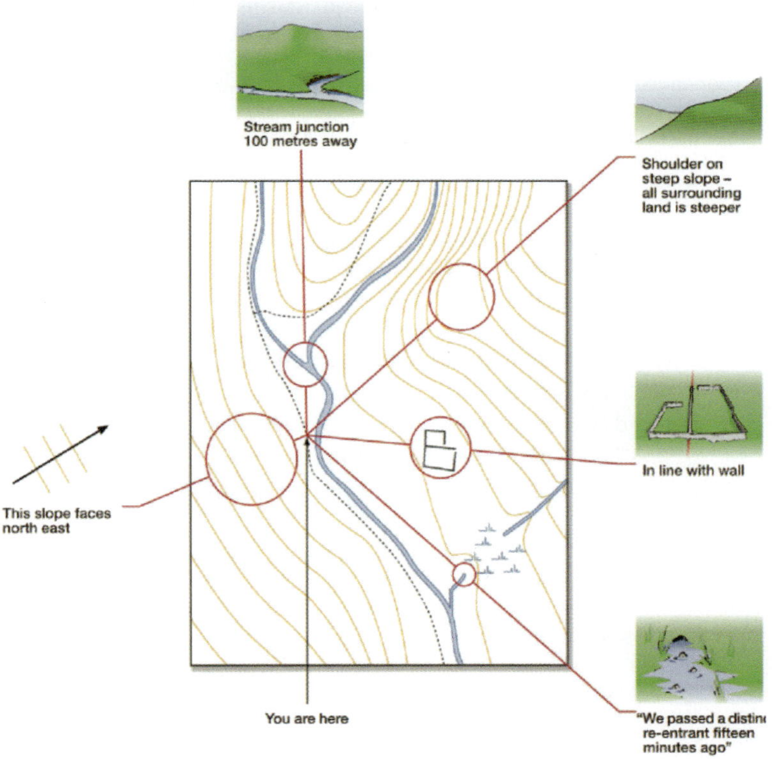

You can do this up to four times using different objects but you are unlikely to be more accurate than to within 100m. One re-section is usually sufficient when you are on a linear feature, a second resection might just confirm your position. If you are in the middle of a moor and not on a linear feature marked on the map then several re-sections are required and you need to draw lines on the map down the side of the compass when all the housing and N/S lines are aligned. When you have two lines drawn which cross each other you should be at that cross on your map.

Estimating Time

Estimating distance on a bike is quite simple provided your cycle computer is working and properly set up. Estimating time is somewhat more difficult and speed varies greatly depending on the variety and type of terrain encountered. For rough estimates, double the time you take to cover the same distance on road for forestry roads and farm tracks, and triple the road time for any length of single track.

Naismith's Rule

Naismith's rule provides a means of estimating how long it will take to travel from point A to point B **on foot**. The rule is based on an average walking speed of 5km per hour, with 1 minute added for every 10m height gained. It is important to be able to use Nasmith's rule should you require to evacuate your party on foot. Although Naismith's rule was originally developed for walking, it can be easily modified for mountain biking.

Experience has shown that the average speed over a 3-4 hour ride can be between 8-12 km per hour, although speed varies greatly on different terrain. When climbing, a mountain biker will only be slightly faster than a walker, about 7kph., plus half an hour for every 300m of climbing. On descents 15kph-30kph can be averaged.

Derek Purdy in his book, *Advanced Mountain Biking*, suggests a modified "Naismith's Rule". The figures used below are for example only; you should establish your own averages for accuracy.

Example of Naismith's Rule for mountain biking

Route 30km, total out and back, rising 600m

Outward leg uphill ***15km/7kph + (600m/300) x 0.5hr = 3.14 hrs***

Downhill home leg ***15km/15kph = 1hr***

Estimated total time: 4.14 hrs or 4 hours 8 minutes

Few routes would be this straight forward but using experience and this method, accurate timings could be achieved. Reasonably accurate estimations will only be achieved by monitoring your own and group performances on a number of routes.

The handy calculator on the opposite page has been devised to help with basic time calculations as mental arithmetic is not necessarily everyone's strength.

Remember too to add "down time" for your group, especially in the early days. A trip planned for one hour of cycling is likely to require two hours of actual time to achieve it. The skill of estimating trip time will become easier with experience of taking groups out.

Bike Time & Distance Calculator														
		Speed												
		5	10	11	12	13	14	15	16	17	18	19	20	
Distance (Kms)	0.1	1	1	1	1	0	0	0	0	0	0	0	0	Time (Mins)
	0.2	2	1	1	1	1	1	1	1	1	1	1	1	
	0.3	4	2	2	2	1	1	1	1	1	1	1	1	
	0.4	5	2	2	2	2	2	2	2	1	1	1	1	
	0.5	6	3	3	3	2	2	2	2	2	2	2	2	
	0.6	7	4	3	3	3	3	2	2	2	2	2	2	
	0.7	8	4	4	4	3	3	3	3	2	2	2	2	
	0.8	10	5	4	4	4	3	3	3	3	3	3	2	
	0.9	11	5	5	5	4	4	4	3	3	3	3	3	
	1	12	6	5	5	5	4	4	4	4	3	3	3	
	2	24	12	11	10	9	9	8	8	7	7	6	6	
	3	36	18	16	15	14	13	12	11	11	10	9	9	
	4	48	24	22	20	18	17	16	15	14	13	13	12	
	5	60	30	27	25	23	21	20	19	18	17	16	15	

FURTHER SOURCES OF INFORMATION

The Bibliography lists several reference books on navigation. A very useful interactive tool to guide you through the principles of navigation with map and compass is "Virtually Hillwalking", available to download from the resource library of the **sport**scotland website www.sportscotland.org.uk.

Weather

By the end of this section Leaders should be able to:-

- Explain why weather should be considered in planning a ride
- List factors influencing local weather conditions
- State appropriate sources of weather forecasts
- Interpret weather forecast information and describe some of the visible indicators of weather conditions
- Describe the safety implications of extreme weather

There is a Scottish saying "if you don't like the weather, wait a few minutes". The only certainty about the weather in Britain, particularly in upland areas, is its instability. Weather systems are constantly passing over the British Isles bringing frequent and sometimes unpredictable changes in weather conditions. The geographical position of Britain makes it subject to several influences on its weather: prevailing south-westerly air flows bringing mild, moisture laden air from across the Atlantic (the so-called Gulf Stream), air flows from continental Europe (generally cold in winter, warm in summer), cold northerly air from the Arctic, and warm southerly air flows. This complexity of influences makes it difficult to forecast both the exact nature and timing of changes in weather patterns. However, local forecasts are usually sufficiently accurate to enable the Leader to make informed decisions when planning and leading a mountain bike ride. Recent weather should also inform decisions on route choice, as factors such as rainfall and temperature will affect ground conditions.

SOURCES OF WEATHER INFORMATION

National weather forecasts on television and radio are most people's source of daily weather information. Although these are usually up to date and therefore reasonably accurate, it should be remembered that national weather forecasts are general forecasts biased towards centres of population and therefore temperatures and wind speeds are given for sea level. Regional TV and radio networks will give more local forecasts, but they are not necessarily detailed enough to predict weather in upland areas. Despite all the technology available to today's meteorologists, predicting the exact timing of weather changes that will result from a developing weather system is difficult. For this reason you should always obtain a forecast as close to your time of departure as possible.

Local bulletins may be posted in tourist information centres, outdoor shops etc. These can be very specific and accurate, and a leader should seek out their whereabouts in advance of a trip.

Telephone/fax weather forecast services are readily available. The UK Met Office's Weathercall service offers 5-day regional and local forecasts for the regions listed in the table below. To use Weathercall simply dial the number for your area and choose the 4-digit location code from the options given when prompted.

Weathercall by phone	
Select a region to view 4-digit location codes	
Greater London	09014 722 051
Kent, Surrey and Sussex	09014 722 052
Dorset, Hampshire and Isle of Wight	09014 722 053
Devon and Cornwall	09014 722 054
Wiltshire, Gloucestershire, Avon and Somerset	09014 722 055
Berkshire, Buckinghamshire and Oxfordshire	09014 722 056
Bedfordshire, Hertfordshire and Essex	09014 722 057
Norfolk, Suffolk and Cambridgeshire	09014 722 058
Glamorgan and Monmouthshire	09014 722 059
Shropshire, Herefordshire and Worcestershire	09014 722 060
West Midlands, Staffordshire and Warwickshire	09014 722 061
Nottinghamshire, Leicestershire, Northants and Derbyshire	09014 722 062
Lincolnshire	09014 722 063
Carmarthenshire, Ceredigion and Pembrokeshire	09014 722 064
Anglesey, Gwynedd, Wrexham and Denbighshire	09014 722 065
North-west England	09014 722 066
York, East Riding, South, West and North Yorkshire	09014 722 067
Durham, Northumberland, Tyne and Wear	09014 722 068
Cumbria, Lake District and Isle of Man	09014 722 069
Dumfries and Galloway	09014 722 070
Central Scotland and Strathclyde	09014 722 071
Fife, Lothian and Borders	09014 722 072
Tayside	09014 722 073
Grampian and East Highlands	09014 722 074
West Highlands and Islands	09014 722 075
Caithness, Sutherland, Orkneys and Shetland	09014 722 076
Northern Ireland	09014 722 077

All of the above area forecasts can be found on-line at www.weathercall.co.uk.

The Internet is possibly the best source of weather information with many sites dedicated to mountain areas. A good starting point is the Met Office's website www.metoffice.gov.uk which provides forecasts for mountain areas including information on hazards (blizzards, persistent heavy rain, gales, storms, extensive hill fog, significant wind chill), the height and extent of low cloud, and freezing level (the level above which you are likely to find ice on the ground, or where any precipitation will be falling as snow. The BBC Weather Centre at www.bbc.co.uk/weather also offers a comprehensive national and local weather forecasting service. Find out the best websites for your intended area in advance. On the hills a web-enabled mobile phone can be used to access some of these websites.

Local radio stations provide updated forecasts at frequent intervals, and some give forecasts for outdoor activities (hill walking, sailing etc). A small radio will allow access to local weather reports when on the move.

INTERPRETING WEATHER AND WEATHER FORECASTS

A basic understanding of some of the features of weather charts will help to make interpretation of weather forecasts easier. The lines seen on a weather map are called isobars and they plot areas of equal air pressure. The spacing of isobars gives an idea of the strength of the wind; tightly packed isobars represent strong winds, widely spaced isobars mean calm conditions. The wind direction is more or less parallel to the isobars.

The two basic types of weather systems which determine our weather in the British Isles are Low pressure (depression) and High pressure (anticyclone). High pressure occurs when the weather is dominated by stable conditions. Because of these stable conditions, cloud formation is inhibited, so the weather is usually settled with only small amounts of cloud cover. As isobars are normally widely spaced around an anticyclone, winds are often quite light. High pressure systems can be identified on weather charts as areas of widely spaced isobars, where pressure is higher than surrounding areas.

In winter the clear, settled conditions and light winds associated with high pressure can lead to frost and fog. The clear skies allow heat to be lost from the surface of the earth by radiation, allowing temperatures to fall steadily overnight, leading to air or ground frosts. Light winds along with falling temperatures can encourage fog to form; this can linger well into the following morning and be slow to clear. If high pressure becomes established over Northern Europe during winter this can bring a spell of cold easterly winds to the UK. In summer the clear settled conditions associated with high pressure can bring long sunny days and warm temperatures. The weather is normally dry, although occasionally, very hot temperatures can trigger thunderstorms.

A low pressure system occurs when the weather is dominated by unstable conditions. The weather is often cloudy and wet. Isobars are normally closely spaced around a depression leading to strong winds. Low pressure systems can be identified on weather charts as an area of closely spaced isobars, often in a roughly circular shape, where pressure is lower than surrounding areas.

MAKING YOUR OWN OBSERVATIONS

Looking at the clouds can help us to predict the weather. High wispy clouds, known as cirrus, indicate changing weather, and an approaching warm front. Cirrus clouds can develop into thin, milky cirrostratus clouds which can produce a ring of light round the sun or moon, a good sign of rain arriving later. Small, white detached puffs of cotton wool type clouds, known as cumulus, indicate stable conditions or light showers. However, if they expand upwards to form towering masses of dark cumulonimbus cloud, this is a sure sign of heavy showers of rain, snow or hail, sometimes accompanied by thunder and lightning. Learning to "read" the sky is a valuable and fun way to make use of the visible clues around us.

The Met Office's website has some useful pages on understanding and observing the weather, including downloadable fact sheets on weather features such as clouds, rainfall and wind, and interpreting weather charts www.metoffice.gov.uk/corporate/library/factsheets.html

LOCAL INFLUENCES ON WEATHER CONDITIONS

The weather experienced in any specific location is a product of the prevailing weather conditions and the effect of various local influences, most important of which are altitude, aspect and exposure. These factors can have the effect of making the prevailing weather either more or less severe. In contrast to the unpredictable nature of the prevailing weather, the effects of altitude, aspect and exposure are more predictable and even follow some easily remembered rules. The leader should have an awareness of these effects and how they should be taken into account when planning a route and preparing for a ride.

Altitude

Air temperature decreases with increasing altitude at the rate of approximately 1^{0}C for every 100 m climbed. This relationship between altitude and temperature is known as the Lapse Rate. In addition to this decrease in temperature, there is an acceleration of winds on high ground. At 600m the wind speed can be three times the wind speed at sea level. The combination of these two effects leads to a much greater wind chill factor. The other effect of altitude is related to the drop in atmospheric pressure as height is gained above sea level which makes it more likely to be cloudy and wet. Low cloud reduces visibility and makes navigation considerably more difficult.

Aspect

The effect of aspect on weather is largely concerned with the timing and amount of sunshine a slope receives. A south-facing slope will always be warmer than a north-facing slope which receives less sunshine. As a result, moisture evaporates more quickly from a south-facing slope and both air and ground temperatures will be higher. In months with snowfall and freezing temperatures, snow will lie longer and the ground will remain frozen for longer periods on north-facing slopes. The other effect of aspect is felt daily as the sun rises in the east and warms an east facing slope early in the day, then as the sun moves overhead, west-facing slopes receive more sunshine later in the day. This daily pattern is felt more acutely in winter when there are fewer hours of sunshine and what little sun there is has a bigger impact on local air temperatures. Camping on a southeast facing slope is the best choice if you want to wake up to early morning sunshine.

Relief / Exposure

Independent of altitude and aspect, the degree of exposure of a slope or open ground will determine how much shelter there is from winds and rain, and from strong sunshine. The exposure factor is effective on a small scale (e.g. leeward side of a single tree) and on a large scale, manifest as “rain shadow”. An area in rain shadow receives ”shelter” from prevailing rain-carrying winds by a mass of high ground forcing the air to rise and cool, thus causing it to deposit its moisture load as rain. As the air descends to the lee side of such a mountain range it warms and dries, so little or no rain falls. An area such as the eastern Highlands receives much less rainfall as a benefit of this rain shadow effect.

Relief can also alter the strength and direction of prevailing winds. Wind can be funnelled through a valley, becoming much stronger than expected, as well as coming from unexpected directions.

EFFECTS OF SINGLE WEATHER ELEMENTS ON THE GROUP

Wind

Wind is the element which has the greatest effect on cycling, both on and off-road. A cooling breeze in summer can be welcome, but a strong gusty wind can be both annoying and dangerous. The strength of the wind will have a big impact on the effort required to cycle and the speed of travel. In general, allow more time to complete a route on windy days, especially if crossing exposed ground where there is little shelter. It may be harder keeping a group together as the wind will take a greater toll on smaller or weaker riders. A strong wind also makes communication within the group more difficult, especially when trying to shout upwind, so a degree of team work is required, and frequent checks to make sure all riders stay together. How to ride as a group on the road is explained in the **Skills & Techniques** section.

The other effect the wind has on mountain bikers, side winds especially, is to make the bike harder to control. The best strategy on a very windy day is to stay low, shorten a route or find alternatives with more shelter from trees, and if possible set off into the wind, returning with a tail wind which is better for safety and group morale. Take advantage of shelter provided by trees, hedges and leeward slopes on the windward leg of a journey.

Anyone venturing out on a cold windy day has experienced the effects of wind chill. A stiff cold wind will whip heat away from a warm body much faster than if the air were still. If clothing or exposed skin is wet, this heat loss will happen even faster. Carrying appropriate wind-proof clothing to reduce wind chill is essential (see **Clothing** section).

Rain

On a short, easy ride on good tracks light rain is not a problem if the group is prepared to get wet. Keeping on the move should prevent anyone from getting cold. On a more challenging ride even light rain can add to the technical difficulty, affecting ground conditions and visibility. Smooth surfaces like slabs and tree roots can become especially slippery. In wet conditions choose a route which keeps to well surfaced tracks and forest roads; not only will this make the going easier, it will minimise damage to soils and vegetation. Persistent rain can take the pleasure out of a day's ride and a good leader should assess group morale with this in mind. Wet weather riding also takes its toll on bikes, wearing brake blocks faster and requiring chains and moving parts to be cleaned and thoroughly lubricated after a day's ride.

Snow

The Winter Conditions Module is an additional module for qualified Trail Cycle Leaders and Mountain Bike Leaders to enable them to work outside the 'summer conditions only' remit of the TCL and MBL qualifications. The module enables TCLs and MBLs to work in defined 'intermediate' and 'winter' conditions, **but operate only in TCL terrain regardless of the level of award they hold**. See the **Winter Conditions Module** section in this manual.

Sun

Strong sunshine is the perfect antidote to cold, wind and rain, but it does carry its own risks, even in Britain. Cyclists are more prone to sunburn than walkers as the breeze created while riding has a cooling effect and burning of unprotected skin in strong sunlight can go unnoticed.

Mist

The obvious effect of mist or low cloud is reduced visibility, requiring an increased level of concentration on the bike and precise navigation skills.

EFFECTS OF EXTREME WEATHER CONDITIONS

Hypothermia

Hypothermia, or "cold exhaustion" is usually brought about by a combination of factors, of which wind chill is highly significant. Coupled with physical exhaustion, being excessively cold and wet can lead to a lowering of the body's core temperature and a disruption of normal bodily functions and behaviour. How to deal with hypothermia is covered in the **Emergency Planning & Procedures** section and the first aid course you attend, but it should be noted that hypothermia cases require hospital treatment, so prevention is far better than cure. Hypothermia can be avoided by use of appropriate clothing, especially wind proof garments in very cold winds, and waterproofs to prevent getting soaked and losing body heat through evaporation. Keep energy and fluid levels up to prevent fatigue and boost the body's ability to deal with the cold. On very cold windy days, a leader should seek as much shelter for the group as possible and limit the duration of exposure.

Heat exhaustion

The combined effects of strong sun, physical exertion and dehydration can lead to heat exhaustion, and eventually sun stroke. Leaders should be aware of the potential for this to occur and be able to recognise the common symptoms – acute headache, nausea and fatigue. Drinking copiously in hot weather is vital to prevent heat exhaustion developing, and exposed skin should be protected from strong sun.

Lightning

The chances of being struck by lightning are relatively small, but the risks are greater when outdoors and can be reduced by taking appropriate action when a storm approaches. The safest place to be is within the area of a conductor which will conduct the lightning to the ground. This could be a mast or tall post which is standing alone. Under a tree or an overhang is a bad place to shelter because the lightning will try to bridge the gap to the ground by the shortest route, which will be through you if you are sitting underneath. You can, however, seek shelter within a wood or group of trees. Although being in a car is a safe place to be, being on a bike is not. If you are caught out in the open the best strategy is to crouch down with your hands on your knees. Do not lie flat on the ground. Stay away from natural lightning rods such as camping equipment, and from rivers, lakes, or other bodies of water.

Emergency Planning & Procedures

By the end of this section Leaders should be able to:-

- Describe how the interaction between external factors and the group characteristics determines the level of hazard
- Explain how planning can play a part in preventing emergencies
- State why it is important to have a strategy for managing an emergency
- Describe how, as a group leader, you would implement an emergency strategy
- List what equipment to carry to be prepared for an emergency

INTRODUCTION

An 'emergency' might be a delay due to minor repairs, a damaged unrideable bike, an injured immobile person or quite likely a combination of these. It does not just affect the group, but also those waiting at base. It will require sound leadership, communication, and planning. If these have been applied before leaving base, then hopefully your emergency procedures are a case of *prevention being better than cure.*

Most organisations will operate to written guidelines in accordance with the Adventure Activity Licensing Service (AALS). This section will add support to those guidelines. 'Late Back' procedures are particularly relevant to mountain biking. There is also guidance on emergency procedures and equipment to be carried.

It is difficult to consider emergency procedures without considering the general management of a mountain bike trip. Before looking at emergency procedures we should briefly consider the range and type of likely problems and hazards.

HAZARDS

Outdoor hazards can be classified into three main groups: weather, terrain and people. They are usually all interlinked and it is commonly leadership, or the lack of it, that determines the effects of any combination of hazards. The mountain bike leader has the additional element of mechanical equipment to contend with.

Weather affects our comfort and environment continuously. Terrain challenges our equipment, skills and experience. The "People" hazard relates to leadership, experience and judgement, with respect to the group, equipment, weather and terrain. Weather and terrain only become hazards when we venture out unprepared, inexperienced and ill-equipped.

Cycling at night should only be planned with Leaders holding a Night Riding qualification, and is only suitable for experienced riders with effective lighting systems. Dealing with emergencies at night as opposed to in daylight is a much bigger challenge. Without the Night Riding qualification, neither TCL nor MBL awards equip a leader for planned group night riding. However some emergencies might mean being out until darkness which will increase the level of difficulty in carrying out planned emergency procedures.

ISSUES OF LEADERSHIP

Good supervision is not about being in the right place to witness the accident, it is being in the right place to ensure it never happens. The majority of accidents are a result of judgement and leadership decisions. Often these are made before leaving base. The mountain bike leader, with the added equipment factor, must weigh up a lot of issues, especially when a group has some individuals producing their own bike for the first time. It is important to consider whether the bike is suitable for the proposed journey. If not what can be done about it? Reaching a solution may lead to a difficult confrontation with an individual or their carer/parent, but the safety of the rest of the group must be considered. **Think, who are you responsible to? Whom are you responsible for?**

If a bike is not suitable for an intended journey, failures of a mechanical nature could lead to serious injury. Whilst a mechanical failure leading to a sudden incident might on the face of it be due to a bump in the track or insufficient bike skills, one might ask was it a reasonably foreseeable accident if the quality of the bike is considered in relation to its rider, the nature of the route selected and possibly the prevailing weather conditions which will affect the terrain? Could a decision to walk a section as opposed to riding it make a difference? If that is the case should you lead by example and walk it also?

Ultimately many of these considerations are linked to experience which the leader will have to rely on to make judgements. Many problems are resolved by firm decision making, based on a weather forecast, previous knowledge of the group and your chosen route. Having alternative route options gives a further safety net for adjusting trip time or avoiding more difficult terrain. A cut off time should be set by which a given route should be started, with an alternative route planned should the starting deadline not be met. These should be marked on the Route Card (see Navigation section). The home base can be informed of any change before leaving or by phone on the way to the start point.

Subconscious, sensible/common sense thoughts need to become conscious thoughts on which the leader can express an opinion and act.

STRATEGIES FOR MANAGING AN EMERGENCY

How is an incident managed in its entirety from the second it happens to the point when the leader finally crawls into their bed at the end of the day? Remember that looking after a casualty is only half of the problem, looking after the rest of the group can be a major part of managing an emergency.

ASSESS THE SITUATION AND MAKE A PLAN

Every emergency is different and there is no set solution. At an incident three main options usually have to be considered before working out a plan:

1. **Self-manage the incident - always preferred, providing no further harm will be done**
2. **Send for help**
3. **Call for assistance and wait for someone to arrive**

In each case there are three basic steps which will dictate the outcome of the incident. They may well happen very quickly but missing one of them could compound the situation considerably.

1. Prevention of any further incident

The situation must be instantly assessed to ensure your own safety, the safety of the rest of the group and also to ensure no further harm can come to those who are injured. For example, if somebody has a crash, it is important not to slam on the brakes and risk crashing or bringing other riders down. It is important to avoid running headlong towards the casualty and risk tripping and injuring yourself. Staying calm can prevent a second accident occurring and can be reassuring for everyone else involved.

If an accident occurs in failing light this can lead to a very serious issues. It is important to ensure that no one else could crash into the scene. People should be placed behind and ahead to warn other users of the hazard. The casualty and equipment must be moved to a safe place off the track (if it is safe to move the casualty), not onto the outside of a bend for example where others might be likely to overshoot.

2. Administer any repairs or first aid

It may be useful to delegate a number of minor tasks to other members of the group to keep them occupied and together. Go up or down the track to warn other users of the hazard, check over the other bikes for any damage, make the casualty comfortable, collect water from a nearby stream etc.

3. Planning for evacuation

All too often a couple of people are sent for help and then the leader realises that they could move the injured party to a more suitable location either for shelter or for ease of access for the emergency services. Not only have those you sent for help then got the wrong grid reference, they are not there to help you move the equipment or injured person either. Taking time to make your plan will, in the long run, save vital time.

Managing the incident yourself

Having made an initial assessment of the situation, the leader may decide to manage the incident him/herself. Self help could include support from your base, for example to collect damaged equipment or assist with a minor injury. It should be stressed that this is only possible when no further harm is likely to be done. An issue often overlooked is the amount of additional equipment each person finds themselves carrying once an injured person is being supported. It is not just the injured person's equipment that has to be passed around but also the equipment of those doing the supporting. Equipment can be left for a while and shuttled along with a casualty or discarded and returned to later once a safe location has been reached. Self help can bring out the best in people, often having a bonding effect on the group.

Sending someone for help

This option needs careful thought. Control of information is vital. Access to a phone is necessary. With a group of minors there is likely to be a second adult in the group available to assist. Either the leader or the assistant should go for help alone or with one other reliable person. Beware of sending a large group of youngsters just to get them out of the way; they can slow the rescue plan down and once a phone is available they may make unhelpful phone calls. In addition, should the emergency services wish to be guided to the casualty by those who have been sent for help they will probably only be able to manage one or two passengers. The group will then be split further which creates other problems and information control / containment.

Calling for assistance to come

This is a serious step to take but might be the only logical decision to take. **Mobile phones, whilst extremely useful for all sorts of reasons do not provide a reliable strategy for dealing with emergencies. Signals may not be possible in remote or hilly areas.**

The standard call for help in the hills is six shouts, whistle blasts or torch flashes, then wait a minute and repeat. The reply is three shouts, whistles or torch flashes. If no one is around, the rescue may depend on the leader having left a **Route Card** with a responsible person back at base who will raise the alarm, based on the organisation's 'late back' procedures.

Alternatively, on well-populated tracks someone may come by who can help. They may have a mobile phone which can get reception or be able to go quickly for help leaving your group intact to look after the injured person. Beware of being overwhelmed by their enthusiasm to assist and letting them rush off for help before you have made a plan. This may also lose the Leader's control of information dissemination to unwanted parties. Your home base contact / employer really needs to hear the facts of the situation from the leader first, not through a parent or, in the worst case scenario, the press.

In reality a combination of the above strategies is often used, with the group making their way with a casualty along the route that the emergency services will approach from.

A MESSAGE FOR HELP

What should go in a message for help?

The sample **Accident Report Form** in The Appendix can be used to record the information which you will need to relay to the emergency services. The sheet can be photocopied and kept in your First Aid pack with a pencil. Carrying it with you is easy and saves you, in what is already a very stressful situation, having to think about what to try and record. Writing the report can also be delegated to someone else in order to involve the group and keep them occupied. It is advisable to record on paper what happens in chronological order.

Sound navigation skills become essential in order to provide an accurate grid reference. A six figure grid reference is accurate to 100 metres which is adequate. Additional information is always helpful e.g. "where the track enters the forest".

Which emergency service should be called?

Help with a casualty requiring evacuation or hospital must be sought through **the police (dialling 999)**, who have statutory responsibility for any accident and co-ordination of rescue. They may call for Mountain Rescue assistance if ambulance access is difficult. Do not rule out helicopter rescue which you may need to get the casualty to an open area. Ensure the number of the phone being used is given and keep it manned until the Rescue Services arrive.

RETURNING TO BASE

Once the casualty is picked up there will be a difficult decision about whether to go with the casualty to the hospital or to stay with the group. If things are working well and there are good procedures in place at base, relatives/friends of the casualty will have been informed and can get to the hospital. People at base should assist with this. It may be that the assistant leader could go to the hospital with the casualty, in which case they may need to be prepared for meeting parents. The leader may have to meet the rest of the waiting parents in order to tell them what has happened. There is also the rest of the group to consider; they may need the opportunity to talk about the incident once they have recovered back at base.

It is advisable to record on paper what happened in chronological order. Though this can be difficult, time should be found to take a step back and note detailed thoughts down. Often delegating minor tasks to the rest of the group keeps them usefully occupied and give some breathing space.

EMERGENCY EQUIPMENT

What do we carry and what can it be used for? A **tools and spares kit** needs to be adequate (see **Trailside Repairs** section), including tools to repair the range of bikes in the group. Various improvised repairs can be made with duct tape, spare cables and zip ties. What and how much equipment to take should be balanced with what can sensibly be carried and what repairs can be done when out on a cold wet day. For dealing with emergencies other than mechanical failure, the following items should be distributed amongst the group:

First aid kit

Include surgical gloves, large wound dressings, bandages and triangular bandages. These are particularly useful for the common injuries which result from unexpectedly parting company with your bike.

Group shelter

This needs to accommodate the entire group. A survival bag or space blanket are not recommended. A Bothy Bag, available in various sizes accommodating from 2 to 12 people, should be sufficient. Next, think about how you might insulate a casualty from cold, wet ground. Using the group's rucksacks leaves a problem of what to do with their contents and what the rest of the group might sit on inside a group shelter. A foam sleeping mat can be cut into sections and carried wrapped around cross bars or lining rucksacks which makes them easily available to sit on. Sections of mat can also be used for splinting. A large piece of bubble wrap (cheap and very light to carry) is great for insulation and warmth when someone is lying on the ground.

Whistle, Map, Compass, Pencil and Paper
All of the above should be in the leader's pack.

Food and Drink
A small thermos flask of hot liquid or a stove and pan with a brew kit can do wonders for morale and warmth under a group shelter. Some high energy bars or gels will prevent blood sugar plummeting and help to maintain concentration and keep people functioning.

Other items
Spare clothing - hats and gloves, waterproofs; torches, mobile phone, money; clean water for cleaning gravel rash.

Improvised stretchers
Improvising a stretcher is only an option when no further harm is likely to be done to the casualty. It can also become a very time consuming affair. In general their use should be limited to moving the casualty to a place that is safer or more sheltered or provides easier access for the emergency services.

If you do decide to make a stretcher whatever is quick and simple is the best solution. Using a group shelter or survival bag is often easiest and requires little explanation. It is possible to construct a stretcher across two bikes using foam sleeping mat and poles of wood, or to make a stretcher which can be dragged along the ground behind a bike. This all takes too long, requires more equipment, energy and skills and carries the risk of causing further injury. It is likely to be safer, quicker and more practical to walk, carrying or supporting the casualty, than to support and push them on a bike, especially up or down hill.

SUMMARY

- **Planning and preparation should reduce the chances of being faced with an emergency**
- **Remember that a leader's responsibility extends beyond those who are being led**
- **Being properly equipped should help to deal with an emergency**
- **Make a plan - no two incidents are ever the same - try to stand back and take time to plan effectively**
- **Control the spread of information**

Bike Set-up, The Safe Cycle & Trailside Repairs

By the end of this section all Leaders should be able to:-

- Explain why correct bike set-up is important for cycling
- Describe the principles underpinning basic riding positions
- List the basic tools required for trailside repairs and explain what repairs they can be used to effect
- Fix a puncture and a broken chain, and know how to adjust gears and brakes
- Demonstrate knowledge of more advanced repairs and their limitations, given the equipment available and remote terrain

MBL

- Effect advanced repairs to enable a bike to be ridden back to base, giving consideration to additional expedition equipment being carried, such as panniers

Expedition

INTRODUCTION

Cycling on or off-road is a marriage between rider and machine. How happy this marriage is depends to a large extent on a good fit between bike and rider, and on having a bike in good working order. Learning how to set-up a bike and repair it when things go wrong are essential skills for any cyclist, and these need to be well developed by a leader in charge of a group.

BIKE SET-UP

To optimise bike-fit to rider the bike must be made to fit the cyclist and not the other way around. The Leader should be aware that a general riding position should fulfil three basic requirements :

1. **Safety – so the cyclist can control the bike at all times, especially the brakes**
2. **Comfort – to enable the cyclist to perform for a given duration through a variety of terrain and conditions**
3. **Efficiency – for optimum power output at any give time**

In seeking a good position, many cyclists use trial and error but few have the sensitivity to judge whether they have achieved their optimum position. They adapt to a position, rather than the position being optimised for them. Young and novice cyclists are those who most need advice - a short session under expert guidance can improve efficiency, safety and comfort.

Saddle position should always be established first, with the handlebar position then being determined in relation to the saddle position for the particular type of mountain biking. Handlebar position must be safe, with easy access to the brake levers.

After cyclists have found their correct position, they should be encouraged to record their individual set-up measurements to make it easy to replicate their position on a new or borrowed bike. With children however, it should be noted that these measurements can change dramatically during periods of rapid growth.

Despite the advice which follows, it is important for the Leader to take into account how a cyclist *feels* on a bike. Everybody is different; no single method can precisely determine bike position. Saddle height preference depends on the type of cyclist, their anatomical geometry, the chosen type of mountain biking and stage of development.

Basic Riding Position

1.1 Saddle height

For introductory or general mountain biking, the saddle height is perhaps the most important adjustment to the bike with regard to *fit* and position on the bike. The height is measured from the centre of the pedal axle up the seat tube to the top of the saddle. Optimal saddle height is a compromise between efficiency, aerodynamics, safety and comfort.

For introductory or general mountain biking, the saddle height is perhaps the most important adjustment to the bike with regard to *fit* and position on the bike. The height is measured from the centre of the pedal axle up the seat tube to the top of the saddle. Optimal saddle height is a compromise between efficiency, aerodynamics, safety and comfort.

A simple approach to finding a good starting saddle height is to sit the cyclist on their bike, set one pedal to its lowest point and place one heel on the pedal spindle (centre). In this position the leg should be straight, without being overstretched. With the balls of both feet on the pedals (correct foot position), the knee will be slightly bent when the pedal is at the bottom of the pedal stroke. Pedalling with the ball of the foot over the spindle of the pedal gives a more efficient and comfortable position.

If this position is found to be too low it may be necessary to raise the saddle; do so gradually a few mm at a time until the correct height is achieved. If there is any rocking of the hips when observing the pedalling action from behind, or if the toes are pointing downwards at the bottom of the pedal stroke the saddle is too high. Novice riders learning to ride a bike may require a lower saddle position that allows them to easily put both their feet on the ground.

1.2 Saddle set-back (fore and aft position)
Having established an acceptable saddle height, the position of the saddle needs to be adjusted to correctly place the rider forward-backward relative to the bottom bracket where the cranks originate. This is important to ensure biomechanical efficiency while pedalling; the rider shouldn't be too far behind or too far forward of the bottom bracket.

Sitting on the bike with pedals level (horizontal) and the ball of the foot centered on the pedal, use a plumb-line hanging from the front of the knee. The line should drop through the centre of the pedal spindle. If the front of the knee lies behind the line move the saddle forward, if it lies in front of the line move the saddle back on its rails.

1.3 Saddle height and setback relationship
Any large adjustment necessary to saddle height will affect saddle set-back (and vice versa) by a ratio of approximately 2:1; for example raising the saddle by 4cm equates to moving the saddle back by about 1.5-2cm because of the angle of the seat tube (commonly 70-73^0 on a hardtail MTB). Similarly, if the saddle is moved forward by say 2cm, this equates to moving it down (reducing the reach to the pedals) by about 1cm, so it may be necessary to go back and alter saddle height, in this case raising the saddle slightly. Always set saddle height first, then setback, then fine tune by going back to adjust saddle height if necessary.

1.4 Saddle angle
The last adjustment which can be made to refine saddle position and which will affect comfort when riding is the angle of the saddle. The starting point is for the saddle to be horizontal. Many women prefer to have the nose of the saddle pointing down slightly, whereas the opposite is true for many male riders. Again, it is a matter of preference, but something worth pointing out to inexperienced riders or any rider complaining of discomfort on the saddle, or lower back pain. Often a small adjustment of saddle tilt can make a big difference.

Handlebar Position
Handlebar position must be safe, allowing easy access to the brake levers. For mountain biking the emphasis should be on comfort and safety, the rider does not want to be overstretched or too cramped on their bike.

It is important that the reach to the brakes is checked during set-up. Children and female riders with a shorter torso will often need a shorter reach than the original set-up on many bikes. It pays to check this when buying a bike and change the stem if necessary, however, it is possible to make some adjustments after purchase.

To check reach to the handlebars sit normally on the bike with hands on the flat part of the handlebars in normal riding position and draw an imaginary line from the shoulder to the hands; the angle between this line and vertical plane should be about 45 degrees. To adjust this angle the stem can be raised or lowered (if spacers allow) and riser bars can be rotated forward or backwards. Most bikes now use “A-head” stems which can be easily removed to add spacers above or below the stem neck. Such stems can also be flipped 180 degrees and mounted “upside down” so changing the effective stem length and height.

Brake levers and gear shifters

To check brake lever position, stand with feet on the pedals with weight shifted a little back, hands covering the brakes. A straight line from shoulders to fingers is aimed for, as the picture shows. Twist levers on the handlebar to adjust position. Lever reach should be set so the finger knuckle sits on the lever, using the small screw which winds the lever in and out. Gear shifters should be in a position that allows easy gear changing while riding.

X INCORRECT

✓ CORRECT

Measurement Card

Once cyclists have found their optimum position, it is useful to record all the important adjustment positions so that the position can be duplicated as and when required. These can be recorded for each rider on a measurement card like the one opposite. The following measurements should be recorded:

- **Saddle height** (along the line of the seat-tube, centre of pedal axle → top of saddle)
- **Saddle setback** (distance, measured with a plumbline, from the nose of the saddle forward/backward to the bottom bracket axle centre)
- **Difference between saddle height and top of handlebar height** (easily done using a spirit level and ruler)
- **Reach** (centre of the saddle → centre of the handlebars)

Remember that during growth phases in young riders these measurements can change rapidly.

Bike Position Measurement Card	
Name	**Date**
Set-up feature	**Measurement (mm)**
Saddle height	
Saddle setback	
Difference between saddle height and top of handlebars	
Reach (saddle to handlebars)	

The information provided so far gives the basic guidelines on establishing bike position. As the type of riding changes or the rider specialises in a particular mountain bike style or discipline the position may change from the basic start position. For downhill or more technical styles of riding a lower saddle height is preferred, whereas longer distance cross-country riding usually results in some fine tuning of the basic position for comfort and efficiency.

BIKE CHECKS

Bikes should be checked thoroughly before setting out so that any obvious mechanical problems can be avoided, and also to ensure that there is a suitable range of tools to fix all bikes in the group. Appendix E contains a **Bike Safety Checklist** which you can use to systematically check every bike before use and record any repairs or adjustments which need to be made. This routine check should be part of a *generic risk assessment* for every planned outing (see **Hazards & Risk Management**).

TOOLS FOR THE JOB

Having the right tools for the job is essential to make a quick and efficient repair. As well as checking bikes before setting out, the condition of tools should also be checked. Using a dirt-encrusted tool is a sure way to wear out the bolts on your bike as the grit acts like sandpaper between the tool and bolt. Metal tools will rust and soon become useless, so keep them clean and dry between rides.

Just as bike technology has advanced in recent years, so has the development of bike-specific tools. Hence, it is generally better to source your tools from a bike shop rather than from a DIY store to make sure you get the right tools for the job. There is a large choice of multi-tools available which combine several tools in one compact unit.

A word of warning about multi-tools: functionally can be compromised by compact and lightweight design. If you opt to carry a multi-tool check that it performs as expected before relying on it to carry out a repair on a ride, e.g. some multi-tool chain tools do not open up enough to insert a Shimano joining pin, and so can be useless for fixing a broken chain.

Always opt for functionality over light weight and aesthetics when it comes to choosing your tools. Sometimes it is worth opting for a sturdier "workshop" tool such as a chain splitter which makes light work of splitting a chain, especially with cold hands when you have a waiting group to manage. Longer Allen keys give you more leverage, and those with "ball" rather than square heads make it much easier to access bolts from awkward angles. A bike mechanic, rather than a front-shop sales assistant, is probably the best person to advise you on tool selection with respect to their functionality and suitability for the job.

Basic tools and spares (All Leaders)

Tools

Pump (should adapt to fit Presta and Schraeder valve types)
Tyre levers
Allen keys (2, 2.5, 3, 4, 5, 6, 8, 10mm)
Torx key T25 (to tighten disc bolts)
14mm socket (for crank bolts)
Chain tool (make sure it will fit a Shimano joining pin)
Crosshead screwdriver
15mm pedal spanner
Spanners (if required for brakes or to remove wheels)
Shockpump (plus adaptors)

Spares

Inner tube(s) (a Presta valve fits any rim)
Puncture repair kit (check it is complete and glue has not set)
Tyre boot/ patches
Lube
Cable (zip) ties
Duct tape
Spare brake and gear cables
Spare chain link and joining pins (for SRAM and Shimano chains)

Additional tools and spares for Mountain Bike Leaders

Tools
Spoke key
Spare spokes or multi-fit Kevlar spokes
Cone spanner
Pliers with cable cutter (a multi-tool such as a Leatherman will have other useful tools too)
Crank remover

Spares
1/2" coach bolt
4" long 9/16 bolt and nuts (emergency pedal)
Spare seat pin bolts (specific to bikes being used)
Spare gear hangers (specific to bikes being used)
Superglue
Bag of bits (SPD cleats, nuts and bolts, Torq bolts etc)

MBL

The lists of tools and spares in the box above and opposite are divided up into basic kit, to be carried by all Leaders, and additional kit which MBL Leaders should carry. The lists are by no means definitive. The **Expedition** section contains more information on expedition kit.

TRAILSIDE REPAIRS

All leaders should be able to effect common repairs to enable a bike to be ridden back to base. These include puncture repair, mending a broken chain and adjusting gears or brakes. The more remote the environment or technical the terrain, the higher the level of mechanical ability required, and the more comprehensive the toolkit and spares list will have to be.

The group leader must not only be familiar with his/her own bike, but must also be confident in making repairs to any bike in the group. It is a good idea to have a training session to demonstrate basic repairs to a group, especially where experience is lacking, and to cover any differences in components of the bikes belonging to individuals. It is good practice to involve each group member in a repair job to encourage team work and to make repairs quicker and a more rewarding learning experience.

It is beyond the scope of this manual to provide a comprehensive guide to carrying out bike repairs. There are many bike repair and maintenance books available which can make even more advanced repairs seem easy (some are listed in the Bibliography). Whilst working on your own bike a lot will be learned about the best way to do repairs and the importance of a bit of prior planning and organisation! Attending a bike maintenance course which some colleges, clubs and bike shops run is a good way to improve in this important area.

The following websites may also be of use:
Maintenance courses www.edinburghbicycle.com
Maintenance tips www.webmountainbike.com

Clothing

By the end of this section Leaders should be able to:-

- List the advantages of cycle specific clothing
- Describe the layering system
- List various ways to control body temperature during a ride
- Describe clothing suitable for a variety of riding conditions

DESIGNED FOR THE JOB

To many people cyclists' clothing may seem strange; it is usually close-fitting to stop garments flapping in the wind or catching on the bike, and made of high-tech stretchy fabrics. You don't have to be an experienced cyclist to appreciate the advantages of cycle-specific clothing. Kitting yourself out with even just the basic items can improve your protection from the elements, your riding comfort and your ability to move around on the bike. A good bike shop, and many outdoor shops, should not only have a range of cycle clothing for you to choose from, but will be able to advise you about the type of clothing suited to your riding and the time of year.

CYCLING SHORTS

If there is one piece of clothing that will really improve your enjoyment of cycling, it is a good pair of cycling shorts. Worn next to the skin, they have a padded insert and flat, well-placed seams to greatly improve comfort whilst riding. They come in a variety of fabrics, but those made of a wicking material offer the most comfort and all round use as shorts in summer and under cycling tights or longs as it gets cooler. Recently, baggy shorts with a padded liner, removable or attached, have become popular as they provide a more socially acceptable look than tight lycra! Women's shorts are also available having a padded insert and cut designed to suit the female anatomy.

HELMETS

Your head is the most vulnerable part of your body when cycling and should always be protected. In some countries it is compulsory. A helmet is especially important when you are riding in rocky, unknown terrain, though you never know when you might crash.

The main things to check when buying a helmet are that it fits properly and meets the safety standards set and tested by institutes such as Snell or ANSI (in the US), EU (Europe), BSI (Britain) or AS (Australia). This will be marked inside the helmet. In order to be effective in a crash a helmet should fit your head like a glove. You should be able to feel the helmet on the top of your head and it should move with your scalp when you wiggle your eyebrows. It should fit low on your forehead without obstructing your vision to the front or side. The more you spend on a helmet the better ventilated it will be and the fit system will probably be more adjustable and more secure too, resulting in increased comfort and better protection should you crash.

Helmets should be replaced regularly, at least every three years from the **date of manufacture** (not the date of purchase - date of manufacture is shown inside the helmet) whether they have had an impact or not as the polystyrene degrades through time, use and contact with UV rays.

In the example above, the dial on the back allows infinite adjustment to give a comfortable and secure fit. The position of the straps can be altered using the locks below the ears.

EYEWEAR

Whilst it is vital to protect your head from a potential crash, it is just as important to protect your eyes from the glare of the sun, flying insects, spray, grit and other debris that can be thrown up from the trail. The sudden impact of an object hitting your eye while riding can be enough to momentarily blind you and make you lose control. Riders who wear contact lenses should always wear protective eyewear, as debris in the eye may mean having to remove a lens as well as damage to the eye. Of course you can spend a lot of money on a pair of shades if you want to make a fashion statement, but you can purchase quite cheaply a frame with a choice of lenses for different light conditions .

BODY ARMOUR
Originally worn by downhill mountain bikers, body armour is now frequently used on cross-country routes, particularly on man made technical trails such as the Seven Stanes. The most common items used are elbow guards and knee/shin protectors. The decision to wear armour is really a personal one, affected by how uncomfortable it is and how frequently you fall off.

FOOTWEAR
Cycling shoes to which cleats which clip into pedals can be attached are recommended. They come in a variety of styles to suit your riding. Cleats offer safety and efficiency advantages; being attached to the pedals by a "ski-binding" type quick-release keeps your feet on the pedals when spinning fast or riding over bumpy terrain. Having a firm attachment to the pedals also allows a better pedaling style to develop, and is more efficient.

The soles of cycling shoes are very stiff to reduce foot fatigue and give more efficient power transfer but there are more flexible shoes available which are a bit more comfortable should it be necessary to walk any distance in them. Finally, cycling shoes tend to have Velcro closures which are safer than laces which can get caught in your drivetrain and cause a nasty accident.

Overshoes, made of neoprene or wind/waterproof fabrics, add the final touch of insulation for your feet during the winter months, when toes are particularly vulnerable to wind-chill.

GLOVES

Gloves are also recommended, enhancing the grip on the handlebars when the hands get hot and sweaty, and in the rain. They protect hands from brushing against trees etc and from gravel rashes during a fall. They vary from (fingerless) track mitts to full winter gloves and are available with or without padding. These days, with suspension forks being almost standard on mountain bikes, the padding function of gloves is not as important as grip.

DRESSING FOR THE WEATHER

In a day's off-road riding you may experience wind, rain, sun and extreme temperature variation as you change altitude and ride through sheltered and then exposed areas. There are many "technical" fabrics and garments, that are designed specially for these varying conditions.

During a ride, many adjustments to clothing may be necessary to maintain an optimum working temperature. There is a tendency to heat up on the climbs and cool down greatly on the descents. Temperature control is achieved through the use of zips, windproof, breathable and wickable technical clothing, and making use of the layering system.

THE LAYERING SYSTEM

The layering system is the term given to a flexible and practical clothing system to which adjustments can be made to allow for changes in both the weather and activity level. The system comprises of layers of clothing which can be put on or taken off depending on the conditions. There are three basic layers in this system and they are:

1. Base Layer
This layer is worn next to your skin and can make a big difference to your comfort. The base layer should be made from a fabric which transports (wicks) moisture away from your skin and helps to keep you dry and comfortable during and after activity. The best fabrics for the job are made from synthetic yarns which have been engineered for maximum performance and are of the type found in sports/thermal underwear.

2. Mid Layer
The mid layer function is to provide insulation from the elements. The most popular modern mid layers are constructed from fleece fabrics which are available in different weights. Fleece is not only extremely warm for its weight, but also allows moisture from the wearer to pass through it readily.

3. Shell Layer
The shell or outer layer is the barrier to both wind and rain. The most effective shell garments are constructed from waterproof and breathable fabrics with taped seams, which not only keep the rain out, but also allow vapour to escape. The price of a shell garment increases exponentially with the breathability of the fabric and the number of features (as each seam/zip has to be individually taped). Only vapour can pass through the fabric, not moisture, so the more breathable and well ventilated your jacket is, the less likely you are to suffer from condensation collecting inside it – it's worth spending the extra if you can afford it.

Access Rights & Responsibilities

By the end of this section Leaders should:

- State the current access legislation in Scotland and where to get information both locally and nationally
- Describe the responsibilities of a Leader when accessing the countryside
- Describe various land use/management practices and how these affect mountain bikers
- Be familiar with the Scottish Outdoor Access Code advice and good practice for off-road cycling
- Describe where to find more information on access, rights of way and off-road routes

INTRODUCTION

Mountain bikers, especially leaders of mountain bike groups, must show consideration for the environment and for others living and/or working in or using the outdoors for a wide variety of pursuits. Public perceptions of mountain biking as an activity which damages the environment and poses a safety hazard to other users may be largely unjustified, but they highlight the need for mountain bikers to demonstrate responsible behaviour at all time times. By doing mutual respect can be cultivated with other land users and the general public, and mountain biking can be shown to be conducted with courtesy and sensitivity. This is particularly important as the countryside comes under increasing recreational pressure and its users need to be sympathetic to environmental concerns and those whose livelihoods depend on the land.

There has been a strong tradition of recreational access to the outdoors in Scotland which has depended largely on the goodwill of land owners and the respectful conduct of walkers and others enjoying the countryside. This voluntary approach has had mixed success, and in some cases has led to a conflict of interest between different parties or even to criminal action.

This section seeks to explain the current access legislation in Britain, provides some guidelines on acting responsibly in accessing the countryside, and gives various sources of further information on access, rights of way and route-finding.

ACCESS AND THE LAW IN SCOTLAND

The **Land Reform (Scotland) Act 2003** has established statutory rights of access to most land and inland water for non-motorised outdoor recreation. These new rights, which are conditional on users behaving responsibly, came into effect on **9th February 2005**. Under section 10 of the Act, the **Scottish Outdoor Access Code** ("the Code") was drawn up by Scottish Natural Heritage who also have a duty to promote understanding of the Code. The Code provides detailed guidance on the responsibilities of those exercising access rights and of those managing land and water. The document is available from www.outdooraccess-scotland.com.

The Code is underpinned by three key principles:

SCOTTISH OUTDOOR ACCESS CODE

- **Take responsibility for your own actions**
- **Respect the interests of other people**
- **Care for the environment**

Some of the key information contained in the Code relating to off-road cycling is summarised in this section.

Everyone has access rights established by the Land Reform (Scotland) Act 2003 provided these rights are exercised responsibly. You have rights of access to be on and to cross over land and inland water for recreational, educational and certain relevant commercial activities. Access rights include off-road cycling, whether undertaken by individuals or groups or as a commercial activity, where that activity could be done by any member of the public exercising access rights. A Trail Cycle Leader or Mountain Bike Leader leading groups on identifiable tracks and trails as a commercial venture would be an example of this.

Access rights apply everywhere as long as they are exercised responsibly, but certain specified areas are excluded. The main exceptions include: houses and gardens, the curtilage of non-domestic buildings, compounds, building sites, demolition and engineering works, quarries and surface mineral workings, sports and recreational fields *while in use*, fields in which crops have been sown or are growing (but access around the field margins is allowed), schools and school grounds, places which charge for entry, and golf courses (except to cross them, although you should never cross greens or tees).

Access rights do not extend to allowing access for any criminal offences or activities, rather the Code should be seen as sitting alongside other legislation concerning behaviour that is classed as a statutory offence. A full list of relevant acts is contained in the SNH publication, "A Brief Guide to Laws Relevant to Outdoor Access in Scotland" (2007) which is available from their website www.snh.org.uk.

Byelaws, management rules or other regulations introduced by local authorities or other public bodies may prohibit or restrict access. For example, byelaws may be in place to protect local nature reserves, or to manage activities which could endanger public safety. Among the public bodies which can create byelaws are local authorities, national park authorities, Scottish Natural Heritage, Forestry Commission and British Waterways – this list should give you an idea of where byelaws might be encountered on land owned by or managed by these bodies. **Infringement of byelaws is a criminal offence.**

RIGHTS OF WAY

Public rights of way have been recognised in Scots law for centuries. A route established as a right of way under common law must connect two public places, follow a more or less defined route and have been used by the public by right for at least 20 years.

Many rights of way exist for walkers; comparatively few have been established for cyclists. Cycling is now considered a separate category of use, and as such, a route used by cyclists for 20 years or more could establish the right to use this route for cycling. Most rights of way in Scotland are not marked on Ordnance Survey maps or signposted, nor is there a legally recognised record of rights of way. The best record at national level is the **National Catalogue of Rights of Way** (CROW) which has been compiled by the Scottish Rights of Way and Access Society (Scotways), in partnership with SNH and local authorities. The latter hold copies of their local CROW record. All recognised public rights of way continue to exist under the Land Reform (Scotland) Act 2003. Where a public right of way passes over land excluded from statutory access rights, such as through a farmyard or field of crops, the route can still be used as a right of way.

CORE PATHS NETWORKS

Under the Land Reform (S) Act, each Local or National Park Authority in Scotland has to compile a **Core Paths Plan** of paths/tracks/trails 'sufficient for the purpose of giving the public reasonable access throughout their area' – which includes a reasonable amount of shared use. Currently Core Paths may not be ideally suited for mountain biking, but an opportunity exists for mountain bikers to influence such developments by getting involved in the planning process. Mountain bikers are encouraged to seek representation on their Local Access Forum which will provide an opportunity to advocate certain design standards of Core Paths for cycling and help address any access issues.

ACCESS LAW IN ENGLAND AND WALES

A different approach to access has been taken in England and Wales. The **Countryside and Rights of Way Act 2000** (CROW Act), the last phase of which came into force in England and Wales in May 2005, gives a new right of public access to "open country" and registered common land. The right includes activities such as walking, running and climbing, ***but does not extend to cycling***, horse riding or driving a vehicle without the prior permission of the land owner or occupier. However, the Act does improve public rights of way legislation, and recognises a new category of right of way called a "restricted byway" with rights for cyclists and horse riders. These access rights have been introduced in England and Wales on a regional basis with a consultation-led mapping of "open country" in each region. The Countryside Agency (now Natural England) and the Countryside Council for Wales have produced a Countryside Code to guide responsible use and management of countryside access – see www.countrysideaccess.gov.uk. The websites of Natural England and the Countryside Council for Wales (www.ccw.gov.uk) both have an on-line map feature showing all the Open Access land in England and Wales respectively; the Welsh maps also show cycleways and bridleways which can be accessed by bike.

Route/Trail	Map feature	On Ground	Access (1:50 000 unless specified)
Bridleway			An extensive network of tracks open to cyclists and horse riders
Byway (open to all traffic)	+-+-+-+-+-+		Open to all traffic, usually unsurfaced tracks. Contact the Byways & Bridleways Trust www.bbtrust.org.uk
Restricted byways			Has replaced "roads used as public paths" (RUPPs)
Towpaths			A British Waterways cycling permit is required by cyclists www.britishwaterways.co.uk
National/Regional Cycle Network			Mapped by Sustrans (see "Finding a Route" below)
Surfaced cycle route			
Off Road Cycle Route			Explorer Series 1:25 000 maps
Broken tracks	= = = = = =		Bikes allowed
Track	=========		Bikes allowed
Unclassified Road			May be narrow road with passing places
B Road			Bikes allowed
A Road			Bikes allowed

The current categories of routes which cyclists *can* access in England and Wales are shown in the table opposite with the map symbol feature as used on Ordnance Survey Landranger (1:50,000 scale) maps. The same features are shown on O.S. Explorer maps (1:25,000 scale), although the colouring used may be different. In addition, Explorer maps show "Off Road Cycle Routes" (marked with a line of orange dots).

EXERCISING ACCESS RIGHTS RESPONSIBLY

All leaders have a duty of care for themself and their group to ensure that the outdoor environment is accessed responsibly and safely. Remember that as a group you will have a greater impact than a solo rider and routes should be planned accordingly. Doing a site-specific **risk assessment** is recommended for every outing. Land managers responsible for the areas your group intends to use may be consulted.

In 2006 Scottish Cycling, in partnership with Scottish Natural Heritage, CTC Scotland and Sustrans, published a guidance leaflet on accessing the outdoors by bike, including a summary of the Scottish Outdoor Access Code's key advice for off-road cycling. Copies of the leaflet can be obtained from Scottish Cycling and the leaflet is available on-line to download at www.scottishcycling.com.

The key messages of the Scottish Outdoor Access Code fall under three headings:

Take responsibility for your own actions

SCOTTISH OUTDOOR ACCESS CODE

- Use common sense to avoid accidents - show care and consideration and make sure your speed doesn't alarm or endanger others
- The outdoors is not risk-free! Be aware of natural hazards such as cliffs, loose rocks, tree roots and ice
- Follow advice on signs advising of activities such as tree-felling, crop spraying or other land management operations - you may need to alter your route
- Take extra care if you are in charge of children to ensure they enjoy the outdoors responsibly and safely
- Take care not to alarm farm animals, including stock on open ground, horses and wildlife; take extra care during the lambing season
- If you have a dog with you, keep it under proper control at all times
- Avoid crossing land when shooting or deer stalking is taking place; try to find out if your planned route will be affected and take account of advice on alternative routes
- Keep access points clear; park your car where it won't cause problems and don't lock your bike to gates

Respect the interests of others

- Respect people's privacy by keeping a sensible distance from houses
- Keep noise levels and potential disturbance to a minimum, especially if riding at night
- Respect people's property, including machinery, gates and fences - leave gates as you find them
- Be considerate to other users of the outdoors such as walkers and horse riders; slow down and alert them to your presence. On narrow paths give way or dismount if necessary

Care for the environment

- Cycling on hard surfaces, such as wide paths and tracks, causes few problems. If going off-trail, especially in winter, avoid wet, boggy or soft ground and don't churn up the surface
- Take care not to disturb wildlife or damage natural vegetation; observe information or signs advising you of sensitive sites
- Take your litter away with you
- A group will have greater impact on the environment, so take extra care and set a good example if you are a Leader

HILLPHONES

Hillphones is a Scottish telephone answer-machine service which provides information on where deer stalking is taking place. The information is primarily aimed at walkers and climbers, but may also be useful to mountain bikers accessing the hills to plan routes avoiding stalking operations. The scheme originated in the Access Forum and is organised by SNH, the Mountaineering Council of Scotland and participating estates. There are some 13 areas where Hillphones operate, but these are by no means the full extent of deer stalking activity in Scotland.

The Hillphones service runs from 1st August to 31st October each year, covering the height of the deer stalking season. If a trip is planned in the hills during this period, it is strongly recommended that the appropriate Hillphone is called to check the location of stalking activities and which routes within the area are unlikely to be affected over the next few days. Stalking may take place any day of the week except on a Sunday.

For maps of the areas covered, a list of the Hillphone numbers and latest postings go to www.snh.org.uk/hillphones. It may be helpful to have a map available when calling the Hillphone.

WHERE TO GET MORE INFORMATION

i. Scotland

Information and advice on access rights and responsibilities, and on who to contact in your local authority is available at www.outdooraccess-scotland.com. You can also contact your local SNH office. The SNH e-mail address for access issues is recreationandaccess@snh.gov.uk.

Local Access Forums (LAFs) have been set up by all local and national park authorities to provide an opportunity for liaison between the public, local authorities and other bodies on any issues concerning the exercise of access rights, rights of way and the development of core path planning. More information about Local Access Forums can be found at www.outdooraccess-scotland.com or from your local authority.

The Paths for All website found at www.pathsforall.org/uk may also be helpful for those interested in paths close to where people live.

ii. England and Wales

Natural England www.naturalengland.org.uk or www.countrysideaccess.gov.uk and Countryside Council for Wales www.ccw.gov.uk carry equivalent information for England and Wales.

The Government Department for Environment Food and Rural Affairs (DEFRA) provides very accessible information on countryside legislation and explains how the Countryside and Rights of Way Act 2000 is being implemented: www.defra.gov.uk/wildlife-countryside/issues/index.htm.

Terrain & Route Selection

By the end of this section Leaders should be able to:-

- Describe the main types of terrain for mountain biking and their advantages and disadvantages
- Demonstrate knowledge of the current trail grading systems in use
- State clearly the terrain criteria for their level of award – TCL or MBL
- Explain how to make informed decisions about what type of terrain is suitable for a group

INTRODUCTION

The choice of terrain for mountain biking in Scotland, and many parts of the UK is very wide. Some classification of the main types of terrain, and of the current trail grading systems in use may be helpful to the leader in considering appropriate terrain to lead groups in.

BASIC TERRAIN TYPES

1. Forestry tracks

Forest plantations, the majority under Forestry Commission management, offer an extensive network of tracks throughout most areas of the UK. The Forestry Commission's website (www.forestry.gov.uk/cycling) has a searchable database of venues; this includes over 100 sites in Scotland alone. Forest or woodland of any type offers shelter from the elements and is usually rideable in almost any weather. Facilities such as car parks and picnic areas are often provided and can make a good place to rendezvous. There are usually a variety of tracks, from forest roads to narrow singletrack, offering a choice of routes of varying difficulty and length. Do bear in mind that forest operations may restrict access to some trails, and that unless otherwise signed, trails will be shared with other users.

2. Open hill country / moorland

In contrast to the forest environment, open hill country or moorland offers advantages of better views and visible navigation features in good

weather, but because of the greater exposure, this type of terrain can be unpleasant or even dangerous in poor weather. Navigation and visibility may be difficult if wet or misty, and the lack of shelter from wind and rain can compromise enjoyment and safety.

Tracks will vary from established paths to narrow sheep tracks, the latter sometimes appearing to be a good route choice, but often frustratingly petering out or disappearing under heather.

Leaders should be aware of access legislation, and respect advisory access restrictions for lambing, deer stalking etc. For more information on checking access restrictions during deer stalking see **Access Rights & Responsibilities**.

3. Shared / cycle-specific tracks / paths
This category covers all recognised routes accessible by bike, from canal tow paths, bridle ways, cycle paths and shared footpaths to minor roads. These routes offer easier riding conditions, with better surfaces, shallower gradients and wider tracks. However, other users must be respected and it may be better to seek quieter times or other areas for group riding. Each local authority in Scotland is compiling a **Core Paths List**, a network of routes which can be used for cycling, walking and other activities. Information on the quality of the riding surface, width, gradient etc of these Core Paths is not always available, but all should be rideable on a mountain bike, although perhaps not suitable for road bikes. For more information on Core Paths see **Access Rights & Responsibilities**.

4. Purpose-built cycle facilities
These include bmx parks, "closed road" circuits and skills loops which may be part of an outdoor centre or sports ground. These are ideal training venues for practicing core skills and offer a leader the chance to assess the abilities of group members. Check whether such facilities have to be booked in advance and what the conditions of use are. Leaders can also construct simple skills tests, as are used by some Tutors during SMBLA courses, using cones, poles etc. Examples of skills courses are shown in the pictures opposite.

TRAIL GRADING SYSTEMS

There are currently several trail grading systems in place, commonly using symbols and colour coding to indicate the difficulty of a trail. CTC, Forestry Commission and IMBA-UK all essentially use the same system, which grades trails as green, blue, red and black, progressing from "easy" to "severe". The descriptions for each grading category can be viewed at the websites of these respective organisations:

www.forestry.gov.uk
www.ctc.org.uk
www.imba-uk.com

However, the relative standards of a grading system may vary from area to area, or depending on the system used. Current signage may not always make a clear distinction between trails graded for cycling or those for walking, so the red cycling trail may be confused with the "red walking route", for example.

The Forestry Commission, in partnership with SMBLA, **sport**scotland, Scottish Natural Heritage, Cycling Scotland, Visit Scotland, International Mountain Bike Association UK and other countryside organisations, is working towards defining a national off-road trail grading standard which will bring consistency to trail grading throughout the UK. This standard will be applied to existing trails, and used to inform on trail building and trail management in Forestry Commission forests and other sites. It will provide mountain bikers, and particularly leaders of groups, with pre-defined information about routes which is consistent across all sites where the system is adopted.

Trail grading criteria are likely to include factors such as trail width, trail surface, average and maximum gradient, natural obstacles, technical trail features, length of trail and remoteness, as well as some indication of the level of skill and fitness required for each trail category. Improved interpretation and signage will make it easy to follow a trail and provide clear distinctions between designated cycle trails and paths marked for walking.

It is important to note, however, that trails are not graded with a view to leading a group down them, and leaders should follow the advice below when deciding on suitability of graded trails for their group.

GENERAL ADVICE ON TERRAIN SUITABILITY FOR GROUPS

Leaders will need to assess their group before taking them on a trail. **The ability of the group decides the terrain, not the ability of the leader**, however, both TCLs and MBLs must be fully aware of the terrain criteria which *limit* their scope of operation (see below).

Trail Cycle Leader

√ public highways, way marked routes, rights of way on which cycles are permitted, identifiable routes, tracks and trails with obvious navigational features

√ routes which are at least 90-95% rideable over their total length

√ terrain **no more than** 30 minutes walk **(or 2km whichever is the greater)** from either:

√ the nearest accessible road (suitable for ambulance access) or

√ a shelter from where it is possible to summon help

√ normal summer conditions, during daylight

√ multi-day trips where the group does not require to be self sufficient

Mountain Bike Leader

√ public highways, way marked routes, rights, of way on which cycles are permitted, identifiable routes, tracks and trails with obvious navigational features

√ routes which are at least 90-95% rideable over their total length

√ terrain **more than** 30 minutes walk from the nearest accessible (driveable) road, or shelter from where it is possible to summon help

√ any height above sea level

√ normal summer conditions, during daylight

√ multi-day trips where the group does not require to be self sufficient

SMBLA TERRAIN AWARD CRITERIA

A Trail Cycle Leader could act as an assistant to a Mountain Bike Leader in MBL terrain, and would be encouraged to do so to gain experience, with a view to attaining the next level of award.

TCL and MBL awards are valid in "normal summer conditions" only. The awards are *not* valid in winter unless the Leader has attended and passed the Winter Conditions module (see **Winter Conditions** for details). This module would enable them to work in defined 'intermediate' and 'winter' conditions, **but only in TCL terrain regardless of the level of award that they hold.**

It should be noted that part of leadership is deciding whether, in the prevailing conditions, a particular trail is suitable for the group being led, irrespective of whatever technical grading that trail might have been given. A guide book description, trail leaflet, or colour coding of a trail can **inform** a Leader but should not be used as a substitute for decision making based on personal experience. The **decision to take a group into any type of terrain, and onto a particular trail must remain with the leader**.

A Rider-defined Trail Definition model

Whereas a trail-grading system based on pre-defined physical criteria can be applied to man-made trails, and may be helpful to the leader in judging the difficulty of a trail in a particular site, what information can a leader use to assess trails in other areas where there is no such grading in place ?

The model below is based on rider-defined criteria and has proven to be a useful tool in assessing trail difficulty in any type of terrain. This model can be used in a number of ways as all the skills required for mountain biking can be condensed into four basic elements: **speed**, **balance**, **line-choice** and **power**. It has a built-in feedback loop: if you can control your speed, balance, power and line choice this will increase your confidence; as your confidence grows your control of these elements will also increase.

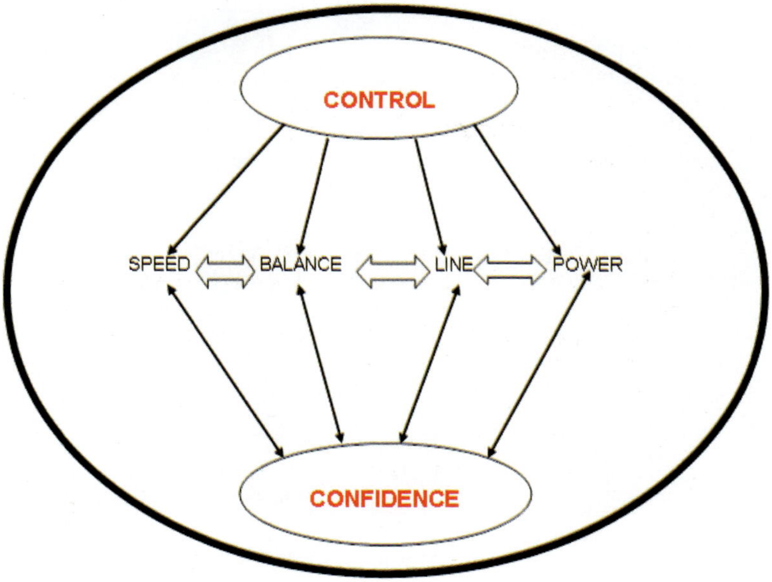

In practice the model is used to assess trail difficulty by scoring how many of the four elements a rider requires to complete a section of trail. If a rider has to be competent in one or two of the model's elements, this can be categorised as easy-moderate, and should be within the scope of that rider's ability. For example, a wide, smooth descent requires a rider to be able to control their speed and possibly understand or be able to weight shift (control balance), thus only two elements are used.

If a rider has to be competent in three or four of the above elements then that trail or section of trail is moderate-difficult and may be outwith the scope of a less experienced rider, but within the scope of a confident and experienced mountain biker. For example, a rolling section of single track littered with rocks and roots would require control of speed, balance, power and line choice.

The model encourages a leader to focus on the ability of the riders in the group when choosing suitable terrain, so echoing the advice given above, the starting point is always the abilities of the group, rather than the nature of the terrain.

As well as helping to match a group's ability to the terrain, the model also allows the leader to modify the degree of difficulty of a trail to meet the group's ability. For example, a twisty descent that requires control of speed, balance and line choice would be moderate-difficult, but if the leader stopped the group and walked them through that section pointing out the line as they went, that would remove the line choice element, so reducing the degree of difficulty of the trail.

Safety and planning

As well as requiring background knowledge of the group, terrain selection and route choice must employ the process of **risk assessment** (see section on **Hazards and Risk Management**). This may involve a specific risk assessment, pre-riding any routes you intend using to identify and record potential hazards, and controlling any risks to your group. If you are taking the group into new terrain, the minimum requirements are for a generic risk assessment, along with an ongoing dynamic risk assessment. As part of the planning process you should select one or more alternative routes, as well as short cuts which can be taken if you have to change your plans due to bad weather, group performance, lack of time or an emergency.

It goes without saying that as a leader you must always ride within your abilities to be able to manage a group off-road; you must have physical and mental energy in reserve to be able to move around the group, make decisions and maintain control of any situations which may arise. If the terrain is too challenging for you as the leader, your ability to lead effectively will be severely compromised. If a group's aim is to challenge their off-road skills on a particular trail, ask yourself honestly, are your own skills and fitness levels suited to this group's aim?

TERRAIN KNOWLEDGE

There are many practical ways to build up your knowledge of terrain and routes which will help you choose what is suitable for the groups you may be leading. You can develop your own database with notes describing terrain type, variation, route length, access points, shelters, riding surface in different weather conditions etc.

Some suggestions for developing terrain knowledge include:

- Personal riding experience
- Riding with a mountain bike club or group of experienced riders
- Assisting other leaders on group rides
- Accessing first hand information on particular routes, e.g. bike shops, bike cafes, mountain bike centres, blogs
- Trail literature, e.g. guidebooks, leaflets, maps
- Recording your own experiences, photographs and annotated maps
- Website information
- Complimentary outdoor activities, e.g. hill walking, orienteering

WHAT MAKES A GOOD TRAIL ?

Though often emotive and very subjective, this is a topic that the Leader should reflect upon. Understanding the basics of good trail design will help the Leader make informed choices to suit the needs of their groups and act as an advocate for better trail design and management.

The International Mountain Bicycling Association provide the best advice on good practice, providing design guidance booklets and information on their websites at:

www.imba.com
www.imba-uk.com

Sustainability is perhaps the most important principle for good trails. A sustainable trail will have the following properties:

- Supports current and future use with minimal impact to the area's natural systems
- Produces negligible soil loss and allows vegetation to inhabit the area
- Recognises that pruning or removal of certain plants may be necessary for maintenance
- Does not adversely affect native wildlife
- Requires little re-routing and minimal long term maintenance

Water management is the principal problem for many trails in the UK and the principal cause of erosion when allowed to channel or flow down the trail. Trails sited on the side of a slope, which drain well, are better than muddy trails at the bottom of the slope where all the water has collected.

Contour trails which gently traverse the hill or slope, with a surface that slopes slightly towards the low side, characterise a trail that stays dry and good to ride. Subtle undulations in a trail create grade reversals and grade dips that also defend against water damage by preventing it from tracking down the trail; they are also fun to ride.

Trail systems with loops are appealing because of the variety they can offer: easy and technically difficult trails, varying distances and different points of interest. The core of a trail system should comprise trails that are wide and smooth and appeal to a variety of users, with more difficult and technically demanding trails branching off the main system. A core trail which is the entrance to the system gets most use; branch loops become narrower and more challenging. Trails can vary from open and flowing to tight and technical. Good trails have a certain flow and rhythm where one turn blends into the next and every descent leads to another rise. Transitions between the different types of trail are important, to avoid cyclists having to brake hard and skid, causing trail damage and requiring additional trail maintenance.

Natural or established routes are likely to have evolved socially and established as Rights of Way, or may be estate roads and access routes for management purposes. It is unlikely that they will always follow the principles of good trail design with respect to cycling. Many of them rely on volunteer management in maintaining or improving these routes. Applying the principles of good trail design to such routes is likely to improve their sustainability and usability. Make sure you get landowner permission before undertaking any "trail improvements", or better still engage in some organised trail building which is a popular activity for groups of mountain bikers.

FINDING A ROUTE

There are many sources of information on suitable routes to ride off-road, for example guidebooks, websites and maps. Investing some time researching a good route when planning a trip is likely to be rewarded. See **Useful Contacts** for *Places to Ride* contact information. Cycle route information is becoming available at an increasing rate as the sport of mountain-biking grows and more and more people wish to access the countryside by bike. Some local councils now have cycle-route information on their websites and tourist information centres usually have leaflets and guidebooks covering parts of Scotland. A good starting point is Scotland's National Tourism Board's website www.visitscotland.com.

The **Cycling Scotland** website has a route-finder with a full description of each route, route-gradings, recommended maps and a list of features such as accommodation and cafés along the route: www.cyclingscotland.com.

The **Forestry Commission** actively encourages cycling in their forests, although forestry operations may restrict access to some routes at certain times. Their website contains descriptions of access points and routes for cycling in the majority of their sites across Scotland and the rest of Britain: www.forestry.gov.uk.

The **National Cycle Network** developed by Sustrans, links towns and cities across the UK using minor roads, cycle paths and other traffic-free routes. Some of these are ideal for leading groups of less experienced riders in non-challenging terrain. Sustrans' website contains maps and information on these routes, www.sustrans.org.uk.

The **CTC** (Cyclists' Touring Club) holds a large UK-wide database on cycle routes which can be accessed (by CTC members) on-line at www.ctc.org.uk or by contacting them to request route information sheets (cycling@ctc.org.uk).

Maps are essential to route planning and can offer alternatives if a planned route can not be followed on the ground. Britain's national mapping agency, Ordnance Survey, has maps covering the whole of Britain at the most popular 1:50,000 scale or at the smaller scale of 1:25,000 offering more detailed coverage. A limited number of OS maps can be obtained through the online get-a-map facility, www.get-a-map.co.uk. Not all cycle tracks are marked on OS maps, but this may become standard on 1:25,000 OS maps for paths which are on the **Core Paths List** (once this has been compiled by each Local Authority). See also **Access Rights & Responsibilities** section.

Mapping software is becoming an increasingly popular and valuable tool for route planning. Digital maps have the advantage of being seamless, i.e. having no edges, and offering the viewer the chance to see a virtual landscape in 3D. Anquet (www.anquet.co.uk), Memory-map (www.memory-map.co.uk) and Tracklogs (www.tracklogs.co.uk) digital mapping software are based on 1:50,000 and 1:25,000 OS maps and include such features as a gazetteer, 3D viewing, route planning tools and compatibility with GPS (Global Positioning System) navigation. Digital mapping products allow updated information on real-life and "virtual" features such as access changes to be available to users more rapidly than printed maps for which reprints take longer to appear.

Fuel & Hydration

***By the end of this section leaders should be able to*:**

- Explain the relative importance of the three main dietary food groups for cycling
- List good sources of carbohydrate and ways to increase carbohydrate intake
- Describe the importance of maintaining hydration and preventing dehydration
- Describe a refuelling strategy for recovery after a ride
- Demonstrate "good practice" in eating and drinking when leading a group

INTRODUCTION

It is now generally recognised that nutrition has a key role to play in influencing an athlete's ability to perform. The concept of optimal nutrition is not as clearly defined as one would imagine, though the basic concepts of good nutrition have remained strong for many years. When people are asked to define sports nutrition, often an image of pills and potions is conjured up; the truth is that optimal nutrition does *not* come in a bottle.

It is not within the scope of this manual to give a definitive guide to sports nutrition. This section will, however, give the sound building blocks of nutrition that you, as a leader and role model in mountain biking, can introduce to your groups. Correct fuelling and hydration are appropriate not only to the performance of the competitive athlete but to the enjoyment of the recreational cyclist as well, whatever their aspirations.

THE BASICS

Mountain biking is a very demanding sport, not only because of the stresses and strains it places on both upper and lower body, but also from the energy perspective. During a mountain bike race a cyclist can expend more than 11.7kcals per minute. For a recreational cyclist this figure would be lower, however compared to many other activities, mountain biking does expend large amounts of energy.

From a practical point of view the concept of energy balance is important to everyone. This is a very simple equation; if energy consumed is equal to energy expended then a person's weight will remain stable. If the energy consumed is less than is expended then a person will lose weight. The converse happens if energy consumed exceeds requirements. This is illustrated by the diagram on the following page.

Energy Balance: Energy Eaten = Energy Expended

ENERGY FOR HEALTH AND EXERCISE

The average daily food intake should provide 2000kcal of energy for females and 2550kcals of energy for males (Department of Health, 1991). A healthy, well-balanced diet must contain the correct amounts of essential nutrients and provide adequate energy.

In terms of providing the body with fuel, most calorie intake should come from carbohydrates, about 60-70% of daily intake, with protein 15-20% and fat 15-20%. In terms of the amount of energy or calories provided, fats are the most concentrated source of energy for their given mass. Fat provides more than double the calories per gram than carbohydrate, giving 9 kilocalories (kcals) per gram, whereas carbohydrate and protein give 4 kcals per gram.

Carbohydrate is the most important fuel for the working muscles and it should make up the bulk of your diet.

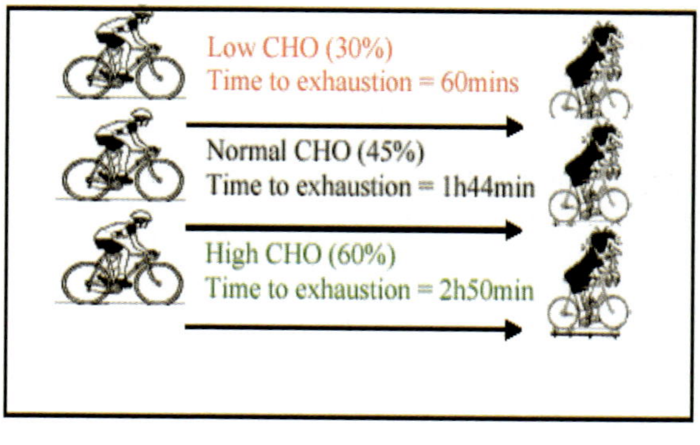

The Effect of Carbohydrate Intake on Cycling Performance

The diagram above illustrates a classic experiment that was conducted to show the effect of different levels of carbohydrate on time to exhaustion. On a diet low in carbohydrate (30% of total intake), the time to exhaustion when cycling is just 1h. With moderate carbohydrate (45%) the time increases to 1h 44 minutes, while a high carbohydrate diet extends the time to 2h 50 minutes.

CARBOHYDRATES

Carbohydrates can be classified into two groups - sugars (simple carbohydrates) and starches (complex carbohydrates). Simple carbohydrates are sweets, sugar, energy drinks, sweet cakes and pastries. They provide an immediate burst of energy, while complex carbohydrates like potatoes, rice, pasta, vegetables, grains and pulses release their energy over a longer period of time.

Carbohydrates are also referred to using the Glycaemic Index (GI) which relates to how quickly foods cause an increase in our blood glucose. GI is rated from 20-100, where 100 is pure sugar which causes a rapid increase in blood glucose, and foods with a GI of 20 have a much slower effect on blood glucose and allow a more sustained release of energy. To give an example, dried dates have a GI of 103, so if eaten on their own will cause a rapid increase in your blood glucose which is relatively short-lived. However, the GI of one food can be altered by eating other foods together with it, for example, by including other dried fruits such as apricots or figs, the combination of foods will lower the GI and keep you going for longer.

Carbohydrates are so important in sports performance because they are a limited source of readily available fuel which is stored in the muscles and liver as glycogen. The average person has approximately 2000kcals of energy stored in their muscles. When this limited source of energy becomes depleted it is often referred to as "hitting the wall" or "getting the knock".

In endurance sports like mountain biking, some muscle glycogen can be spared by providing an additional readily available energy source such as a carbohydrate drink or high carbohydrate snacks

The Balance of a Healthy Diet

The diagram above illustrates the types of foods, and the relative proportions of each, which make up a balanced diet. Fruit and vegetables and complex carbohydrates (the two biggest segments of the "pie") make up more than half, with smaller proportions of protein and fats.

GOOD SOURCES OF CARBOHYDRATE

Good sources of carbohydrate to provide energy for cycling include:

- ✓ Wholegrain breakfast cereals—porridge, muesli, Wheetabix, Oatabix, Special K, oatflakes
- ✓ Bread – all breads especially wholemeal, pitta, rolls, muffins, bagels
- ✓ Crackers—Ryvita, rice cakes, oatcakes
- ✓ Pasta – all varieties
- ✓ Rice – brown & white
- ✓ Potatoes – including sweet potatoes, boiled, mashed, baked. Roast potatoes or chips are high in fat and less suitable
- ✓ All types of beans – baked, kidney, black eye, butter beans
- ✓ All pulses - lentils, peas, chickpeas, barley
- ✓ Fruit – fresh, dried, canned, frozen, juiced, smoothies
- ✓ Vegetables all types – frozen or fresh
- ✓ Cakes – although some are high in fat. Low fat options include fruit cakes, malt loaf, scones, gingerbread, pancakes
- ✓ Biscuits – low fat options include Rich Tea biscuits, plain Digestives, Fig Rolls, Ginger Nuts, Jaffa Cakes
- ✓ Low fat puddings – fruit crumbles, baked fruit, bread puddings, custard, rice pudding
- ✓ Cereals bars – some are high in fat, sports bars are best (look for less than 10% fat)

If exercising regularly, and especially when planning an extended day's bike ride or several consecutive days biking, carbohydrate intake should be increased in order to keep muscles well fuelled and allow good recovery. It is often easy to underestimate the amounts of carbohydrates which have to be consumed for cycling, especially by those who are newcomers to the sport.

Below are some practical hints for increasing carbohydrate intake.

- ✓ Eat plenty of bread and cut thicker slices
- ✓ Try different types of bread
- ✓ Be continental by having bread with meals as well as rice, pasta or potatoes
- ✓ Add beans, chickpeas, lentils or broth mix to soups tomato sauces and salads
- ✓ Breakfast cereals are a good source of carbohydrates and can be eaten at any time of the day
- ✓ Add fresh or dried fruit to breakfast cereal
- ✓ Snack on fruit scones/breads or toast with jam or honey
- ✓ Make starchy foods the main items in each meal, together with plenty of fruit and vegetables

DIETARY FATS

Fat is also essential for a balanced diet. As well as providing energy for endurance exercise and helping to keep us warm, it provides a medium for allowing various micronutrients into the body.

Unlike glycogen, fat storage is not a limiting factor for exercise. Even the leanest of athletes has a large reserve of fat for energy, so there is no need to consume a lot of fat. Aim for around 15-20% of total dietary energy to be from fat. A low-fat high-carbohydrate diet is best for both health and performance. Of fat intake the proportion of poly- and mono-unsaturated fat (sunflower and olive oils, raw nuts and seeds and their oils, and oily fish should be higher than saturated fats like lard, processed meats, cakes, biscuits, pastries and fried foods). Also be aware of "hidden" fats as these are often saturated (e.g. creamy and buttery sauces, mayonnaise-type dressings, pastries, cheesy foods and the above mentioned foods). Avoid hydrogenated fats as these are chemically altered and behave just like saturated fats in the body, and are again found in processed and convenience foods.

PROTEIN

Protein is made up of small building blocks called amino acids some of which can be manufactured by the body and some of which are essential and must be provided by dietary sources. Good sources of protein are meat, fish, dairy produce, seafood, tofu, eggs, soya, quorn and pulses.

One of the most common myths is that sports people who exercise regularly require extra protein in their diets. The scientific evidence to date suggests that this is not the case and that the very small increase in protein requirements is easily met by the protein intakes in most diets. Therefore dietary supplementation is not required or recommended.

Strict vegetarians or vegans need to ensure a good variety of protein foods as no single (non-animal) food contains all of the essential amino acids.

FLUID AND EXERCISE

The body produces heat as a result of exercise and to dissipate this heat the body sweats. A lot of fluid can be lost by sweating and through respiration, especially when exercising hard and/or in hot conditions. It is especially important to be aware of this in children who might not know the importance of hydration or the symptoms of becoming dehydrated.

When the body starts to dehydrate several functions are compromised; severe dehydration results in death. **Losing even 2% of body weight in fluid, about 1.5 kg, can impair performance by as much as 10-20%**. The ability to keep riding, to co-ordinate movement and maintain concentration are all reduced with even mild dehydration. This is potentially dangerous when mountain biking and could lead to loss of control and at worst an accident.

A leader should be able to recognize the symptoms of dehydration:

- Light-headedness
- Weakness
- Nausea
- Headache
- Muscle cramps

Preventing dehydration is much easier than trying to cure it. The advice which follows explains how to avoid dehydration occurring.

PRACTICAL ADVICE FOR STAYING HYDRATED

- ✓ It is vital to be well-hydrated prior to exercise – pale and plentiful urine indicates a good level of hydration
- ✓ Aim for a minimum of 2 litres a day, starting the day with a big glass of water or fruit juice
- ✓ Alcohol is NOT a suitable fluid, it acts as a diuretic (makes you pass more urine) so save it for post-event celebrations!
- ✓ Reliance on tea, coffee and caffeinated soft drinks (like Coke) for hydration is not recommended as again they have a diuretic effect. Try using de-caffeinated varieties
- ✓ Try drinking fluid immediately before starting to cycle and continue to drink small amounts regularly throughout the ride
- ✓ Get used to drinking during training sessions or solo rides and only use the drinks you are used to
- ✓ Thirst is NOT a good indicator of hydration – by the time you feel thirsty you are already dehydrated
- ✓ Remember that as soon as the ride is over it is essential to rehydrate and begin replenishing glycogen stores to promote good recovery. A good sports drink, smoothie or fruit juice is ideal

FLUID REPLACEMENT

Water is adequate fluid replacement in some situations (where sweat loss is minimal), but when sweating a lot or after a longer ride drinks containing some carbohydrate and electrolytes are better.

Suggestions for replacing fluid during and after exercise include:

- ✓ Water (still / mineral / plain tap water)
- ✓ 4-8g glucose powder or glucose polymer (maltodextrin) per 100ml water + pinch of salt (makes a 4-8% solution)
- ✓ Fruit juice (one part) diluted with water (2 parts) with a pinch of salt
- ✓ Fruit cordials diluted with water and a pinch of salt
- ✓ Carbohydrate drink (e.g. Lucozade, High-5, SIS PSP22, Gatorade)
- ✓ Isotonic drink (e.g. SIS GO Electrolyte, Isostar, Lucozade Hydrate)

Note: it is important to observe the dilution factor when making up carbohydrate drinks, as a solution which is too concentrated will delay hydration as the body can not absorb the fluid from the stomach fast enough. For rehydration, solutions should be *no more than* 10% strength (i.e. 10g carbohydrate in 100 ml or 100g in 1 litre).

You can weigh yourself before and after exercise to see how much fluid you are losing.

Weight lost in kg x 1.5 = number of litres of fluid needed to rehydrate

For example:

Pre exercise weight = 70kg
Post exercise weight = 69kg
Loss of 1kg in weight
1kg X 1.5 = 1.5 litres of fluid needed to rehydrate.

During a ride it is important to maintain hydration by having regular drinks breaks, especially for less experienced riders who may not be in the habit of taking on enough fluid on the go. A leader must take responsibility for ensuring everyone drinks enough to be able to cope with the day's ride and avoid the risk of dehydration.

Aim to consume 1 litre each for every hour of riding, or up to 2 litres in hot weather or strenuous riding. This represents 1 large or 2 small sized water bottles or a full hydration bladder which can be worn on the back or stored in a rucksack. The latter makes taking regular sips easier, especially when mountain biking, as only one hand is off the handlebars briefly. If enough fluid can not be carried for the intended duration of the ride, plan places where fresh supplies can be obtained.

Decide if the length and demands of the route require additional fuel, a particularly important consideration when leading children as their glycogen storage is considerably less than an adult's when relative muscle sizes are compared.

As a leader it is important that you maintain your own fluid and fuel intake. If you fail to do this then your concentration, perception and judgement can be impaired as a result of dehydration and fuel depletion, thus compromising your group's safety.

In summary, being properly fuelled and maintaining hydration can enhance both your and your group's enjoyment of a ride. A well fed and watered group is a happy one!

REFUELLING

After exercising there is a window of opportunity to refuel your muscles, often known as the "glycogen window". This window last for about 2 hours and it is when the muscles can replace glycogen (muscle carbohydrate stores) at double the rate it can normally. It is therefore very important to eat the correct foods and in the correct quantities during this time, especially when you will be riding again later in the day or the following day. The graph below illustrates the effect of exercise on muscle glycogen.

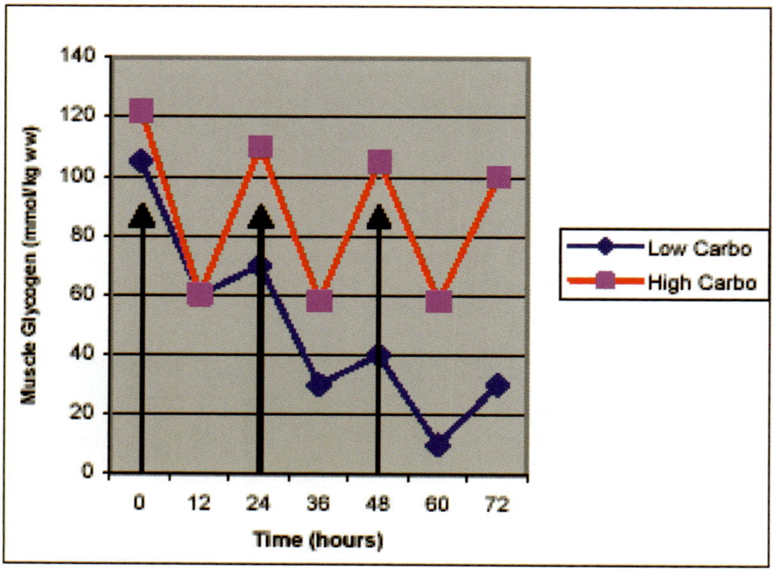

The Effect of Exercise on Muscle Glycogen (Costill et al ,1980)

It is clear that after each period of exercise (illustrated by the black arrows) muscle glycogen is depleted. On successive days of exercise the graph shows that even with immediate and appropriate refuelling (high carbohydrate) it becomes difficult to fully replenish your glycogen stores. This is why it is so important to start refuelling as soon as possible after the activity has finished. With a low carbohydrate diet the depletion of muscle glycogen is even more drastic and progressive increasing susceptibility to injury, fatigue, illness and poor performance the following day.

If possible, it is a good idea to top up glycogen levels during activity. Some examples of good snacks that can be eaten during activity are fruit (fresh or dried), sport/cereal bars and sandwiches. Energy drinks will supply a readily absorbed source of carbohydrate, however it is important not to make these too strong, as too concentrated a solution will compromise hydration.

When activity ends try to eat as soon as possible and practical. Often people do not feel hungry immediately after exercise as the hormone adrenaline, which is secreted during exercise, remains high for a time after exercise has finished. However, it is important to teach the body to accept food gradually or try using smoothies, fruit juices and sports drinks to get some easily digestible carbohydrate into the body. Foods that are high in carbohydrates and low in fat are best.

Examples of foods good for refuelling are:

- ✓ Fruit, especially bananas and dried fruit
- ✓ Fruit juice and smoothies
- ✓ Sandwiches with fillings such as honey, banana or tuna
- ✓ Breakfast cereals
- ✓ Toast with fruit spreads or honey
- ✓ Jaffa cakes, Fig Rolls, low-fat cereal bars
- ✓ Pasta with low fat sauce
- ✓ Soup with bread/rolls
- ✓ Scones, pancakes, fruit breads, crumpets

GUIDELINES TO REFUELLING

Start refuelling as soon as possible after activity has stopped. Plan ahead and have suitable food and drinks available at base or in your vehicle. Carbohydrate drinks and sugary food may provide a practical and compact carbohydrate source. Small frequent meals may assist in achieving a high carbohydrate intake. Alcohol is *not* recommended to refuel the body, if planning to consume alcohol then make sure that the refuelling and rehydration process begins first.

PUTTING IT ALL TOGETHER

- **Increase intake of carbohydrate rich foods**
- Bread, rice, pasta, noodles, corn, potatoes, oats, breakfast cereals, fruit and fruit juice

- **Eat a variety of protein foods**
- Lean meat, poultry, fish, pulses (peas, beans, lentils), nuts, seeds, eggs, reduced fat milk, cheese, tofu, quorn

- **Increase intake of fruit and vegetables**
- Aim for at least 5 portions of fruit or vegetable (not including potatoes). This includes fresh, frozen, tinned, juiced and dried, but must be from different sources, so 5 glasses of orange juice is just one portion!

- **Be properly hydrated before exercise**
- Thirst is a poor indicator of dehydration, so keep drinking during exercise

- **Rehydrate and refuel as soon as possible after exercise**
- Maximise recovery by consuming high carbohydrate foods and plenty of fluids

VITAMINS AND MINERALS

With a well-balanced healthy diet, supplementation with vitamins or minerals should not be necessary. Although supplement manufacturers offer all sorts of claims, including that they can increase physical performance, prevent injuries, provide more energy or build muscles, *excess* vitamins or minerals will offer no competitive edge.

There are two classes of vitamins – water soluble and fat soluble. People often imagine that taking in extra vitamins is beneficial, or at least harmless. In fact, large doses of fat soluble vitamins are not eliminated from the body and can be toxic. Both classes of vitamins may cause gastro-intestinal upsets and so could potentially have a detrimental effect on health and performance.

The same advice is largely true for mineral supplementation, the possible exceptions being iron, especially in females, and minerals which are required for healthy bones (principally calcium and magnesium).

Unless a medical condition or an illness causes susceptibility to vitamin or mineral deficiency, taking supplements as an "insurance policy" is not advisable. Anyone who thinks they may be suffering from a vitamin or mineral deficiency should seek medical advice, or consult a dietician who can carry out dietary analysis.

Many people lack confidence that their diet is always well-balanced. Hectic lifestyles can leave little time and energy to shop, cook and eat properly. However, with a little thought and organization it should be possible to eat healthily and support a high level of activity.

PRACTICAL TIPS FOR THE GROUP

Get a good breakfast

Breakfast is essential to set you up for the day. Blood sugar levels fall overnight and need to be topped up upon waking. Eating a hearty breakfast of cereals, porridge, toast, fruit and plenty of fluid will boost energy levels for several hours' riding.

Out on the trail

Each individual should have their own fluid supply. If the bikes have bottle cages fitted then each person should have their own bottle; if not they should be carrying a hydration bladder in their rucksack.

Everyone should also carry some snack food, whether that is a sandwich, muesli bar or dried fruit, even on a short ride. If an emergency occurs, returning to base could be delayed and this will lead to people getting hungry, a situation which is going to hamper the recovery plan. On longer rides or expeditions a leader must plan how much food will be required so that everybody has sufficient rations.

Setting a good example

As the leader, you are setting an example with what you choose to eat and what you do out on the trail. Out on a ride, when the leader has a drink or something to eat often the group does the same. A leader who chooses bananas or dried fruit rather than a bar of chocolate (less good as an energy source) may influence others to do likewise. So set an example of good practice.

Food and fluid stops are an opportunity to talk about nutrition. Explain the importance of fluids and make sure the participants are eating sufficient to provide enough energy for the day's activity. There is no need to go into great detail about diet; just highlighting the importance of nutrition and possibly talking about the importance of starchy foods like bread, potatoes, pasta and rice along with eating plenty of fruit and vegetables will get the group to think about what they are eating.

Be aware of individual's needs and monitor the group

Remember that everybody is different with respect to food and fluid requirements. Some people are very tolerant of sugary foods, for example, some are not, so monitor the group and look out for signs of hypoglycaemia or low blood glucose - a condition in which the level of glucose (sugar) in the blood, drops below normal levels. Exercise lowers the blood glucose level but will normally not cause hypoglycaemic episodes in otherwise healthy people. For people prone to hypoglycaemia during exercise it is especially important to eat some low GI carbohydrates before exercising (e.g. apples, oranges or baked beans), and to consume moderate to high GI carbohydrates during exercise (e.g. bananas or cereal bars).

Hypoglycaemia and diabetes should be covered within a first aid course. The Leader should always have prior knowledge of any medical conditions such as diabetes within a group (see **Planning & Group Management**).

People will have varying knowledge of sports nutrition and it is important that as the leader that you lead by example. Sport is an excellent way to encourage people to change dietary habits for the better and of course to get fitter! Remember to look out for changes in behaviour that might be attributed to lack of fuel or fluids.

Catering

Some outdoor centres do not always have an understanding of what food is required for outdoor groups as many have come from mainstream catering. So give them a helping hand by making suggestions of what meals and snacks are suitable for your activity in advance. You can influence what is provided.

References

Bergstrom J., Hermansen L., Hultman E., Saltin B. Diet, muscle glycogen and physical performance. Acta Physiologia Scandica 1967; 71: 140-50.

Costill D.L. & Miller J.M. Nutrition for endurance sport: CHO and fluid balance. International Journal of Sports Medicine 1980; 1: 2-14.

Leadership Skills & Styles

By the end of this section all candidates should be able to:

- Describe different leadership approaches
- Describe how these approaches affect the ways in which people learn

***By the end of the TCL course leaders should be able to*:**

- Effectively apply the Action Centred leadership model

***By the end of the MBL course leaders should additionally be able to*:**

- Effectively apply the Hersey Blanchard situational leadership model

WHAT IS A LEADER?

A Leader is someone who exercises a definite and particular role in relation to others

A Role is a set of expected behaviours associated with a position in a group

A leader will have a range of skills or general functions specifically pertinent to effective leadership. The more important of these are:

- Responsibility
- Control
- Care
- Support
- Setting and maintenance of standards and limits
- Decision making
- Sustaining the group's energy
- Engagement and commitment of personal energy to the group's aims
- Awareness of and responsiveness to one's own feelings, wants and needs, and those of the group as individuals and as a whole

To carry out these functions effectively a leader needs to be able to call on a range of both technical and relationship skills. The technical skills are presented in the other modules of this manual. Some of the more important "people skills" are trainable and can be acquired to assist the leader in performing their role. These skills should be developed from conscious skills into ingrained habits (i.e. from awareness phase through practice phase until they are acquired).

LEADERSHIP QUALITIES

Leading skills can be viewed along a spectrum, where at one end all responsibility rests with the leader, and at the other end, decision making is devolved to the learner. As the relationship between the leader and group develops it becomes possible, sometimes necessary or desirable, for the leader to use alternative ways of exercising control.

The leader has to decide which particular approach to use. Leadership is an interactive, two-way process involving both the leader and the learner in decision making and responsibility.A leader requires a wide range of competencies to fulfil the role successfully. The Leadership Competencies list on the following page shows a "top 10" of the skills, behavioural qualities and knowledge which candidates felt were important to the role of Trail Cycle Leader. Candidates on a training course will be asked to fill in a similar sheet . An example of a skill might be "Navigation", behaviour qualities might be "calm in a crisis" and knowledge might include "awareness of access issues".

LEADERSHIP MODELS

There are a number of leadership models which have been used in leadership training. They have become more generally known in outdoor activities since the late 1970's. They are helpful and useful as aids to help leaders to think and develop their own ideas about leadership.

Two models of leadership are described; you will be introduced to one at each level (TCL and MBL) of the award. The first one, "The Action Centred Leadership Model", is included as an early aid for Trail Cycle Leaders. Generally, inexperienced "leaders", "coaches" and "teachers" can easily focus most of their attention on the task rather than on other leadership functions.

SKILLS	BEHAVIOUR/ QUALITIES	KNOWLEDGE
Planning	People Skills	Underpinning Knowledge
Bike Skills	Patience/Tolerance	Health and Safety
Navigation	Motivational/ Enthusiastic	Routes and Terrain
Teaching	Sense of Humour	Weather
Organisational	Confidence	Research
Delegation	Empathy/Compassion	Group Dynamics
Decision Making	Observant	Access
Communication	Good listener	Conservation
Group Control/ Management	Flexibility	Emergency Procedures
Emergency repairs	Judgement	Hazard Awareness
First Aid	Trust	Repairs
Teambuilding	Self Discipline	Risk Assessment
Goal Setting	Responsibility	Escape Routes
Incident Management	Assertiveness	Leadership Styles
Judgement	Calm in Crisis	Fitness
Motivation	Sense of Fun	Nutrition
Leadership	Time Management	Clothing
Bike Maintenance	Sensitivity	Local Routes
Road Safety	Problem Solving	N.G.B.
Risk Assessment	Well Prepared	Natural History
	Diplomatic	Working with Children
	Honesty	Highway Code
	Communication	Environmental Protection
	Approachable	Setting up Bike
	Role Model	Relevant Legislation
		Flora/Fauna
		Bike Maintenance
		Local History
		Local Geography
		Cadence
		First Aid
		Rules/Bye-laws

TCL

LEADERSHIP MODEL 1 – The Action Centred Leadership (TCL)

John Adair suggests that the three main aspects a leader will constantly have to keep in mind and cope with to achieve a particular task are:-

- The Task
- The Team
- The Individual

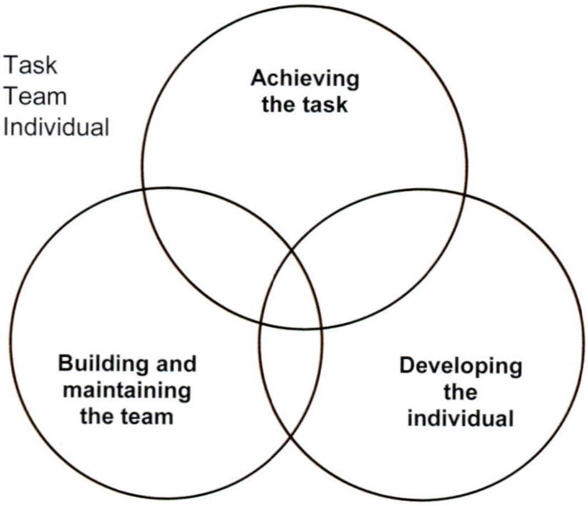

Adair's Action-Centred Leadership Model

This model should be used following a period of leadership to check where the leader's focus of attention has been. Over a period of time (e.g. a half or whole day session) it would be expected that a leader would spread their focus between the task, the team and the individual.

All three areas should be regarded as interlinked in that an over-concentration on one will be to the detriment of the other two. For example, a single-minded concentration by the leader on the task is likely to result in a breakdown of communication with the group. Conversely, concentrating too much on individuals within the group could mean that the attainment of the group's goal is put in jeopardy or never achieved.

This model provides one way for the leader to identify and decide which of the three areas most requires immediate attention in a working situation.

The following checklists are designed to help apply the 3 areas of the leader's responsibility.

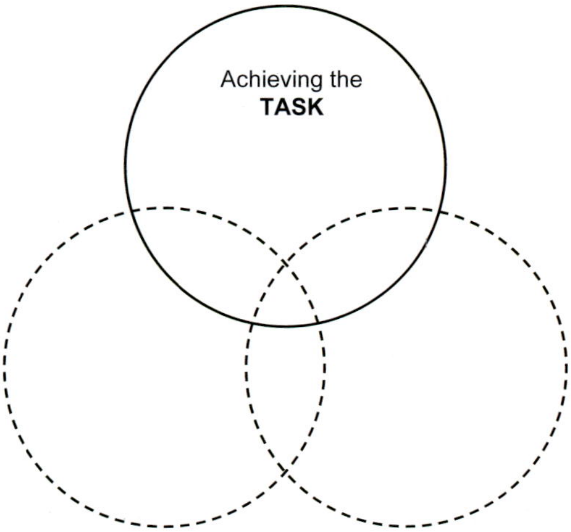

TASK

Purpose:	Am I clear what the task is?
Responsibilities:	Am I clear what mine are?
Objectives:	Have I agreed these with the person accountable for the group?
Programme:	Have I worked one out to reach objectives?
Working Conditions:	Are these right for the job?
Resources:	Are these adequate?
Targets:	Has each member clearly defined and agreed them?
Authority:	Is the line of authority clear?
Training:	Are there any gaps in the specialist skills or abilities of individuals in the group required for the task?
Priorities:	Have I planned the time available?
Supervision:	In case of my absence who covers for me?
Example:	Do I set standards by my behaviour?

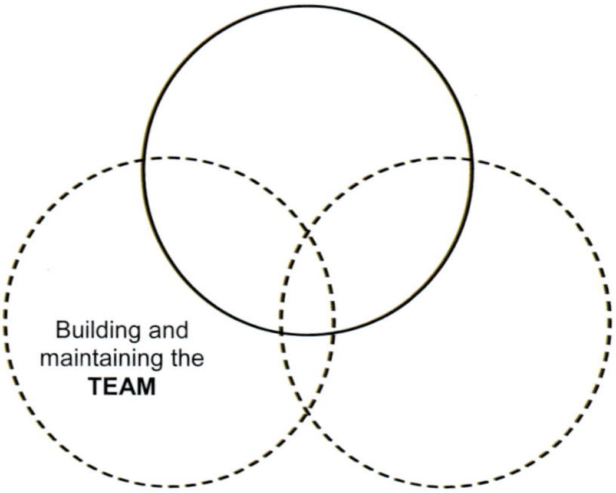

TEAM

Objectives:	Does the team clearly understand and accept them?
Standards:	Do they know what standards of performance are expected?
Safety Standards:	Do they know the consequences of infringement?
Size of Team:	Is the team size correct?
Team Members:	Are the right people working together? Is there a need for subgroups to be formed?
Team Spirit:	Do I look for opportunities for building teamwork into jobs? Do methods of instruction help to develop team spirit?
Discipline:	Are the rules seen to be reasonable? Am I fair and impartial in enforcing them?
Grievances:	Are grievances dealt with promptly? Do I take action on matters likely to disrupt the group?
Consultation:	Is this genuine? Do I encourage and welcome ideas and suggestions?
Briefing:	Is this regular? Does it cover current plans, progress and future developments?
Representation:	Am I prepared to represent the feelings of the group when required?
Support:	Do I encourage individuals when the team is not working well together?

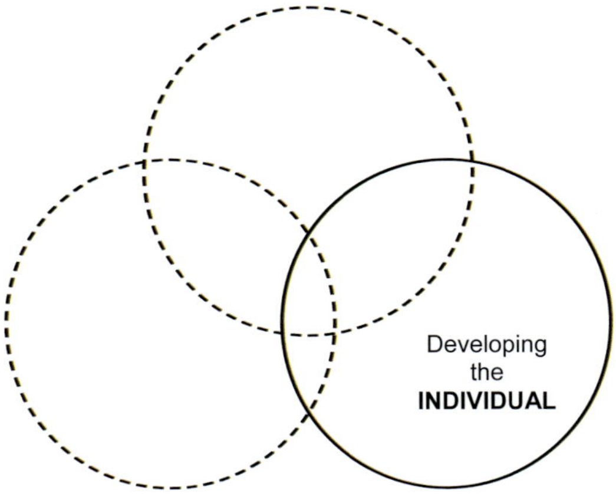

INDIVIDUAL

Targets:	Have they been agreed and quantified?
Achievement:	Does he/she know how his/her work contributes to the overall result?
Responsibilities:	Has he/she got a clear and accurate job? Can I delegate more to him/her?
Authority:	Does he/she have sufficient authority for his/her task?
Training:	Has suitable training been provided ?
Recognition:	Do I emphasise people's successes? In failure, is criticism constructive?
Growth:	Does he/she see the chance of development? Does he/she see some pattern of improvement?
Reward:	Are work, capacity and reward in balance?
The person:	Do I know the person well? What makes him/her different from others?
Time/Attention:	Do I spend enough time with individuals, listening, developing, counselling?
Grievances:	Are these dealt with promptly?
Security:	Does he/she know about safety arrangements?
Appraisal:	Is the overall performance of each individual regularly reviewed?

OBSERVATION OF THE LEADER

One way of helping course members develop their awareness of leadership behaviour is to review a session after someone has been leading the group. Imagine there are 100 points to be allocated amongst the three overlapping circles. How many points would be allocated to each one?

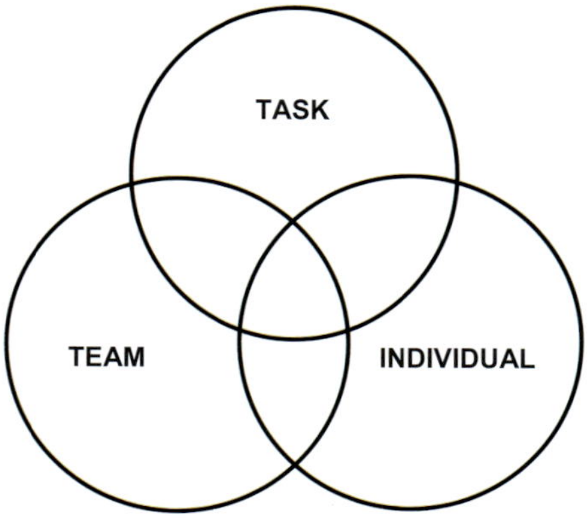

If the leader focused largely on one task to the exclusion of the other two areas, most of the points would be allocated there. If there was equal emphasis then the points should be spread more evenly between the three circles. Reviewers should be able to justify their allocation of points by giving clear examples of how the **task** was achieved, how each **individual** was developed and how the **team** was built and maintained. If the leader had decided, or was required, to focus on one particular area and this was also highlighted in the way the group allocated their 100 points then clearly the intention of the leader will have been successful. This method of review can identify mismatches where a leader thinks they are operating in a particular way but this is not actually what is perceived by the group.

During a period of leadership, all three areas would be expected to have received a balance of the leader's attention.

ASSESSING LEADERSHIP ABILITY

An attempt has been made to create a tool for assessing leadership competence. This was prepared for the SMBLA when it began mapping TCL competencies to National Occupational Standards. The table on the following two pages is set out in that style, where the unit of "leadership" is expanded into 6 key elements. Each element has performance criteria which should be achieved before the unit of leadership can be passed. This work is presented to assist in understanding of the leadership competence required to undertake any leadership role whether it is on a bike or under other circumstances.

LEADERSHIP ELEMENTS	PERFORMANCE CRITERIA
1. Managing a Group Safely and Effectively	1. Obtains sound relationship 2. Takes sensible decisions on safety 3. Keeps control 4. Keeps everyone informed 5. Keeps in touch with whole group
2. Making Decisions	1. Considers all relevant factors 2. Doesn't avoid difficult/unpopular decisions 3. Listens to opinions when relevant 4. Is decisive when required 5. Consults as appropriate
3. Setting and Maintaining Standards	1. Establishes ground rules 2. Enforces ground rules 3. Leads by example
4. Using a Range of Styles	1. Selects style appropriate to circumstances 2. Exhibits use of range of styles
5. Showing Concern for the Group	1. Reach agreement on objectives 2. Encourage group to work together 3. Involve everyone 4. Control the group
6. Achieving the Task	1. Be successful in achieving objective 2. Work to the plan 3. Take the whole group along 4. Keep to time

LEADERSHIP MODEL 2 – Situational Leadership (MBL)

For years, when people talked about leadership style, they identified two extremes – an autocratic (directive) leadership style and a democratic (supportive) leadership style. Autocratic leaders used position, power and their authority to get results, while democratic leaders used personal power and involved others in participative problem-solving and decision-making processes.

Hersey and Blanchard in "Leadership and Administration of Outdoor Pursuits" by Phyllis Ford and James Blanchard (1985), tell us that the continuum between human relationships and the accomplishment of tasks, one's leadership style, will depend on two variables: the *level of maturity* of the group of followers and the *demands of the situation*.

The *demands of the situation* relate to the task to be accomplished. In outdoor pursuits the situation may range from formal to informal, tense to relaxed, dangerous to safe. It may demand a great amount of leader control or little or no control.

Situation demands little leader control	Situation needs some leader control	Situation demands complete leader control
Cycling in playground, checking that bike gears are working	Cycling at moderate speeds along an easy trail	Descending a steep rocky section of single track trail

Further research showed that leadership styles tend to vary considerably from situation to situation, and that it is not helpful to think of leadership style as an *either/or* continuum. While the behaviour of some leaders is characterised mainly by directing their followers' activities in terms of task accomplishment (directive behaviour), other leaders concentrate on providing socio-emotional support and on building personal relationships between themselves and their followers (supportive behaviour). In other situations, various combinations of directive and supportive behaviour are evident. Thus, it was determined that directive and supportive leader behaviours are not either/or leadership styles. Instead, these patterns of leader behaviour can be plotted on two separate and distinct axes.

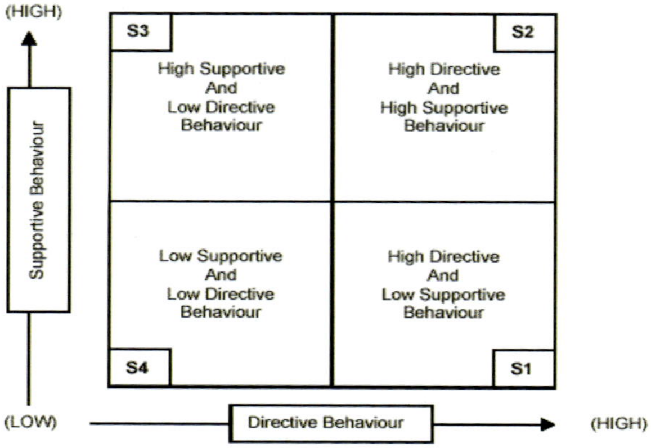

Figure 1.

DIRECTIVE AND SUPPORTIVE LEADER BEHAVIOURS

MBL

Directive behaviour is defined as:
The extent to which a leader engages in one-way communication; spells out the follower(s) role and tells the follower(s) what to do, where to do it, when to do it and how to do it; and then closely supervises performance.

Three words can be used to define directive behaviour: structure, control, supervise.

Supportive behaviour is defined as:
The extent to which a leader engages in two-way communication, listens, provides support and encouragement, facilitates interaction and involves the follower(s) in decision making.

Three words can be used to define supportive behaviour: praise, listen and facilitate.

In *style 1* (S1) (figure 1.) a leader is high on direction, low on support. He/she defines roles and goals, provides specific instruction to the follower(s), and closely supervises task accomplishment. When using *style 2* (S2) the leader is high on both direction and support. He or she explains decisions and solicits suggestions from the follower(s), but continues to direct task accomplishment. *Style 3* (S3) leader behaviour is characterised by high supportive low directive behaviour. The leader and follower(s) make decisions together and then the leader supports the followers' efforts toward task accomplishment. In *style 4* (S4), a leader provides low support and direction. He or she turns over decisions and responsibility for implementation to the follower(s)

Styles of Leadership

Each of the four leadership styles outlined above can be identified with a different approach to problem solving and decision making as illustrated by the diagram below.

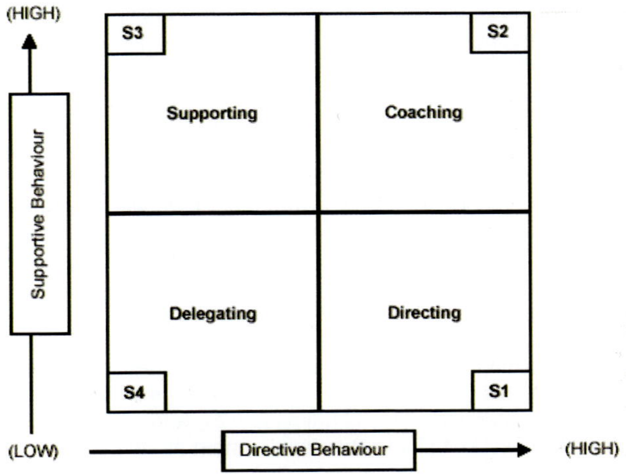

Figure 2.

The styles of leadership model explanations are amended and reproduced with the author's permission from "Leading and Managing Groups in the Outdoors", by Ken Ogilvie.

S1- Directing High directive/Low supportive leader behaviour
This style is well illustrated in the early stages of a group's life when the members are uncertain of each other, not too sure about the leader and a bit hazy about the objective. The important thing is to get the task moving by feeding in much information and perhaps imparting a lot of skill. In this situation the leader will be doing a lot of telling and directing and staying in charge. Personal feelings and group needs will be secondary to the achievement of the task. Emergencies would come into this category. The maturity (development stage) of the group is low and the leader may well have a very impersonal relationship with the group.

S2 – Coaching High directive/High supportive leader behaviour
In this situation the leader will be active and visible but not necessarily directive. A lot is going on, such as in the "early" phase of a new group's life. Questions to do with 'why' rather than 'what' are being asked, so reasons and explanations are required in order to persuade and convince e.g. Why do we have to go up this trail rather than down that one?

Good relationships are as important as getting on with the job because at this juncture if the relationship becomes soured the task may not be achieved. At this stage the leader's role tends to become political and diplomatic in essence, particularly when conflicts, a feature of this phase, have to be resolved positively. In other words, to be effective, the leader has to be flexible in order to be able to adapt to a variety of conditions or situations. The sustained exercise of a single leadership style here might well be disastrous.

S3 – Supporting High Supportive/Low directive leader behaviour
Here, roles have been assigned to, or assumed by, group members with the skills and ability to undertake them. Control of some things is moving naturally away from the leader. But it is important that, with the removal of this cohesive influence, group harmony is maintained so that various parts continue to work together. In order not to become too distant from the group, it is now possible for the leader's focus to move away from the task, and concentrate more on the needs and wants of the group and individuals within it. The leader will thus participate on a level nearer to the group by joining, sharing, testing and consulting. On some expeditions leadership never gets beyond this phase because of a leader's need to feel that his/her group remain dependant. This is a limited view and can be considered as unjust or selfish in that it blocks the development of others.

S4 – Delegating Low supportive/Low directive leader behaviour
In this situation the leader allows his/her role to become low key in order that the group is able to become self functioning to the extent that it, or individuals in it, can see what needs to be done, set up tasks, take most of the decisions and carry them out. The leader will be mostly delegating, consulting a little, supervising a lot and monitoring all the time. A physical example of this sort of situation would be a group well on the way to self sufficiency as say with an established, fairly well trained and experienced group, preparing to go on a semi-accompanied expedition as part of the training for the Duke of Edinburgh Award Scheme.

There is a possibility of becoming confused here: within the expedition group there will need to be high supportive behaviour in order to carry out a task that may be simple at times and complex at others. So how does this fit into a category of Low supportive/Low directive behaviour? The distinguishing feature here is that the relationship between leader and the group needs to be less involved.

Relating situational demands to group maturity or development tells us that the leader's style will change depending on the task/relationship orientation as well as group maturity.

To further illustrate the four dimensions above, assume a group of adults is starting their first mountain-biking excursion. As a whole, the group's knowledge, skills, and ability to take responsibility for itself is very limited (immature), and safety is a prime concern of the leader who would use a directive approach with little interaction with the learners. However, leadership style would change to a point where it might even be participative, as the learners develop their skills and maturity in the activity and become as adept as their leader.

Some leaders' own behaviour may be 'locked' at the outer edge of the two axes in figure 1. In other words, leaders who 'need' to be 'in charge' at all times may find it uncomfortable to develop a 'supportive behaviour' role. Similarly, some leaders may find it hard to take control and this may not be advantageous in certain situations where safety is an issue.

There are some psychometric tests which can be used to determine a leader's comfort zone and some people require to make a considerable effort to operate as a well rounded leader who considers and achieves group development, as well as task achievement.

Irrespective of the leadership model selected or leadership style used a competent leader will have the following said about him/her:

- Is human and treats team members as human beings
- Has no favourites and doesn't bear grudges
- Is easy to talk to and you can tell they listen
- Keeps their word and is honest
- Doesn't dodge unpleasant issues
- Explains why or why not
- Is fair with praise and criticisms and criticises without making enemies
- Is fair to everyone
- Drives him/herself so hard you don't mind them expecting the best of you

Teaching & Learning

By the end of this section all candidates should be able to:

- State teaching principles
- Identify a range of teaching styles
- Sate how they might be used

INTRODUCTION
Before designing a learning experience for an individual or a group it is important to set a good learning environment. Take a moment and reflect on two situations where learning took place (one a successful learning experience and the other an unsuccessful learning experience).

If you were to turn the unsuccessful one into a successful one what would you do? Make a note of your top tips for creating a good learning experience.

LEARNING PRINCIPLES
Current research has shown that people learn best when:

- Given time to **practise**
- It's **relevant** to their own situation and session outcomes
- They are **involved** in their own learning
- In a non-threatening and supportive **climate**
- There is **enjoyment** and they have fun
- It is **learner** centred — at their own pace and in their own way
- Their skills, knowledge and **experience** are respected
- They are encouraged to **self reflect** on their own behaviour
- They have **success** and their self esteem is raised

The aim of this section is to consider teaching "approaches" or "styles". It may be appreciated that an effective teacher adopts a flexible approach in common with an effective leader. The skilled teacher will use judgement and experience to decide how much responsibility to delegate and when the time is "right" to do so.

Whilst quality demonstration, analysis of performance, selection of terrain, and good clear management are vital skills to possess, so too is the ability to teach using various "approaches" or "styles" and to constantly evaluate the success of each style used with both individuals and groups.

In all forms of modern education, the emphasis is increasingly on encouraging a more participative approach, with students becoming actively involved in learning. This section will focus on the work of a noted American Physical Educationalist, Muska Mosston. He has provided a model for studying teaching approaches which offers a useful framework for our purpose. This framework is known as "Mosston's Spectrum of Teaching Styles". Many national governing bodies of sport have now adopted Mosston's teaching styles as the basis for their coach education programmes.

One important area we are not directly considering is how individuals will learn. There are vast differences in how individuals learn, some are much more receptive to auditory signals, others are predominately visual learners, whilst some learn most through active practice. Also, most individuals learn differently under different circumstances and at different times. By being able to teach or lead in a range of styles, leaders can greatly improve their chances of success with most individuals.

In his work Mosston makes it clear that each of his eight styles possesses key features and particular strengths and weaknesses. The spectrum is not presented as a hierarchy of style, and one is not necessarily better than any other. The best style is the one which will be most effective for the learners during any particular teaching episode.

Spectrum of Styles

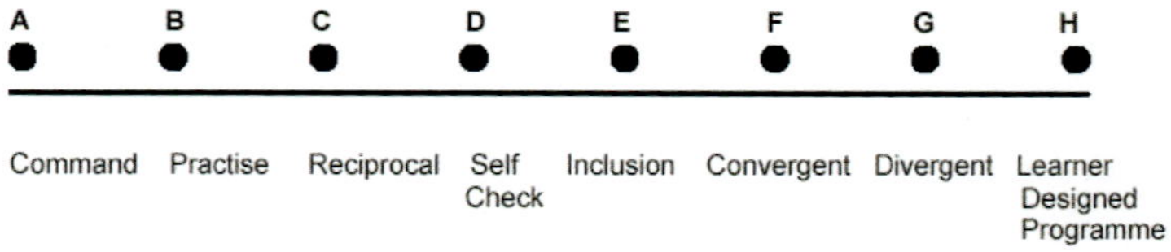

THE ESSENCE OF EACH STYLE

Style A – "Command Style" In this style, the teacher directs the members of his/her class in all their actions; a clear comparison being possible with a sergeant major controlling a group of recruits on a barracks square.

Key Features of the Command Style are:
To learn to perform a task accurately and efficiently. It provides for teacher control and learner compliance. The learner does not take any active decisions except consenting to take part.

Implications

- Subject matter is fixed, a single standard to be followed
- The teacher's demonstration of the skill establishes the model to be copied
- The teacher's commands must be obeyed with great care in performance

- The teacher's decisions cannot be questioned
- Individual differences in the abilities of learners cannot be taken into consideration

Style B – "Practice Style" This style enables the teacher to provide the class with a model of performance, probably by demonstration, which the student then tries, with repetition, more or less at their own pace. It is perhaps the style of teaching most frequently employed by teachers of physical activities particularly when introducing a new technique.

Key Features of the Practice Style are:
It provides for near maximum opportunity to practise the task at hand and to receive feedback individually and privately.

TCL & MBL

Implications

- Students learn to make certain (not all) decisions about performance and to accept the consequences of those decisions
- They learn to perform tasks within constraints of time and space
- They learn to accept private and individual feedback

Style C – "Reciprocal Style" In this style the teacher divides the class into pairs, whose members work together as "performer" and "observer" in turn, providing each other with immediate feedback according to clear criteria provided by the teacher.

Key Features of the Reciprocal Style are:
By working co-operatively, partners provide each other with immediate, one-to-one feedback. Evaluation of the performance of a skill/activity are shifted from teacher to learner who observes a partner's performance and also provides feedback on the basis of criteria laid down by the teacher.

Implications

- This style promotes a new kind of relationship among learners
- Patience and tolerance are developed and exhibited
- Reciprocation of giving and receiving feedback is developed and exhibited
- Precision in offering feedback by criteria is developed
- Learning the task itself is facilitated due to immediate feedback from the partner
- The teacher can stand back and monitor the work of the observers as well as the developments of the whole group

Style D – "Self-Check Style" Whilst operating in this style, the teacher enables the class or group to work individually to analyse and reflect upon their own performance. However, the correct direction and guidelines are still provided by the teacher.

Key Features of the self-check style are:
The self-check style provides opportunities for self-assessment. By a further shift in decision making, a situation is created in which the learners' skills in analysing performance are enhanced, and they are required to apply those skills to analyse their own performance rather than that of a learning partner.

Implications

- Learners expand their experience in working privately
- They learn to "feel" and "sense" their own performance
- They learn to use criteria to improve their own performance
- They learn to be honest and objective about their own performance
- They learn about discrepancies and their own limitations
- They learn to be more independent of the teacher as the sole source of feedback
- There is more individualising than in previous styles. Learners make individual decisions about themselves both in the "performance" and "reflective" phase

Style E – "Inclusion Style" In this style learners are again allowed to operate individually, but are provided with more opportunities for selecting the level at which they attempt a particular activity; more or less demanding according to choice.

Key Features of the Inclusion Style are:
The Inclusion Style provides the opportunity for each learner to be included in the task at hand. In each of the styles identified so far, the task had been thought of in terms of a single standard and no consideration has been given to individual differences amongst learners. Up to this point, the teacher has the opportunity to alter the nature of the feedback in accordance with the learners' performance but this does not alter the fact that learners have been working towards a teacher-determined level of performance. Style E addresses this problem which is of crucial importance to all teachers.

Implications

- The learner is given the opportunity to select a standard that suits his/her abilities
- The teacher's main task is to ensure that there is a sufficient range of options available
- Opportunity is provided to choose the standard of performance where success can be "guaranteed"
- There is the opportunity to take a step backward in order to succeed in the activity
- There are options to move on if one wishes to do so
- Promotes learning of self-assessment and deals with the (frequent) discrepancy between aspiration and reality

Style F – "Guided Discovery" (Convergent Style) Here, the success of the style rests on the effectiveness of the teacher in asking questions of the learner or learners. The questions may be posed verbally or by setting problems, but should result in the learners reaching a similar conclusion to the teacher, "converging" in their thinking.

Key Features of the Guided Discovery Style are:

None of the styles identified so far have made significant demands of learners in terms of their ability to understand and think more deeply about performance, rather they have been concerned with reproduction of knowledge as given by the teacher. To develop situations wherein learners have a different relationship to that knowledge, Mosston claims that learners have to go beyond the discovery threshold. The first of two styles (F and G) which takes learners beyond this discovery threshold is based on the notion of "guided discovery" and the process of CONVERGENT THINKING.

Performance: teacher presents a situation to create a thinking process in the learner which, when resolved, becomes subject matter (e.g. "Which is the more effective brake on a bike?)

Evaluation: when feedback information is fundamental to the task, the learner can evaluate their own responses, otherwise the teacher provides the feedback.

Style F is dependant on the teacher's skill in asking appropriate questions, in sequence, during the performance phase.

Implications

- Develops a precise relationship between the learner's response and the stimulus (questions presented by the teacher)
- Develops a relationship between the teacher and the learners which is based on discovery by a learner (this is fundamentally different from the stimulus–response relationship that occurs in Command Style A)
- Develops sequential discovery skills that logically lead to the discovery of a concept
- Develops the patience (in both teacher and learner) required during the discovery process

Style G – "Divergence Style" While the teacher still poses the question or sets the problem in this style, in contrast with the previous (Convergent) style, the answer or answers may be varied and unexpected. In others words, the learner is required to both understand more and be more creative than previously.

Key Features of the Divergence Style are:

This style of teaching is based on the process of divergent thinking. The shift in decision making which identifies this style of teaching is outlined as:

Performance: learners create subject matter by discovering alternative solutions to questions posed by the teacher (e.g. cornering on bike)

Evaluation: depending on subject matter, learner verifies own solutions or receives feedback from the teacher

This style requires the teacher to consider and use something called the "PFD reduction process", which can be defined as, "the successive use of criteria to reduce a given number of solutions". For example, is a particular day's ride possible for a given group given the constraints of fitness, terrain, weather, time of year, equipment, group skill etc? Is it feasible with the time available? Is it the "best" and most rewarding route for the group?

PFD Reduction

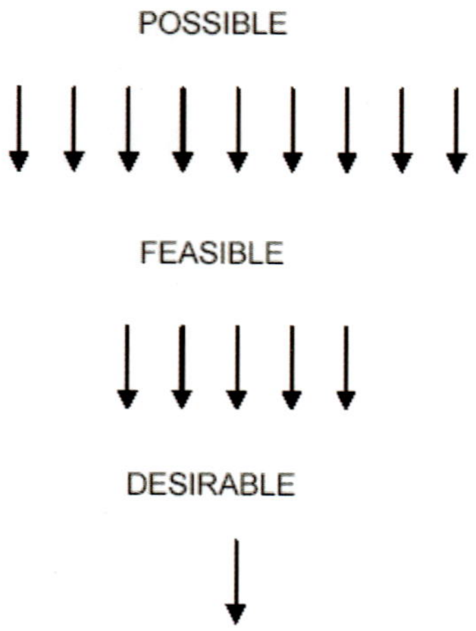

Implications

- To tap the thinking capacities of the teacher in designing problems in a given subject matter area
- To tap the thinking capacities of the learners in discovering multiple solutions to any given problem
- To develop insight into the nature of the activity and discover possible variations
- To reach the level of effective security which "permits" the teacher and the learner to go beyond accepted responses, i.e. to go beyond the conventional
- To develop the ability to confirm solutions and test them in context

Style H – "Learner Designed Programme" Although the teacher may still prescribe the general area of enquiry for the learner or learners, it would be up to the learners to identify the specific problem to be solved or design the programme to be followed. Perhaps, if they wish, they could call upon the teacher for advice, guidance or even direct instruction.

This style requires the learner to use the skill and understanding developed earlier, and apply them in a context in which work is undertaken much more independently of the teacher. In style H the learner identifies the questions or problems prescribed by the teacher.

The style, which can only be followed over a series of episodes, is dependant on the learner having a sound understanding of the subject matter. Only then can the learner identify relevant questions in a highly disciplined manner and thus avoid the situation in which "anything goes".

Style H provides opportunities for students to develop initiative and be guided and reminded, if necessary, during the progress of a self-motivated project. The main limitation is that the project has to be undertaken within the parameters of the teacher's knowledge, conditions, time etc.

SUMMARY
Styles and their use have to be judged on how appropriate they are. Decisions about their suitability can only be made by the teacher whilst taking into account:

- Maturity of the learner
- Nature of the activity (complexity, danger element)
- Confidence/competence of the teacher

Expectations of the learner in terms of how the teacher will operate are a significant factor in any teacher/learner situation. It is important, therefore, that the respective roles are clarified before any teaching episode begins and re-enforced as the episode progresses.

Research has shown that "Spectrum" Teachers display the following qualities:

- Exhibit flexibility in different use of styles
- Give more individual attention to students
- Spend less time dominating discussions
- Use time more efficiently, evidenced by:
    - students pay more attention
    - more time is spent on work
    - less time is spent on distractions
    - less time is spent on discipline
    - more subject matter is taught

And "Spectrum" Students show corresponding characteristics:

- greater flexibility in coping with learning demands
- more independence and responsibility
- posses a clearer idea of tasks and roles

APPLICATION OF VARIOUS TEACHING STYLES (MOSSTON) IN THE TEACHING OF MOUNTAIN BIKING

The following is intended to provoke thought among those teaching and leading mountain bike groups.

A Command Style

Suitable for the following:

- Teaching basic skills such as setting up a safe bike or braking
- Leading in hazardous positions on, for example, a steep slope
- Coping with an unforeseen crisis

B Practice Style

May be employed to gain maximum class activity when the class size is large or the range of abilities is great. The class may be split so that each part may try an appropriate manoeuvre. Suitable for teaching, for example:

- In a wide area, use of gears
- Attempting to manoeuvre round obstacles

C Reciprocal Style

Useful at a stage when it is desirable to increase analytical skill, e.g. for aspiring leaders. Pairs can work on "bunny hops" or some other technical aspect, where one or two clear "points for observation and feedback" are used. Simple instructions on cards could be useful here.

D Self Check

Individuals can work on refining own skills as determined by the teacher.

- Body positioning on steep descent or ascents
- Braking without skidding

E The Inclusion Style

Programme level is determined by choice of each learner. For example, ascent or decent of a bank where there is choice in selecting the slope angle and length.

F Guided Discovery

Employs the use of exercises to assist in discovering "correct" position on the bike, or technique to be used.

- Selection of gears for optimum performance
- Determining which is the more effective brake (front or rear)
- Climbing a steep slope (body position)

G Divergent

Students make, for example, choices over equipment, line of slope, type of turns, speed etc. Decisions are made according to equipment, experience, fitness, conditions etc. They choose the route for the day, length of outing and type of terrain.

H Individual Programme Student's Design

Learner has achieved almost total independence. Learner decides how they wish to use the expertise of the teacher or trainer, and may seek assistance when required. For example, a trainee racer may decide the type of discipline and even the training schedule, possibly with advice from a trainer. Advice from the teacher on which area, trails and types of terrain offer the greatest challenge, as well as the greatest aesthetic rewards.

CONCLUSION

The role of teacher or leader can be particularly challenging, and carrying out this role effectively is vital. Initially there is likely to be the desire to operate in a "command" style of teaching and the similar "directing" style of leadership. As confidence and experience grow, the teacher/leader is likely to experiment with the ranges of "styles" outlined in this section. Such experimentation is normal and should be evaluated for effectiveness. Eventually, the complete range of styles should be well within the repertoire of skills which the effective leader can employ. As more and more responsibility is undertaken by group members and as their skills develop, the leader must avoid "holding on" and recognise that such a development can be considered the result of effective instruction.

LEARNING

Rather than focus on learning styles it is useful to remember that learning takes place at different rates. However, we all go through a process of stages which have been identified by Fitts and Posner and described by them as a "learning cycle".

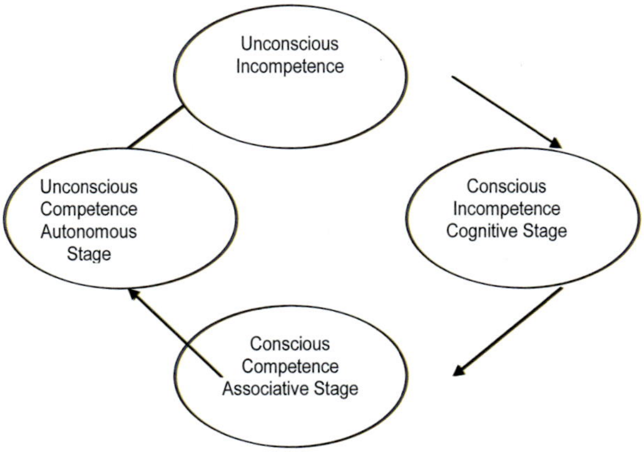

At the start of a new learning experience we are all "unconscious incompetents". In other words "we don't know what we don't know". Once something new is explained or a demonstration given we become "conscious competents", or we know what it is but we don't quite know how to do it yet. As practice begins we have some successes which is the "conscience competence" stage and finally the new skill can be performed under any conditions and in any circumstances without thinking about it—"unconscious competence". This process can be translated as shown below:

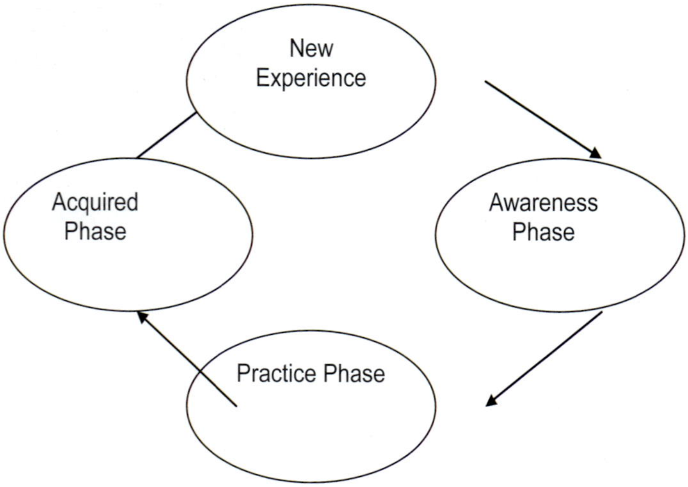

During TCL and MBL training courses candidates may be at any of the above stages. It is anticipated that everyone will leave the course at the practice stage phase of most of the course content. Some skills will require to be at the acquired phase for the assessment whilst others can remain at the practice phase. For example, Mosston's teaching styles will be included at TCL training but are not assessed at TCL assessment. This is to allow sufficient practice to develop competence in this area which is assessed at acquired phase at MBL assessment.

Planning & Group Management

By the end of this section Leaders should be able to:-

- Describe the types of prior knowledge required of a group leader about the group
- Describe how this knowledge might be put to use in planning a group session
- State the Leader:Group size ratio from an insurance and advisory perspective
- Describe why it is important to establish aims for each session

INTRODUCTION

Mountain biking can be a tremendously sociable experience, and one which many people engage in as a group activity, especially when they are just starting out and discovering new routes. Having someone within a group who has local knowledge of access, routes, weather and the sort of challenges a ride can throw up is always helpful and can enrich the riding experience for all. Equally useful is having somebody who can demonstrate riding skills, show riders the best line on a trail and provide encouragement and motivation when needed. A competent leader must be all these things and above all, be prepared for what is planned, and plan according to the needs of the group and the specific conditions of the trip.

1. THE GROUP

To operate as successful leaders of groups it is fundamental to recognise and plan for the wide range of abilities, expectations and responses individuals have to the challenges of cycling. It would be unrealistic to expect a cross-country racer to have the same expectations of a group-led session as someone who has never ridden a mountain bike, for example.

Within every group the combination of age, fitness, experience and skills provides a challenge for the leader trying to meet the needs of everyone all of the time. A skilled leader could find themselves employed to run a taster session in a forest park for a local school one day, and guide skilled recreational riders the next. The delivery repertoire of the leader must be flexible to meet the very different needs of each group, and the most important aspect of this flexibility is planning. This section describes the vital ingredients which go into the mix to make a successful off road session.

Prior knowledge
Having knowledge of the needs and abilities of your groups is a fundamental starting point for the session plan that follows. You need documented participant information which includes names, ages, addresses, next of kin, any medical issues and the background of your group (youth/school/leisure) as a starting point. You also need to ascertain the same detailed information for any accompanying staff and leaders. The medical information of a 50 year old sedentary classroom teacher is as important to the party leader as the 14 year old(s) he or she may be responsible for.

In order to deliver the outcomes of the session to an acceptable standard the leader also needs to clarify the group's expectations and any outcomes requested by the organiser. Is the session fitted into a framework of a residential personal development course, is it tied into training for the Duke of Edinburgh Award scheme or are the group expecting a challenging ride designed to develop their off-road riding skills?

Armed with the group's expectations, it is necessary to assess their abilities and behaviour before the session. Do their expectations outweigh their abilities? At what point does adventure become misadventure for a group of novices wanting to ride technical singletrack, or at the other end of the spectrum, are the group of skilled adventure racers going to get sufficient stimulation riding the local towpaths?

Group Size
"What is the ideal group size?" is always a difficult question to answer. Leader/Group ratios must be based on risk assessment and also need to take into account prior knowledge (see above) as well as the duration and location of the trip, the conditions overhead and underfoot, the ages, personal capabilities and characteristics of the participants and

expectations of reasonable behaviour. It is more important to meet these criteria rather than to simply work with an established fixed ratio. However, clarification is often sought on ratios and the following information is provided by way of guidance.

SMBLA Leader ratios would not normally exceed 1:8. This would require a Leader to be covered by their employer's insurance, which may be a Local Authority. **If a Leader is depending on British Cycling insurance through Silver or Gold membership the maximum ratio is 1:6.**

Two leaders for a group of 12-16 participants gives a workable situation for most outdoor centres. To work with larger groups than this can cause its own problems; educational and development agendas can be hard to deliver as 'crowd control' becomes the order of the day. The impact on other trail users and the environment is increased with larger group sizes and effective management is impaired and it is doubtful if appropriate learning takes place.

Equipment

What to carry on an off-road cycling venture is a topic which provokes much discussion and the finer points and preferences will largely depend on the type of journey and the terrain to be crossed. A leader must issue a "what to bring" list to his/her group in advance, and make plans to borrow or hire equipment which individuals can not provide. The "what to bring" list can also act as a check list to use before the ride.

A minimum list of equipment broken down into leader, group and personal equipment is supplied below. It should be noted that there are different trailside competencies for each of the SMBLA awards. For example, at TCL level there is no requirement for spoke keys or crank extractors to be carried. For a day journey all equipment can be carried in a small rucksack or similar. Expedition Leaders or those assisting an expedition should see the **Expedition Module** section for more information on equipment needs for an extended self-supported trip.

LEADER EQUIPMENT (in addition to personal equipment)

- ◊ Adequate tool kit, to include:
  - *Multi-tool or equivalent*
  - *Tyre levers*
  - *Puncture repair kit*
  - *Spare Tubes (X2 with presta type valves)*
  - *Pump*
  - *Chain tool*
  - *Zip Ties (various)*
  - *Spoke Key(s)* - **MBL**
  - *Chain Lube*
  - *Tyre Boot or Patch*
  - *Superglue*
  - *Crank extractor*—**MBL**
  - *Adjustable spanner*
  - *Knife*
  - *Duck Tape*
  - *Brake pads/blocks*

LEADER EQUIPMENT cont. (in addition to personal equipment)

- ◊ First aid kit
- ◊ Compass
- ◊ Whistle
- ◊ Map (and waterproof case)
- ◊ Mobile phone
- ◊ Head torch
- ◊ Polythene Survival Bag
- ◊ Spare warm clothing (for group members)
- ◊ Emergency food
- ◊ Extra fluids

PERSONAL ITEMS

- ◊ Helmet
- ◊ Gloves
- ◊ Eye protection
- ◊ Windproof/Waterproof jacket
- ◊ Suitable footwear
- ◊ Clothing suitable for the environment/season/weather
- ◊ Food
- ◊ Drink
- ◊ Medication (inhalers etc)

GROUP EQUIPMENT

- ◊ Emergency Group Shelter
- ◊ Extra spares for longer / more remote trips (pedals, tyre, cables etc)

Fitness

Cycling off-road places a different set of demands on the body to many other activities and it is of primary importance that any planned session operates within the abilities of the whole group. When a cycling group becomes energy depleted their concentration may lapse and skill on the bike is likely to deteriorate with a corresponding effect on safety. Also, an exhausted group will become more prone to cold injury (potentially leading to hypothermia) and will become debilitated very quickly.

The endurance fitness so critical to cycling is something that develops over years of riding and it is easy for a leader to underestimate the physical challenges experienced by their group. Sessions should be progressive with plenty of time allowed for refuelling and resting. Strategies for managing disparity of fitness levels in the group should be prepared and routes planning should always take account of the ability of the weakest member.

Working as a team

Cycling in a group provides a great opportunity for working in a team and working as a team. In the **Leadership Skills & Styles** section the Action Centred Leadership model suggests that one of the key roles of an effective leader is to 'build and maintain the team'.

Initially a group may be given an opportunity to ride in formation, outlined in the section on **Skills & Techniques** (Riding in a group on the road). This can be developed through practising 'transitioning' (changing places in a structured, controlled way). A tired rider 'resting' at the back of the group can also be assisted by being in the group and being pushed along. Pushing can also be carried out (on safe forest tracks) by getting into a triangle formation and the two at the rear pushing the middle cyclist by putting their nearest hand on their lower back.

The group can be additionally equalised by allowing the more tired cyclists to select a suitable gearing ratio but challenging the fittest to cycle for a given distance in their granny ring and easiest gear. This tactic generally ensures the fittest and the less fit arrive at the same point equally challenged. Working in pairs (on a safe forest track) using a towing technique with a rope, less able/less fit cyclists can be towed by a fitter partner. All of these techniques can contribute to a co-operative approach so that everyone completes the trip successfully.

Aspirations

It is a commonly held belief that everyone can ride a bike. This misconception both helps and hinders the Trail Cycle / Mountain Bike Leader. It gives confidence and encourages young people into the activity, but it can allow individuals to ride in an unsafe way whilst being led as part of a group. Before embarking on a cycling session it is important that a leader evaluates his/her plans against the stated aims of the session. This gives perspective and rigour to the plan and checks that the aspirations of the leader are in tune with the outcomes for the group. I might like to ride miles of sinuous singletrack, but is that the right experience for a group working on gear selection and cadence during their first sessions of a programme? The aspirations of the leader must match the abilities of the group in his/her charge. If there is a mismatch in this relationship then the group could become demotivated or put off if the challenges set by the leader are either too high or too low .

2. AIMS

The information on leadership in the **Leadership Skills & Styles** section focuses on providing some form of cycling activity. Whether that activity involves providing an experience of the outdoors, allowing a process of personal development or increasing the skills of a mountain biker, one thread underlies all. Each session delivered by a Mountain Bike Leader or Trail Cycle Leader must have an aim. To have an aim in mind when planning a session allows outcomes to be assessed more accurately, it creates focus and should give direction to the experience provided.

"Why am I doing this?" should be the first question a leader asks themselves before planning their session. If the answer is "I don't know" then an alarm bell should start to ring! As leaders on mountain bikes we have responsibility to our groups to ensure that they leave us with a positive experience and motivated to continue the activity of biking.

Some aims will be consistent in each session. "To provide a safe and enjoyable session" for example would be applicable to all. Some other more specific examples are given in the list which follows:

Examples of session aims

1 If a session was to be delivered to support the skills development of a group then the aim could be communicated with the statement "By the end of the session the participants will be able to *change gear smoothly and accurately*" This could be tested and the aim could be assessed as either met or not.

2 A group of 14 year olds on a residential outdoor course might be expected to develop their abilities to work together as a team. To assess the successful outcomes a review of the students' experiences would be appropriate.

3 A team of 16 year-olds undergoing Duke of Edinburgh Award training to use mountain bikes as part of their Silver Expedition need to develop their navigation skills prior to embarking on their venture. Using a route card and allowing them to lead sections would allow abilities to be assessed and provide opportunity for navigation coaching.

4 Eight colleagues have come away for the weekend to the mountains to have an adventurous and exciting holiday on mountain bikes. To send them away technically better bikers, safe and covered in mud would be an appropriate outcome in this situation!

Although basic, each of the above four statements easily demonstrates some of the wider aims of a mountain bike session and how a leader would employ different strategies to meet those aims and assess or evaluate their success. With a clear set of aims a leader is better equipped to deliver the session, has the ability to make clear and purposeful decisions, and to effectively assess the effectiveness of the session.

'Failure to Plan means Planning to Fail'

3. TERRAIN

Planning where to take a group and what sort of terrain will be suitable depends on having prior knowledge of the group as well as the logistics of transport, costs, and accessibility of the area and facilities you are seeking to use. Plans should also reflect time of year and both overhead weather and underfoot terrain conditions (as affected by the weather). For guidelines on terrain choice see **Terrain & Route Selection**.

4. ROUTE PLANNING

A detailed route plan helps identify any potential problems to be encountered in advance. The plan should include escape routes in case of injury, bad weather or exhausted group members. Working out escape routes in advance performs two functions – they can be worked out without stress, and it may help someone to find you in an emergency. A route card should be small enough to be accessed easily but should not be relied on alone – a map and compass should always be carried.

The Appendix contains a sample route card (see **Navigation** and **Emergency Planning** for further information on the use of route cards).
A route card can be used to work out distance, height, estimated time and to adjust plans if necessary according to ability, fitness and the prevailing conditions. Mapping software can also help with this type of planning, See **Terrain & Route Selection** for some examples of mapping software which can be used to produce your own route cards.

A home based contact should be appointed for each trip. A copy of your route plan should be left with the home based contact who will know what to do if you have not returned by a specified time. Don't forget to inform them of your safe return by a specified time in line with best practice.

5. COMMUNICATION AND DECISION MAKING

The **Leadership Skills & Styles** section describes leadership models which provide guidance on when the leader retains decision making (i.e. the leader takes all decisions), when to involve the group and to what extent the group will have decision making responsibility.

During the planning phase the leader should similarly decide on what stages, if any, can involve the group. The stages listed below should be included by the leader in the planning phase.

Planning tasks

1. Collect information on the group, including age, gender, fitness, , any special needs, previous experience and the group's expectations for the session. (i.e. why do they want to do it)

2. Obtain parental consent forms for under 16 year olds (under 18 if in full time education), which should include details of any medical conditions, special needs and current medication being taken. Sufficient information should be supplied so that parents can make an informed choice

3. An emergency contact list should be prepared and a copy given to your base contact person

4. A detailed route should be prepared for the session taking into account the aspirations of the group, their ability and level of fitness

5. A risk assessment should be prepared for the session related to the group's abilities, weather conditions and time of year (see **Hazards & Risk Management**)

6. Equipment for the group (whether shared or personal) should be checked for safety, functionality, suitability and size/weight

7. Meeting arrangements should be communicated to participants and parents/guardians, including, location, start time and planned finishing time

8. Information should be given to participants about what to bring including food and drink and what to carry it in

9. The leader's repair kit and first aid kit should be checked to ensure its suitability for the session and that nothing is missing.

At the start of the session the leader should brief the group on the session and confirm agreement on the aims of the session.

On return, contact should be made with the home base so that your late back procedures are not activated.

Finally, a good leader will review the session and note any lessons to be learned which could inform the planning and organisation in the future.

Communication aids

The use of mobile phones is referred to in **Emergency Planning & Procedures.** A leader should carry a mobile phone at all times, but remember that mobile phones can not be relied on in all areas; reception depends on the topography and proximity to a transmitter. A leader carrying a mobile phone and emergency contact list should include his/her own emergency contact on this list. He/she should also advise 'appropriate' members of the group of the location of this phone and list so that they could be accessed should the leader be involved in an accident.

2-way radios are an alternative option, although their range is relatively short, typically up to 3km. They are a popular communication aid in the outdoors with skiers, climbers, event teams etc. Radios have the advantages of being fixed-cost (i.e. no call charge), and being generally reliable within their range of operation. Two or more radios can be used to communicate, providing they are within range and using the same channel. With advance planning, a leader could arrange for radio communication between the party and one or more bases within range of their location en route. Leaders of two or more groups within the same area could use radio communication to relay information about their group, navigation features, trail conditions, weather etc., allowing for a degree of remote teamwork.

Hazards & Risk Management

By the end of this section Leaders should be able to:-

- State the principles of risk assessment
- State what the three levels of risk assessment are and when each is applied
- Describe the types of hazards encountered while mountain biking
- Explain how the interaction of hazards can increase the degree of risk to the group
- Carry out a risk assessment for a group ride

INTRODUCTION

In order to maximise the enjoyment of a mountain bike ride it needs to be challenging but safe. A well prepared leader and a motivated group should be able to experience excitement without danger, and adventure without hazard.

Some degree of risk is associated with all activities, including mountain biking. Assessing and managing identified hazards which could cause harm is the process described by **Risk Assessment**. In simple terms, it means looking at what could go wrong, and deciding how to prevent or minimise any problems.

A leader in charge of a group needs to understand how to carry out a full risk assessment and how to modify a previous one. Although a leader's principle concern is the safety of the group, a risk assessment should also seek to minimise any risks to other outdoor users whom the group may come into contact with.

- **What are the identified hazards?**
- **Who might be harmed by them and how?**
- **What safety measures need to be in place to reduce the risks to a reasonable level?**
- **How will the group leader implement the safety measures?**
- **How effective are the safety measures, and should any proposed changes be made?**

THE PRINCIPLES OF RISK ASSESSMENT

Carrying out a risk assessment is a relatively simple task once the basic principles outlined below are understood and applied to the context of a mountain bike ride.

1. Hazard – anything that could cause harm or injury

In the context of mountain biking a hazard could be physical, e.g. frozen ground, sharp rocks or fallen trees; mechanical – e.g. faulty brakes, a loose headset or worn tyres; or human – e.g. fatigue, inappropriate clothing or an existing injury or physical disability. Some hazards can be identified by checking out a route, pre-ride bike checks and monitoring the condition of group members before and during a ride. Other hazards can be predicted, for example through the use of weather forecasts.

2. Risk – the likelihood that someone will be harmed by a hazard

Once the hazards have been identified, they must be evaluated. How likely is it that the hazard will lead to an accident or harm to any group members? What is the degree of risk for each hazard? In the context of mountain biking, harm could occur to an individual directly through slipping or hitting an obstacle, or indirectly through faulty brakes or a sudden puncture resulting in a loss of control. Either way, not only is an individual hurt, but the ability of the group to continue will be affected.

3. Risk management – taking action to reduce the degree of risk

Any risks which are determined to be **high** must be considered significant and require action to be taken to reduce the risk to **low** or to an acceptable level. For example, the risk associated with extreme cold is high; somebody could easily get hypothermia, but the risk can be reduced to low by taking account of weather conditions to avoid exposure and by ensuring adequate clothing is worn or carried and energy levels are maintained.

There will be a risk rating for every hazard, but it is also important to consider the interaction of two or more hazards which may be individually of low or medium risk, but collectively pose a medium or high risk. For example, a section of trail with slabs of rock may be low risk in the dry, but high risk when wet. The group factor must always be bourn in mind; even one ill-prepared rider or faulty bike in a group poses a risk to the entire group, and increases the chance of an accident or bad experience for everybody.

4. Review and appraise risk-controlling measures
Having carried out the risk assessment before an excursion, after the event you need to assess your control measures, comment on their effectiveness and record any changes which are required. A written risk assessment needs to be dated and signed, with any reassessment date stated.

Almost everyone is now familiar with the requirement to carry out a risk assessment which is no more than common sense. There are three types of risk assessment:

1. **generic risk assessment**
2. **specific risk assessment**
3. **dynamic risk assessment**

a) Generic Risk Assessment
As the name implies, a generic risk assessment concerns the general risks associated with the activity wherever and whenever it takes place. For mountain biking these would include safety of bikes and clothing. An example of generic risk-control measures would be bike safety checks and mandatory wearing of helmets.

Local authorities and some outdoor centres may have their own generic activity risk assessments, and would normally want to check any generic risk assessment prepared by an external individual or organisation. Centres licensed under the Adventure Activity Licensing Regulations 2004 should be considered safe in the leading, instructing and equipping of the activities stipulated on their licence, which may include mountain biking (see Legal Issues & Liability).

b) Specific Risk Assessment
Specific risk assessments will differ from place to place and group to group. They require more detailed knowledge about the hazards which may be specific to the location and to the individuals in the group.

Examples of location hazards include potentially dangerous sections of trail, river crossings, roads, electric fences etc. Hazards specific to the group could be medical conditions, behavioural problems or inexperience in mountain biking.

Physical hazards can be identified by a reconnaissance ride, which together with "local intelligence", can help to inform risk control measures. For example, local information can be obtained on the safest places to cross streams or roads, the timing of movements of farm animals, likelihood of sudden weather changes in the mountains, or ice affecting roads in frosty weather. Control measures for group specific hazards would include ensuring adequate supervision, having an agreed code of conduct and taking necessary precautions to deal with medical needs.

At this stage a leader should draw up a Plan B in case Plan A becomes too hazardous, incorporating an alternative route and time schedule for the ride.

c) Dynamic Risk Assessment

While the first two levels of risk assessment are concerned with all hazards which can be identified or reasonably predicted, and as such are pre-recorded, dynamic or ongoing risk assessment is about making judgements and decisions to cope with changing levels of risk or unpredicted hazards. Examples would be worsening weather, injuries or illness, fatigue, inability to access a trail due to forestry operations or a road closure due to flooding or an accident. This is where Plan B may come into use.

A leader must be able to assess the situation which is facing the group and make a decision based on best judgement and the knowledge he or she has about each individual, even if it means making the unpopular decision to end the ride in the interests of safety.

WHY CARRY OUT A RISK ASSESSMENT ?

It should be clear by understanding the principles of risk assessment what the leader's responsibilities are with respect to the safety of the group. Fundamentally, risk assessment is just one element of a systematic approach to the management of safety, a "safety culture", whether operating as an individual or as part of a large organisation. However, carrying out a full risk assessment can fulfill several purposes beyond legal and moral responsibility.

Carrying out a risk assessment can:

- **Help prevent any accidents or emergencies occurring**
- **Avoid any costly damage to bikes, clothing and equipment**
- **Help allay the concerns of anxious parents / teachers / carers**
- **Increase the chances of all participants having a positive experience**
- **Identify and increase knowledge of individual needs and differences in ability**
- **Give a leader greater confidence in his / her ability to supervise the group**
- **Improve a leader's leadership and group management skills**
- **Protect the reputation of the leader and of mountain biking as an activity**
- **Facilitate future group leading exercises**

HOW TO CARRY OUT A RISK ASSESSMENT

The Health and Safety Executive's (HSE) Guidance on Adventure Activities Licensing Regulations (2004), states that "the scope of the risk assessment should be sufficient to identify the significant (non-trivial) risks arising from the activity". It should enable a leader to identify and prioritise the measures that need to be taken to ensure the safety of participants or others who might be affected. The scope of the planned activity must not be wider than the terms described by the risk assessment.

There are five steps to carrying out a risk assessment:

1. **Look** for the hazards
2. **Evaluate** the risks
3. **Record** the information
4. **Act** to reduce all risks to low
5. **Review** the risks

1. Look for the hazards

A **specific risk assessment** should be carried out in advance of every group ride. It is a good idea to do this with another leader or somebody who can help you record your findings.

The ideal time for a reconnaissance ride would be a week or two before your planned trip. If done too far in advance it is possible that some features may have changed by the time you take your group out. On the other hand, if you do not leave sufficient time between your risk assessment and your group ride you may not have enough time to evaluate the risks and adjust your plans according to your assessment.

Pre-ride the route(s) you plan to use. Look for any physical hazards along the route – rocks, loose gravel, tree stumps, gates, steep slopes. Record any fixed features on a route map with symbols to identify the feature and notes explaining what the hazard is. Some hazards might not be apparent at the time of this initial assessment. Changes in weather can create new hazards, or change the nature of a hazard unexpectedly. Specific location hazards might include a stream which you wish to cross becoming a small torrent after heavy rain. A road or track may be safe without traffic, but at certain times of the day or at a weekend it might become busy and possibly dangerous. So try to think about how changing conditions could change the nature of the hazards you encounter. Seek local knowledge or information sources on factors such as weather, deer stalking, visitor usage etc. Find out if there are any other events taking place on the same day as your planned trip, such as other sporting events, a country fair, a public rally etc, which would make it safer for you to change the time or date of your of your ride.

Consideration also needs to be given to the group, including any medical or behavioural issues identified at the planning stage. These might include group size, experience, fitness and skill levels, medical and/or behavioural issues.

2. Evaluate the risks

Think about each hazard you have identified. How might it cause harm to your group, who is most likely to be harmed, and what is the degree of risk? When doing this you have to try and anticipate how the risk rating might change in different conditions, as outlined above. For example, you may have a parallel risk rating for each hazard in dry and wet weather conditions.

By this stage you should have built up a picture of what and where the significant hazards are and identified the risks which will need to be controlled.

The table below gives examples of hazards in the three key areas (terrain, location and human) and the types of action which may be taken to reduce the associated risks. This list is an example and by no means exhaustive, and leaders should expect to identify all the foreseeable hazards for their trip.

Hazards	Who could be harmed and how?	Risk-control measures
TERRAIN		
Steep descents	Brake failure or loss of control resulting in fall and injury to participant and/or others close by	Bike safety check prior to trip Progressive practices on steep descents and controlled braking as part of program provided by qualified leader
Gravel and/or loose rock	Loss of control resulting in fall and injury to participant and/or others close by	Practise on varied surfaces as part of training program
Tree stumps and roots	When wet, risk of skidding/slipping on roots and/or hitting them. Injury to participant and/or others close by	Avoid rooted tracks and paths when wet. Leaders pre-ride route and identify possible problem sections. Point out specific hazards during outing, get off and walk if necessary
LOCATION		
Horse riders on trail ahead	Horses could be spooked by bikes and rider(s) thrown off and/or bikers kicked by horses. Injury to horses, riders or bikers	Communicate code of practice to stop when horse riders sighted. Group leader responsible for talking to horse riders and asking what action to take to allow horses to pass safely
HUMAN/GROUP		
Behavioural problems / conflict within group	Group members could go off alone with possible risk to those individuals	Establish good knowledge of group members prior to trip and agree ground rules. Gradually increase length of trips. Ensure sufficient additional adult helpers, with biking competence, are present to assist. Alter ratios as necessary.

3. Record the information

Record your findings using a risk assessment form. The Appendix contains a sample **Risk Assessment Form** which could be used, or adapted to suit. The **Bike Safety Checklist**, also in the Appendix, could be used as a part of an equipment risk assessment. You can return to this form if the risks change and your assessment needs to be modified. Your employer, insurance provider, a site owner or others involved with your group may wish to see a copy of your completed risk assessment. A sample of a part completed risk assessment using some of the details from the above examples has been prepared below

RISK ASSESSMENT FORM					
Date		Leader		Start location / venue	
Reassessment date		Signature			
Hazards		Risk Evaluation		Controlling measures	
Location / Map ref.	Description of Hazard	Potential risk & who might be affected	Risk Rating H/M/L	Control measures to reduce the risk	Assessment of effectiveness or proposed amendment
Gartmorn	Tree stumps and roots	Front wheel hitting stumps and/or skidding on exposed roots – all participants and leader	Low	Avoid this route when too wet. Leader points out hazards, gets groups to focus on good control skills on this section	Effective to date
Devilla Forest	Horses being ridden in forest	Horse startled, throwing rider Horse rearing or running off injuring rider and/or participants and/or leader	Low	Leader communicates rule to group to STOP when horses are seen Leader speaks to horse rider and asks what they prefer to do to allow bikes to pass Leader qualified and trained in effective group management	Effective
Whole trip	Group members getting lost	Member(s) of the group could take wrong turning either accidentally or deliberately	Low	Good group management and leadership style used, with appropriate leader decisions on how to manage the group. Route well known to leader	Effective to date

4. Act to reduce all risks to low

Now you have gathered your information and evaluated the risks, what can you do to minimise the risks and prevent harm occurring to any of your group? What type of action you might take will depend on the nature of the hazard, and to a certain extent, when it is encountered.

Hazards identified in advance of a ride must be reduced or eliminated at this stage. For example, any mechanical problems with the group's bikes need to be attended to immediately. Anyone who does not have a helmet and appropriate clothing will need to acquire some, or be able to borrow from others who have spares. These basic safety points should be part of the **generic risk assessment** and should be routinely addressed before every outing.

If you have identified potentially dangerous sections of trail on your reconnaissance ride you need to decide what actions will be necessary to reduce the risk of anyone coming to harm here. Control measures will include briefing the group about these hazards and issuing instructions such as “dismount” or “slow down” well in advance.

A leader needs to know how to practice good **group management** in this respect. Your position within a moving group is going to be important in preventing any accidents due to riders getting too far ahead or losing control. Being at the front of the group can be useful for slowing the group down before a steep descent or tricky section, controlling the pace of over enthusiastic riders, navigating, and showing a good line to take on single track. Leading from the rear of a group may be best when the group is tiring or when individual members need encouragement.

5. Review the risks
A crucial stage of risk assessment is reviewing the risks. Even the best risk assessments involve a degree of prediction and informed guess-work. and the experience of the leader is important in this respect. The environment and the human condition are dynamic, not static, and unanticipated changes can occur. In particular, you need to monitor the condition of the group and continually assess their safety by observation, communication and asking questions about their well-being. How are the group’s energy levels, morale and comfort? Is the weather taking a turn for the worse? Have the riding conditions been harder than expected? As a leader, you will have to think on your feet and make decisions to prevent risk levels from increasing due to changes in the factors you are monitoring. This is the process of **dynamic risk assessment**.

After a ride, review your risk assessment, and in particular your risk control strategy. Make notes and try to use your experience, positive and negative, to help you with future planning and risk management. Record your findings using a risk assessment form

TCL v MBL considerations
Leaders should be fully aware of the competencies of a Trail Cycle Leader and Mountain Bike Leader (see **SMBLA Scheme**) which define their respective operating environments. These criteria have been devised against a risk management background to place safe and realistic limits on where and when (time of day and season) groups can be led.

A group operating in more remote MBL terrain is potentially exposed to greater risks, than a group in TCL terrain. These risks must be controlled by matching the experience, abilities, motivation and equipment of your group to the terrain and routes you choose. This is a critical part of controlling the risks when planning any ride.

The ability of the leader (either TCL or MBL) to take appropriate leadership decisions is a significant part of the assessment, as using good judgement is crucial and frequently called on when assessing a route or part of a route to be used.

Legal Issues & Liability

By the end of this section Leaders should:-

- Describe their principal responsibilities with respect to good practice, including ethical leadership and child protection
- State where to obtain further information and help
- Explain the implications of insurance, duty of care and parental consent for safe and legal leadership practice
- State the operating boundaries/limits of the TCL and MBL awards in relation to competencies defined by the Adventure Activities Licensing Service required for leading groups off-road

INTRODUCTION

Leaders, being in a position of responsibility, must have an awareness of their moral and legal responsibilities to others who may be affected by their actions. This is as much about setting personal and professional standards of good practice as it is about simply fulfilling legal requirements. Therefore, a leader who wishes to take pride in his or her work and to set a good example of leadership should be willing to accept and embrace their legal responsibilities for their own protection, and the protection of those whom they are leading. This section outlines the main issues which a Leader must have an awareness of and how this understanding should inform SMBLA Leadership practices. Some of these issues are large topics in their own right and can not be covered in detail within this manual, however references are given which provide further sources of information.

ETHICAL LEADERSHIP

Participation in outdoor activities, especially as part of a group, can have major impacts on people's health and wellbeing, offering tremendous opportunities for social interaction and shared fun and challenges. Everyone who is involved in facilitating this, including leaders, has a responsibility to ensure that the activity is safe and enjoyable for those taking part. This is important not only for the Leader's personal reputation and the reputation of the organisation which the Leader is representing, but also to ensure that ethical values are upheld and no member of the group, or the communities they represent, are treated unfairly.

What are these ethical values and what are the implications for leadership practices?

Ethical values in the context of sport are no different from those in any other area of life and can be simply defined in application as: Fairness, Integrity, Respect and Equity.

Legislation exists to promote certain standards of ethical behaviour. Much of this legislation originates from equal opportunities in relation to employment and the protection of human rights, including the protection of children and vulnerable adults. However, recent changes have extended the scope of this legislation to cover the provision of goods, services and facilities, with the aims of ensuring that everyone has equal access to services and no one is discriminated against on the grounds of age, race, religion, gender, sexual orientation (or assumed sexual orientation) or disability.

Discrimination or unfair treatment can take many forms, including harassment, abuse, assumptions, exclusion, unfair allocation of rewards or resources, jokes and innuendo. A point to remember about discrimination is that even if a particular behaviour was not intended to be discriminatory, an individual or group whom the behaviour was directed towards or a third party who witnessed the behaviour may perceive it to be. Leaders must be very aware of the potential for discrimination to occur and be prepared to challenge behaviour which is discriminatory or in any other way unethical. A "nip it in the bud" approach can often prevent what could otherwise be an unpleasant and potentially damaging situation from developing. The best way to do this is to take the group member aside and ask them if they are aware of the consequences of their behaviour or language. In many cases it is found that discrimination happens through ignorance and is unintentional, but it does nevertheless need to be pointed out to someone to avoid reoccurrence.

Being prepared to deal with potential discrimination within a group also means knowing something about the make-up of the group in advance. Some of this information, such as age, gender, learning difficulties and disabilities might be routinely collected to help plan activities, but other information about people can be more sensitive and if it is collected, it should be done on a voluntary basis with clearly explained reasons for asking.

Whilst anti-discrimination has a defined legal basis, equitable leadership is more than just staying within the law. It is about respecting all individuals and treating people fairly, no matter what their cultural, social, economic or physical characteristics. This does not necessarily mean treating everyone exactly the same, but according to their individual needs, in order for them to be able to participate fully and have a positive experience within a group. Finding out what these needs are and how to manage them should be part of the planning process. To address the needs of an individual with a disability, for example, the Leader may need to talk to them or to a carer to find more about their needs and the support available. No leader should find themselves in a position where they are unaware of or ill-equipped to deal with a need which should have been previously identified and addressed.

Fair play is a familiar concept in competitive sports governed by rules and officials. The same concept applies equally well to group activities such as mountain biking where there are rules in place to ensure people's safety and agreed roles for individuals. Fairness, or lack of fairness, can significantly impact on the dynamics of the group. A leader must make sure that rules and roles are very clearly explained to the group. The standard for behaviour and consequences of breaking the rules must apply equally to all and it must not be influenced by differences in individuals' level of skill, background, experience or popularity within the group. Consistency in approach may be challenging at times, but is vital to achieve.

Fairness is very often promoted by a **code of conduct** that describes good practice in a particular context such as sport. Leaders should be aware of Scottish Cycling's Code of Conduct to which leaders are expected to adhere.

There is a large volume of resources, particularly on-line, providing information on equity, research reports, links to equity organisations and to specific projects and support available. A good place to start is your Sports Council and links therein: www.sportscotland.org.uk or www.sportengland.org or www.sports-council-wales.org.uk

Leaders wishing to develop their awareness and understanding of equity issues and good practice are advised to undertake sports equity training and do further reading in this area. A useful training resource has been developed by Sports Coach UK and is listed in the Bibliography.

Integrity

Integrity covers a number of issues such as confidentiality and data protection. A leader may hold or have access to personal details for clients, parents, payees etc. The Data Protection Act (1998) applies to everyone and aims to protect individuals from misuse or insecurity of personal information stored on computer, paper, video, mobile phone or other media. This responsibility for integrity also applies to the issue of disclosure in relation to child protection which is discussed below.

DUTY OF CARE

"Duty of Care" refers to the responsibility of a leader to look after a person in their charge. There are two aspects to Duty of care:

1. **Legal** Duty of Care
2. **Moral** Duty of Care

Legal Duty of Care

The most obvious example of Legal Duty of Care is in the context of Health and Safety. The Management of Health and Safety Regulations 1999 require that employers must carry our risk assessments and specify measures to reduce the risk of their activities. All Leaders need to risk assess their activities (see **Hazards & Risk Management**) and when doing so pay attention to the requirements relating to duty of care and other aspects of health and safety.

There is obviously a higher duty of care owed to children and young people and a Leader must be prepared for a child to be less careful than an adult in a similar situation, particularly so if there are medical or social factors which make the child more vulnerable to foreseeable risks. For the purpose of these guidelines the definition of a child is "A person under the age of 18" (Protection of Children [Scotland] Act 2003). Liability for the Legal Duty of Care would only arise if no action was taken to remedy a foreseeable risk of harm.

Moral Duty of Care

Moral Duty of Care can be described as the responsibility for safety and welfare, in the context of leadership, for those people who are being led. In a specific activity like mountain biking, the qualified instructor or leader has the Duty of Care for all those taking part, irrespective of age or position.

However, Leaders in charge of children have an additional moral responsibility, that of acting as "in loco parentis", meaning in place of the child's parent or guardian. A person "in loco parentis" owes a duty of care to the child equal to the duty of care owed by a *reasonable* parent, not necessarily the actual parent. A reasonable or careful parent will avoid activities and situations likely to cause harm to a child in his or her care and ensure the child's safety and welfare. This duty requires careful thought and forward planning.

To determine a breach of Moral Duty of Care ordinary civil law of negligence is applied. The question is whether the accused in acting, or not acting, has failed to reach the standards of a reasonable person?

Scottish Cycling's **Code of Conduct** and **Child Protection Policy** (see "Safe in Care Guidelines") contain further advice on how to act responsibly in a position of care and fulfill both legal and moral Duty of Care standards.

CHILD PROTECTION AND GOOD PRACTICE

One of the most important legal issues which Leaders must be informed about is Child Protection. Leaders have a legal and ethical responsibility, firstly to protect children they may come into contact with from any form of abuse, and secondly, themselves from wrongful accusations.

Mountain biking is just like any other sport or outdoor activity in that opportunities exist for abuse and bad practice to occur. Leaders must be aware of this potential in planning and assessing their own leadership practices. They must also be able to recognize the signs of potential child abuse and take appropriate action when a child discloses information to them, or when there is suspicion of abuse or evidence of bad practice by a colleague or another adult known to the Leader.

Anybody working with children or vulnerable adults has an important role to play in ensuring good practice is adhered to and in helping to identify and eliminate to child abuse.

Child Protection and Good Practice Training

It is beyond the scope of this manual to give more than an introduction to the issue of Child Protection. However, Scottish Cycling and British Cycling strongly recommend that all Leaders undertake Child Protection training by attending an approved course provided by an employer or organisations such as **sport**scotland or NSPCC, e.g. "Safeguarding & Protecting Children" (see Useful Contacts for details of these course providers). Leaders are expected to operate within the guidelines of Scottish Cycling's **Child Protection Policy, Code of Conduct**, and **Equity Policy**, or the policies of your employer under whose authority you are working.

Scottish Cycling Child Protection Policy

The full Scottish Cycling **Child Protection Policy** is available to Leaders on request or from the Scottish Cycling website www.scottishcycling.com. All Leaders should familiarise themselves with the Policy and know a Leader's responsibilities with respect to protection of participants and themselves.

The three key responsibilities are summarised below. All these issues should be covered in more detail in an approved Child Protection training course.

1. **Be able to recognise the signs and indicators of child abuse**
   There are four main kinds of child abuse: physical, emotional, sexual, or neglect. Abused children may display a variety of behaviours; they may be aggressive or withdrawn, they may be nervous and are often reluctant to take part in group activities. Physical signs of injury or neglect may or may not be apparent; a child will often try to hide these. Bear in mind that children can show disturbed behaviour or have bumps and bruises for any number of reasons and these signs do not necessarily indicate abuse. Children's behaviour must be viewed within the context of what is normal for that individual child and physical signs with reference to other activities they are involved in. However, such signs should give you grounds for concern, especially if the child is reluctant to

talk to you when questioned about the underlying causes. If a child whom you work with shows one or more of the possible indicators of abuse then there are reasonable grounds for concern over their safety and well-being.

2. Follow the policy and procedures of Scottish Cycling or your organisation for dealing with suspected child abuse

It is NOT a Leader's responsibility to determine if a child or vulnerable adult is being abused, it is however, their duty to report any such concerns. You should take steps to inform others about your concerns so that appropriate actions can be taken. Your organisation should have a designated Child Protection Officer whom you can speak to in confidence. They will advise on whether to involve parents or guardians or social services. Only where a child requires urgent medical attention should the situation be treated as an emergency.

3. Reduce the risk to yourself of potential accusations of child abuse and promote good practice in working with children

As child abuse is a highly emotive issue and public awareness is being raised in trying to tackle the problem, anyone working with children is at risk of being falsely accused of abuse. To protect yourself from this risk you must adopt good practice and implement a plan to follow procedure.

Good practice for working with children

The following advice is reproduced from Scottish Cycling's **Code of Conduct** for the Protection of Children & Vulnerable Adults:

- Make sport fun, enjoyable and promote fair play
- Always work in an open environment e.g. avoid private / unobserved situations and encourage an open setting for activities
- Treat all children and vulnerable adults equitably, with respect and dignity
- Put the welfare of each child or vulnerable adult first before personal achievement or performance goals
- Give enthusiastic and constructive feedback rather than negative criticism
- Ensure that if any form of manual or physical support is required for a child or vulnerable adult, it is provided openly, the individual is informed of what is being done and their consent is obtained
- Involve parents/guardians/carers/support-workers wherever appropriate
- Build balanced relationships based on mutual trust that empower children and vulnerable adults to share in the decision making process
- Recognise the developmental needs and capacity of children and vulnerable adults, avoid excessive training or competition and either pushing them against their will or putting undue pressure on them

In addition to the above Code, the following guidelines for working with groups of children should be applied:

- Avoid situations where you are the sole adult in the company of a child
- Always obtain parental consent for minors (see later section)
- Address all safety issues through a full risk assessment (see Hazards & Risk Management)
- Meet the physical needs of children in your care for food, water, warmth and rest
- Ensure all adults who may be assisting you with supervision adopt the same practices

The **Child Protection Checklist** in the Appendix can be used to record useful information for you to have readily available when working with children. Finding out this information in advance will allow you to act more quickly and confidently should the need arise.

Vetting suitability – Disclosure checks

In addition to Child Protection training, leaders working with children may be required by law to have an **Enhanced Disclosure Check**. The Disclosure service is provide by the Criminal Records Bureau (CRB), CRBS in Scotland, to employers and voluntary organisations to enable them to check records which may make an individual unsuitable for working with children or for working in certain roles. The role of leaders and those supervising or managing them would normally come within the definitions of positions requiring Enhanced Disclosure.

There are some circumstances in which a local authority or staff in charge may decide that a Disclosure Check is not necessary. An example would be a one-off or short-term involvement by an individual with a group of children in an activity, where the group continues to be supervised at all times by a member of staff who is Disclosure Checked and trained in Child Protection. In other circumstances a Disclosure Check will be judged mandatory, such as a residential excursion, or leading a group of children with special needs. Any Leader should seek the advice of the organisation they intend to work with well in advance, as Disclosure Checks can take several weeks to process.

These requirements will be affected by the Protection of Vulnerable Groups Act 2007, and leaders should make themselves aware of these changes when this act is implemented. Further advice can be gained from Disclosure Scotland, www.disclosurescotland.co.uk

PARENTAL CONSENT

Parental consent must be sought for any activity or outing planned for anyone under 16 years or under 18 if in full time education in Scotland, or anyone under 18 in the rest of the UK. A leader will be acting "in loco parentis" (as a parent) for any young person defined as a "minor" in law.

A consent form will clearly outline your planned activities, start and end time, location and inherent risks. The consent form is your "contract of agreement" with a parent or guardian, so it must give sufficient detail about what is planned, and you must not stray outside of this plan once it is agreed to.

There is a sample **Parental Consent Form** in the Appendix with the basic information which must be provided. Your employer may issue a standard form for you use, but you should provide supporting information for parents so that they can make an informed choice for their child.

Providing comprehensive information to parents will help to reassure them, give the Leader confidence that he/she has their support for the activity and reduces the possibility of any claims of negligence.

LEADER INSURANCE

All Leaders should have some form of insurance cover for their own protection. Membership of British Cycling (see **Introduction**) at Silver or Gold level provides entitlement to Third Party (Public Liability) insurance, free legal advice and assistance for members resident in the UK. Entitlement to Professional Indemnity insurance for registered British Cycling Leaders who are Silver or Gold members is dependent on evidence of Leaders having attended Child Protection training. To gain automatic entitlement to Professional Indemnity insurance, Leaders should submit evidence of Child Protection training to Scottish Cycling.

Leaders who are working for a Local Authority, outdoor centre, or some other organisation may be covered by their employer's insurance policy. It is important to check this and to check the details of the policy so that all conditions are met.

It is the responsibility of every Leader to check the details of the insurance policy (or that of their employer) under which they are operating, and abide by the conditions, adjusting practice and factors such as group size where necessary.

ADVENTURE ACTIVITIES LICENSING

The aim of the Adventure Activities Licensing Scheme is to give assurance that good safety management practice is being followed so that young people can experience outdoor activities without being exposed to avoidable risks. The licensing scheme is founded on good safety management and the principles of risk assessment - also the basis of the Health & Safety at Work Act 1974 which applies to all the activities subject to licensing, whether the activities are within the scope of the licensing scheme or outside it.

The **Adventure Activity Licensing Service** (AALS) is the body responsible for inspecting adventure activity providers and Local

Authorities whose provision falls within the scope of The Activity Centres (Young Persons' Safety) Act 1995, on behalf of the Health and Safety Executive (HSE). Providers which meet the appropriate standards of good practice will be issued with a licence for these activities by the Licensing Service. Most Local Authorities recognise this official approval and consider AALS licensed centres safe in both leading and equipping of activities on their license.

The Activity Centres (Young Persons' Safety) Act 1995 only applies to Scotland, England and Wales, and does not extend to Northern Ireland, the Isle of Man, the Channel Islands or elsewhere outside Great Britain.

Mountain biking is an AALS licensable activity, coming under the category of "Trekking", which also includes walking, pony trekking and off-piste skiing. Under the Adventure Activities Licensing Regulations 2004, licensable trekking activities are defined as:

"those which take place in moorland or more than 600m above sea level, and from which it would take more than 30 minutes travelling time (on foot using the standard Naismith's Rule) to reach any accessible road or refuge"

- **Moorland** is defined as: ***open uncultivated land at any height above sea level***
- An **accessible road** is defined as: ***a road which is, at the time in question, accessible to ambulances which are road-going vehicles, not specially adapted for rugged terrain***
- A **refuge** is defined as: ***a building offering shelter for the party in an emergency, which is either occupied or has some means of summoning help***

The Mountain Bike Leader award was designed to operate within the scope of adventure activity licensing, whereas the Trail Cycle Leader award was designed to operate outwith licensing conditions.

Who requires a licence?
According to the Adventure Activities Licensing Regulations 2004:

Anyone who provides, in return for payment, adventure activities covered by the Regulations to young people under 18 years of age must have a licence and abide by its conditions.

This includes **local authorities providing the facilities to an educational establishment in respect of the pupils of such an establishment**.

A licence is ***not*** required by voluntary associations offering activities to their members, or, by arrangement, to the members of another voluntary association, or by schools providing activities to their own pupils, or where young people taking part in the activities are accompanied by their parents or legal guardians.

The aforementioned is a summary of the relevant Regulations, and anyone who may potentially require a licence is strongly advised to consult the full Statutory Instruments relating to this legislation, available from the Adventure Activities Licensing Service (www.aals.org.uk). The publication ***Guidance from the Licensing Authority on the Adventure Activities Licensing Regulations 2004*** details the licensing scheme and safety standards which providers must meet for granting a licence, and is available from the Health & Safety Executive www.hse.gov.uk.

What level of competence is required to lead activities which are licensable?
The SMBLA awards, while not the only qualifications in mountain bike leadership recognised by AALS, are the only national governing body (NGB) awards. Local authorities or other organisations would generally seek an NGB qualification as a measure of competence for leaders of activities which are licensable. The licensing authority in carrying out its functions will take into account guidance published by the relevant NGB , for example in considering applications for a license, specifying leader-group ratios, or where there are concerns about the safety of activities, including those outside the Regulations. The SMBLA Manual would be considered published guidance in the context of mountain biking.

It should be noted that with respect to assessing competence to lead licensable activities, a local authority, school or other organisation may seek, in addition to paper qualification(s) (SMBLA certificate, first aid qualification, governing body membership) references, verification of personal skills and relevant experience.

SMBLA Tutors, recognised as "Technical Experts" for mountain biking by AALS, may be nominated to perform the following services by a facilities provider:

- clarify areas of uncertainty which neither the provider nor the instructors involved have suitable knowledge of, are experienced or qualified to address, e.g. advise on particular venues and or equipment to be used, conditions prevailing, required competence levels for given circumstances
- ratify the competence of their non-NGB qualified staff or conduct staff training
- be consulted on any issues identified by AALS inspection, and contained in a report issued to the provider

Details of the AALS interpretation of the scope of SMBLA awards can be found on the AALS web site:
www.aals.org.uk/guidance_details.php/pArticleHeadingID=138

Expedition Module

EXPEDITION: ***A journey or voyage with definite purpose***
Whatever the purpose, a journey over more than one day by mountain bike is likely to require participants to pull together their cycling and other outdoor skills, allied to their knowledge, understanding and appreciation of the outdoors. In this context, it is assumed that mountain bike expeditions will be undertaken by groups of comparatively inexperienced cyclists, led by very experienced leaders.

The great mountaineer and sailor, the late Bill Haman once commented, 'If an expedition cannot be planned on the back of an envelope, it is too big'. However, before undertaking a mountain bike expedition, a group leader needs to ask many questions and make many decisions, even if the final plan is in fact succinct enough to fit on the back of an envelope!

THE PARTICIPANTS
"Who is going to take part in the journey?" is the first, and probably the most important question to be asked by the leader(s) of any expedition. Also to be decided is the size of the group and the personnel who are to be involved in assisting in leading the party during the journey. As a general rule, smaller groups experience fewer problems en route and make less impact on the environment than larger groups.

THE PURPOSE
It is vital that the purpose of the journey is agreed by all and that everyone feels that they wish to commit themselves to its achievement. The more that all members of the group are involved in planning and preparation from the earliest stages, the more likely they are to be fully committed if circumstances become testing.

THE ROUTE
The route must be designed with considerable care so that it enables all members to achieve their aims without being excessively demanding for anyone. Previous experience by the Leader of the intended route or area to be visited is likely to be very valuable. Bearing in mind the time of year, an initial assessment of the possible environmental impact of the group on the area should be made at this stage.

HAZARDS AND RISKS
An assessment must also be made of the hazards which are likely to be encountered on the route and of the risks that these could pose for members of the group if the right precautions are not taken (see **Hazards & Risk Management**).

If some members are not sufficiently able or fit enough as cyclists to attempt the journey, or they lack the necessary expedition skills, it will be necessary to arrange training sessions to help improve their level of fitness and competency. Skills and fitness levels must be matched to the hazards and risks which the route and expected conditions are likely to present.

PERMISSION

In addition to full consent from the members of the group, permission for the venture may also have to be sought from parents or guardians (see the **Legal Issues & Liability** section), employers, an education or other authority, land owners, and other countryside users. The leader should check in advance of any route plan whether there might be any land management activities or events which will restrict access to the area they wish to use (see the **Access: Rights & Responsibilities** section).

BIKES AND OTHER EQUIPMENT

If the leader is relying on group members to bring their own bikes it will be necessary for rigorous checks to be made of the safety and efficiency of all machines well in advance of departure. It is also important at an early stage to make an assessment of the likely requirements for continuing maintenance and of the provision of tools and spares during the expedition, as well as the capacity of the bikes for carrying extra load. Depending on the anticipated nature of the journey, it will be necessary to judge what other gear and provisions may be necessary, such as equipment and food for camping, or severe weather clothing. In most cases, members will need to carry more cycle luggage than usual for day-long ventures with additional attention to requirements for extended travel in what might be a remote area.

TRANSPORT

Although the expedition may be wholly self propelled, it is probable that the group will need to make arrangements for travel to and from the expedition area. They may also wish to arrange some sort of vehicle support during the journey.

Carrying Bikes on Cars

What is the best way to transport bikes by car? Whatever method you choose it must be safe, secure and legal. If the bikes are being carried outside the car make sure you remove all attachments (pumps, water bottles, saddle bags, lights etc) which could potentially fall off or become detached during transit. Tighten all straps and fixings fully and double check them just before you leave and at intervals on your journey.

Rear-mounted bike racks, particularly hatch or boot-mounted types, are extremely popular, but when laden with bikes there is usually some obstruction of the car's lights and registration plate. When it is dark this is barely noticeable because the lights shine through the spokes, but there is still a problem with the number plate which must be legally displayed at all times. You can overcome this to some extent by attaching a spare rear plate with rubber bungees. However, to be totally law-abiding and comply with the Road Traffic Act, the Road Vehicles Lighting Regulations and the Road Vehicle (Registration and Licensing) regulations, you need a fully functioning trailer board with all the attendant supplementary vehicle electrics. In the absence of a trailer board you can remove the bike wheels and position the bikes so the rear derailleur doesn't get in the way. Or, alternatively, resort to using a roof rack.

PLANNING RESPONSIBILITIES OF THE EXPEDITION LEADER

The leader of a mountain bike expedition has to fulfil multiple responsibilities to ensure the success of an expedition. He or she must:

- identify the purpose and aims of the expedition
- complete and record an assessment of the hazards, and risks which the group will face
- have knowledge of current legislation for adventurous activities
- obtain parental consent, clearance from the authority, and relevant personal and medical information if appropriate
- work out a budget for the trip and ensure that personal/equipment/ travel insurance arrangements are made, if necessary
- plan an appropriate route for the group, including alternatives and escape routes
- ensure that bikes and other equipment are prepared and maintained in expedition ready condition
- obtain and take account of local weather forecasts
- prepare a base contact communication plan
- brief the group before, and at relevant points during the expedition
- arrange and organise transport to the start and from the end point of the journey, if required
- have sufficient experience of extended journeys by mountain bike to ensure he/she is confident that all eventualities can be dealt with
- recognise his/her responsibilities to parents/guardians, individuals of the group and the group as a whole, any sponsoring authority, employer or manager, local residents and landowners, as well as to other outdoor users and to the environment

PERSONAL AND GROUP EQUIPMENT

Clothing (see also **Clothing** section**)**
Two sets of clothing are recommended, one set of cycling clothing to ride in and another that is always kept dry to use at the campsite or if the other set gets too wet. This would imply that both sets of clothing can be used for cycling, even if one set is not perhaps cycling specific. It is better to start off in damp clothes and keep the dry stuff dry than to risk ending up with no dry clothes at all. It is important that the leader checks the clothing of the group before setting out that day. Even when using waterproof panniers/rucksacks, clothes and other items that need to be kept dry should be routinely stored in sealed plastic bags . Heavy items should, if possible, be placed at the bottom of panniers, but those items that may be required during the ride or when first reaching a stopping point should be placed on top or in side pockets so they are more accessible.

Carrying kit
There are three main ways of carrying kit, either on your body, on the bike or in a trailer. As the amount of gear carried increases, the ability to successfully negotiate technical terrain decreases. Routes should therefore be planned with this in mind.

(i) Rucksacks
Gear carried on the body can either be in a rucksack or bumbag. Carrying much more than can be accommodated in a 25 litre rucksack is going to severely limit your riding ability and will dramatically increase the potential to cause injury either to your back, or to some other part of you when you fall off. It is probably better to carry most of your stuff either on your bike or in a trailer.

(i) Panniers
Two small panniers firmly attached to a rear rack is possibly the best method. The rack should be strong and secured to the bike in four places by bolts secured by locknuts. A rackpack could be attached to the top of this. A traditional saddlebag is a favoured method of carrying gear by many. If you need to carry more gear than this then front panniers could be considered if the forks allow them to be fitted. Most experienced off road riders have found front "lowrider" style panniers to be too close to the ground, and easy to snag on the narrower trails. Again, the strength and fixing method should be as the rear rack. Some find handlebar bags useful, others find that they obstruct the view of the trail and can interfere with steering. If used, limiting the weight they carry is essential.

(iii) Trailers
Most riders who have used trailers report that a single wheel trailer is the only design worth considering off-road. Tandem riders and those travelling with young or much weaker riders have found them especially useful, as carrying kit for two people on one bike is more difficult. Trailers can be useful for hauling in heavier gear to base camp. However,

consideration should be given to the reasons for the trip and the environmental impacts of creating longer term, larger base camps.

Tents

There are many tent designs available, from the more traditional ridge or tunnel design to more modern dome and geodesic designs. Dome, Tunnel and Geodesic tents are very lightweight with the poles being made from very light and flexible fibreglass or, more commonly, aluminium wands (tent poles) which slot through sewn sleeves in the tent itself. The design of these tents maximises the use of floor space due to their steep walls, and makes them easy to move if you decide to change your campsite to another spot in the immediate locality. These tents are also incredibly strong as they are designed to flex with the wind rather than try to stand up to it and eventually buckle.

Ridge tents are classic pieces of camping equipment and still remain popular today. Although heavier and usually bulkier than the other three types of tent, they are incredibly robust and durable which makes them a good choice for group and extended use when the tents may be up in one place for a number of days. Ridge tents can be pitched flysheet first in a storm, so are a better choice for wet weather.

Ideally all tents should be lightweight, waterproof (even under heavy rain), condensation free and fitted with a sewn-in ground sheet and down to the ground fly sheet. Modern single skin breathable tents can be very light, however they are often more fragile, condensation can be more of a problem and they can leak after a season or two. A two layer tent, outer flysheet and inner, is heavier but can be more reliable, as well as often providing more room under the flysheet for cooking and gear. A tent with a covered porch is great for storing grubby panniers, and may also provide a shelter to cook under in bad weather. Tent areas used for cooking should be easily vented to avoid build up of steam and therefore condensation, as well as build up of toxic gases. The entrance to the tent should be large enough to allow you easy access to the inner tent and should be designed to keep out driving rain and snow.

Most lightweight tents suitable for mountain bike expeditions will be classified as 1-3 person tents. One-person tents are designed for the solo camper, whilst the two-person tent is designed for the very comfort-conscious solo camper or a duo. Two-person tents offer the best compromise in terms of weight, space and pack-size. It is probably not worth trying to carry a tent for more than two or three people, as even splitting it between this number, the parts will be quite heavy. Similarly, a 3-season tent is probably the most versatile for UK conditions, being fully waterproof and tougher than a 2-season tent. Only if you expect to be camping in winter conditions or high winds do you need a 4-season tent.

In summer you can get by quite adequately using bivvi bags. This may be a useful fall back if your intended campsite is a mountain bothy that might be full when you get there or if you don't make it there before nightfall.

Sleeping bags

These come in many shapes, sizes, fabrics and weights. The most important feature to consider is the bag filling which gives the bag its insulating properties. There are two main types of filling: synthetic and down. Synthetic filled bags are generally cheaper, heavier and bulkier but can retain warmth when wet. Down bags are generally more expensive, lighter and pack smaller. They have the best warmth:weight ratio, but their main disadvantage is they must not be allowed to get wet, as they become almost impossible to dry and start to rapidly loose their insulation qualities. Synthetic fillings such as "hollofill" are now very advanced and approaching the qualities of down. Some bags now use a combination of synthetic and natural fillings.

Sleeping bags have a number which is based on a seasonal rating. 1-season bags are suitable for warm summer use, while 4-season bags are suitable for winter use, and 5-season bags can cope with high mountain use. The choice is baffling but if you set a budget and know the most suitable season rating for your bag you cannot go far wrong. As you may have a bag for a long time it is worth spending as much as you possibly can to ensure comfort on your expeditions. However, when choosing a sleeping bag it is important to remember that the stated insulating qualities of the bag are a guide only. Factors such as altitude, expected weather conditions and site exposure are obvious factors to help you decide. People of different ages, sizes and outdoor experience vary greatly in what they require in terms of insulation. A 1-season bag can be fine for one person, but may feel uncomfortably cold to another in the same tent. If you tend to feel cold at night go for a bag with a higher season rating than you think you might need, and/or purchase some thermal sleeping wear.

The shape and size of a bag will also affect its comfort. Some bags are body-hugging “mummy style”, others are rectangular in shape with more room to move about. Those with a full length zip offer greater ventilation, but will be slightly more bulky to pack. There are now women-specific sleeping bags which are slightly shorter, wider at the hips, and have extra insulation around the hood, middle and feet.

Using a sleeping bag liner made of silk or microfleece can increase insulation and help to protect the inside of your bag.

Sleeping Mats
These are very important items which will greatly improve your comfort in two ways. The first is to add a padded layer between you and the ground, and the second and more important, is to insulate you from the ground which will suck heat from you as you sleep.

Mats come in two main forms; either a closed cell foam pad, or a self-inflating open cell pad which affords more protection in both areas. The foam pad is significantly less expensive than the inflatable pad. People often compare the difference between the ground and a foam mat to the difference between a foam mat and an inflatable mat. For this reason, many people are now using inflatable mats which provide an even greater degree of comfort and insulation; the three-quarter length one is smaller and lighter than a full size foam mat.

Stoves and cooking fuels
Food must be prepared on a small, reliable and lightweight stove which is capable of heating up quantities of food and water quickly and efficiently Stove stability and properties and availability of the fuel the stove uses are the main things to consider when choosing a cooking system. There are three main types of stove: gas, pressurised liquid fuel and spirit stoves.

Gas stoves are the most popular type amongst the vast majority of campers as they offer a simple, clean and easily adjustable way to cook. The drawbacks are the expense and the availability of suitable gas cartridges in some remote areas. The performance of gas stoves can decrease markedly in cold conditions, and when the gas canister is getting empty. More recently, gas mixtures have gone a long way to solving some of these problems. Mixed gas fuel is easy to use and burns very cleanly.

Pressure stoves are the cheapest type of stove to run but are generally the most expensive to buy. They require a certain amount of delicate and practised handling in order to get them working, but once mastered they are very efficient, but noisy! Refuelling is not a problem no matter where you are, as many will burn on any combustible fuel such as petrol or paraffin (but not camel methane). They are reasonably controllable for simmering, but a close eye must be kept on them. The fuel must be carried in a crack-resistant container, as it is both smelly and messy.

Spirit stoves or meths burners, in particular those made by Trangia, offer a very compact and light set of stove and cooking pots in one unit and are the preferred choice for many groups of less experienced campers, especially young people. The fuel is easy to use and they work well in windy conditions, an important consideration when trying to discourage people from cooking inside tents. Meths burners are cheaper than gas stoves and pressure stoves and there is also much less that can go wrong as they have no delicate moving parts. The invisible flame of a meths burner can be a hazard which has to be managed carefully. Again, carrying the fuel in a suitable crack-resistant container is essential as it can be messy.

Solid fuel stoves, the most common being the Hexamine, are little used as they require some time to heat up and do not produce any heat worthy of note. A recent development which no self-respecting expeditionist should go without occasionally is a disposable barbecue which will make you the envy of everyone else on the trip! Do be aware of the environmental impact of where you place these when lit.

Whilst deciding which stove will suit you best do not forget the humble match or lighter without which the only option may be the old boy scout stick rubbing trick.

General kit

It is important to carry bags etc to enable rubbish to be carried out, as burning and burying is unacceptable in most areas. However, it may be important to be able to start a small fire, so matches and firelighters should be carried, especially if the intended destination for the night is a bothy. A torch is essential for the leader, and at some times of the year for all group members. It may be a good idea to have bike lights for all in case the group is delayed, and these can double up as torches.

EQUIPMENT CHECKLIST

Equipment needs to be suitable for the location, weather conditions and time of year, e.g. a tent suitable for camping in summer valleys may not be suitable for more exposed high level sites or other times of the year. More spare clothing may need to be carried, or less, depending on conditions.

Individual equipment	Shared equipment	Leader equipment
♦ helmet	♦ torch / bike light	♦ group first aid kit
♦ gloves	♦ map	♦ larger tool kit / spares etc
♦ warm hat	♦ compass	♦ group shelter
♦ food / water for the day	♦ stove	♦ flares / mobile phone
♦ whistle	♦ spare stove seals	♦ spare batteries
♦ cycle shoes	♦ fuel and bottles	
♦ 2 pairs socks	♦ cooking pots	
♦ 2 pairs trousers / tights / shorts (quick drying for washing)	♦ camp food	
♦ 2 base layers (one can be washed overnight)	♦ water purification tablets	
♦ 2 mid layers	♦ tin opener	
♦ waterproof / breathable top	♦ pot / dish cleaning kit	
♦ toiletries	♦ toilet paper	
♦ travel towel	♦ matches	
♦ sleeping bag	♦ small shovel	
♦ mug / plate / knife, fork	♦ tent	
♦ polythene bags	♦ small toolkit / spare tube	
♦ watch / cycle computer	♦ insect repellent	
♦ personal 1st aid kit		

Keeping kit dry

This in an area where people often have difficulty. It is wise to carry a few polythene bags or dry bags in which to place wet items to separate them from dry. Do not get into your sleeping bag with wet kit on as you will only succeed in getting your bag wet. This is vitally important in a down bag for reasons described earlier. Store anything that does not require to be kept dry under the fly sheet, such items include stoves, pans and water bottles.

A full list of **Tools and Spares** is given in the **Bike Set-up, the Safe Cycle & Trailside Repairs** section and should be included in an expedition equipment checklist. It is important that the correct tools are carried to repair every bike in the group. Tools and spares which can be shared amongst the group include:

Shared Tools

- adjustable spanner
- allen keys
- chain tool and spare links
- pliers
- mole wrench
- Swiss Army knife
- Hypercracker
- spoke key

- **Shared Spares**
- brake and gear cables
- spare tyre
- brake blocks
- seat pin bolt(s)
- 4" bolt and nut (emergency pedal)
- Lube
- zip ties
- spokes (to fit each bike)
- electrical tape

When using panniers on an expedition it is well worth carrying some pannier spares in case anything breaks: spare hooks (for attaching pannier to rack), zip ties (various sizes) and spare fixing bolts for the rack.

EQUIPMENT CHECKS AND MAINTENANCE

All bikes should be thoroughly checked in advance of the expedition, allowing enough time for any repairs or maintenance to be carried out. When on your trip, daily checks should be carried out on each bike, paying particular attention to:

Daily bike checks

- wheels – check spokes are tight and wheels true
- brakes – check adjustment and replace worn blocks or pads if necessary, check condition of brake cables/hoses
- tyres – check for bald patches, condition of tread, any damage to side walls, correct tyre pressure
- gears – check all gears are reachable and changing smoothly, check for condition of gear cables
- bearings - check for excessive wear
- pannier rack - check all fixing bolts are tight
- chain - check for stiff links and excessive wear, lube if necessary

Making regular adjustments and carrying out maintenance after each day's ride can prevent a small problem becoming worse or in the worse case scenario a mechanical failure which could cause an accident and lead to the expedition being cut short.

Remember to check the condition of tents and all camping equipment as well as bikes daily. Tents can rip in strong winds and this is not an uncommon occurrence. Carry a few extra items to enable a tent repair to be carried out on-site.

Ensure that all kit is checked for damage, cleaned, dried, repaired if necessary and put away as soon as practicable after returning from an expedition so that it is in a condition to be used for the next trip without the frustration of discovering a broken sleeping bag zip, rip or burn hole in the groundsheet of the tent

CAMP CRAFT

Choosing a camp site

It is important to seek the permission and approval of the landowner before choosing any site to camp on. On arrival at the proposed venue several requirements should be considered; a camp site meeting these standards should ensure a comfortable night and a better ride the following day.

(i) Shelter

Shelter is a very important factor in allowing you a good night's sleep. Many a sleepless night has been passed in tents pitched in areas with little or no shelter. Interrupted sleep can be caused by something as trivial as the continual flutter of the tent fabric, or as major as chasing a tent around a hillside in the middle of the night. Large boulders or a wall can act as a wind break.

A block of trees provides shade in hot weather and protection from driving rain. However, do not pitch your tent directly underneath large trees. After rain has continued for a while or even after it has abated, large drips will fall on the tent which can keep you awake, and are often successful at penetrating the fly sheet. Depending on the time of year and the condition of the trees, windy weather may bring down branches from the trees, creating an obvious hazard to tents below.

(ii) Water supply

Having a good water supply close to hand is essential for cooking and for matters of personal hygiene. The supply should be free-flowing and water should be taken upstream of any suspected pollutant. If the quality of the water is at all suspect then the use of various water purifying methods is recommended. These consist of tablets, mechanical devices, and of course boiling. All water for consumption or cooking should be taken from above the area designated for personal hygiene. Great care should be taken to avoid polluting water courses with waste foodstuffs and personal hygiene items (soaps, toothpaste, washing up liquid etc).

(iii) Drainage

It is critical that your site is dry and will remain so in the event of heavy rain. Therefore choose a site which is naturally freely draining and not in a hollow. The ideal site is a slight slope which allows drainage. Do not camp in a dry river bed or a narrow valley which may be susceptible to flash flooding. Do not try to improve the drainage of a site by digging drainage channels around your tent as this is destructive to the environment.

(iv) Topography

Wherever possible avoid camping in hollows if the temperature is to be low at night. Cold air sinks below warmer air, thus hollows collect sinking cold air and could make for an uncomfortable, shivery night. For the masochists amongst you choose a boulder field but otherwise choose a site which has an even surface and is rock / pebble free.

Toilets

Ensure that all party members are familiar with where the toilet is going to be. This is particularly important with regard to location which should be at least 60 metres from the nearest water and should always be downstream of the water supply for the camp. "Packing out" is best practice as our countryside comes under increasing pressure from recreational users. This involves removing all solid bodily waste from these areas and disposing of it in a waste bin. If this is not to be adopted then the waste should be buried at least 30 cm underground.

Biting insects

Awful is the fate of the one who camps in a midge infested area during the summer months. Avoid conditions which attract dense swarms of midges – standing water, nearby cattle or sheep.

Pitching the tent

When you have found a suitable area to camp, you must then pick out a specific spot within that area on which to pitch your tent. Conditions to take into account are: wind direction, cooking, and view. Quite often people will place view before wind direction as they enjoy opening the tent in the morning and having the best view possible. When rain and wind are forecast try to pitch your tent with the door in the lee of the wind to avoid rain driving through the door zips. This will also allow you to cook in the door of the tent without the tent filling with wind and taking off with you in it.

In the main, if your initial assessment of a suitable site has been good you can pitch your tent anywhere in that general location and you should remain comfortable.

When pitching a tent begin by pegging it out from the windward end and be careful to ensure that it remains neat and wrinkle free. More often than not this will only be a problem with ridge tents and is caused by over tightening guys and fly sheet pegs. It is important that you are well practiced in pitching your tent as it is significantly more difficult to pitch any tent in a howling gale than it is to pitch it on a still summer's day in your back garden. The more time you save here the drier the tent inner stays and the drier and less frustrated you will be once you've finished.

CAMP COOKING

Cooking a meal adequate for replenishing used energy and preparing the body for exercise the following day is an essential skill for the mountain bike expeditionist.

Pots and pans come in all shapes and sizes for camping. Most important is that heat is distributed evenly throughout the base of the pan so as to ensure that you use fuel most efficiently. This will get your cooking done quicker and so deliver a hot meal faster and will give you that extra brew when you need it. Cooking receptacles should also be easily washed and light and compact for transporting on your bike. If you choose non-stick items cleaning will be much easier, especially when using cold water.

Carrying three or four pots to cook with in a camp is impractical due to the implications of space available, therefore the expeditionist must be able to cook well with just one or two pots. This is possible only if you are either cooking a very basic meal or if you are well organised and you plan the order in which items should be cooked. Using old tricks such as boiling rice then leaving it while you cook the main sauce on the burner are very helpful. The rice will continue to cook and swell as long as it remains in the hot water. After the rest is cooked, finish the rice off on the burner again.

Always remember that if you can not eat all the food you cook then you should dispose of any excess. If you are conscientious this will mean packing it out twice as heavy as it was before cooking, not to mention the mess if the bag it is in bursts! Try to cook what you will eat and then cook more later if you need it. This avoids food wastage and disposal problems.

Be aware of food hygiene issues to avoid health risks associated with contaminated food or water supplies. It is best to avoid cooking meat for a group, unless it can be bought tinned or fresh locally. Remember, the "shelf-life" of any perishable foods stored in panniers will be much less than if kept in a refrigerator. Cooking only what you need will also avoid the dangers associated with re-heating foods.

The most practical ingredients for camp meals will keep well, be light to carry, and have minimal but burst-proof packaging. Porridge oats are a great carbohydrate source which will keep you going for hours. Dried fruit and nuts can be used to enrich any meal or used as snack foods. Powdered milk and soups can be used to make an instant hot drink, or sauce for pasta or rice. There are all kinds of dried packet foods which can provide a complete meal by just adding boiling water. However, if you are camping for more than a weekend you will probably appreciate some fresh foods which may be available locally from villages or farm shops.

SHELTERS

Huts & Bothies

These are extremely useful to know about in advance when expeditioning, especially if the weather turns particularly nasty and you decide to retire to one for shelter and to allow kit to dry out. The Mountain Bothies Association welcomes cyclists at its bothies, of which there are over 100 in more remote locations across the UK www.mountainbothies.org.uk. A night in a dry, warm shelter can make all the difference to moral and boost the group's spirits before the next leg of the expedition.

Bivouacs

Planned bivouacs can be amongst the most pleasurable of expedition nights out. They allow sleeping under the stars in a controlled environment. These can only be highly recommended as multi-day options when the weather is, as far as possible, guaranteed to be fair. A good Goretex (or similar) bivvi bag is recommended in case of rain. Emergency and unplanned bivouacs can be very uncomfortable and can prove a very negative experience. To ensure that you will survive in relative comfort, think carefully about what you carry on your expedition by way of emergency gear. If somebody loses the tent off the back of their bike and you get to your camp site at 10 pm in the rain before you realise, could you fudge a shelter?

SUSTAINABLE CAMPING

Ensure that you and your companions look after the area you cycle through. This is everyone's responsibility and by doing your bit, no matter how inconsequential it may seem at the time, you can sometimes leave a site in better condition than when you first encountered it. As expedition cyclists, we should adopt a policy of sustainable camping so as to raise the profile of mountain biking as an activity responsible for its actions.

Scottish Outdoor Access Code advocates that anyone accessing the outdoors should care for the environment and help to protect the natural and cultural heritage which we enjoy.

The key points of the Code with respect to wild camping are:

- Take care not to damage or disturb wildlife, vegetation or soils
- Take all litter away from your site (even if it is not yours!)
- Follow any signage aimed at protecting plants or animals, geological or archaeological features
- Do not camp or light fires on any cultural heritage site
- Help to prevent erosion by avoiding sensitive habitats such as loch shores, riverbanks, dunes and marshy ground
- Do not move, disturb or deface walls or other structures

For more information on the Scottish Outdoor Access Code visit www.outdooraccess-scotland.com (see also the **Access Rights & Responsibilities** section).

The advice of the Scottish Outdoor Access Code and Countryside Code for England and Wales is commensurate with the principles of **Leave No Trace**, guidance widely recognised in the outdoor world and endorsed by IMBA (International Mountain Bike Association). Would be expeditioners are advised to research these as part of their planning (see www.lnt.org).

Actions that would promote sustainable camping include:

- Plan your expedition to avoid times of high usage. Large groups will inevitably have a greater impact than smaller ones.
- Plan your campsite carefully. It may be better to use a well established site which is already damaged environmentally. If choosing virgin ground be sensitive to flora and fauna. Consider dispersing pitches over a wide area but beware of tramping out pathways, particularly if staying more than one night.
- "Pack it in, pack it out" is the basic principle of Leave No Trace. Apart from human waste, everything you take in should be brought back out. This includes toilet paper, unless it can be safely burned after use.

Views are evolving as far as "crap carrying" is concerned. Generally it is safe to bury human waste. If operating in ecologically sensitive areas you may consider carrying waste out. Do not compromise personal hygiene.

Before having a fire anywhere you should ensure that any landowner approves of this and when doing so you should be extremely sensitive to the environmental implications of having that fire. Ask yourself - do we really need a fire?

With a little research before your trip you can find out what, if any, conservation significance an area has, not only so you are aware of any restrictions on access or permitted activities, but so you can increase your awareness of the natural and cultural interest of the area which you can share with the group.

To find out local environmental and conservation information you can contact one of the Scottish Natural Heritage Area Officers www.snh.org.uk

As environmentally responsible bikers we should also think about sustainability, not just in relation to any particular expedition, but also in relation to equipment purchases and resource use. Expeditioning can be a materialistic and energy consumptive activity, so think of ways to reduce your consumption and minimise your impact in every aspect of your planning. Remember that what you do to protect the environment can be appreciated by future generations, but what you take away or use up is gone, to the detriment of others and the planet.

Expedition Module Learning Outcomes

Session	Learning Outcomes
Introduction	By the end of this session leaders will be able to recall: • The structure of the course • The requirements for assessment
Tents	By the end of this session leaders will be able to: • Describe the physical aspects of a good site • Discuss the pros and cons of common tent design • Pitch and repack a tent • Describe best practice in terms of the Access Code
Expedition Food, Stoves & Cooking	By the end of this session leaders will be able to: • Discuss the pros and cons of different types of camping stoves • List foods that can be easily prepared in a wild environment • Employ techniques to maximise safety and efficiency of camping stoves
Expedition Clothing & Equipment	By the end of this session leaders will be able to describe: • The clothing necessary to cope with varying conditions • The protective clothing that should be worn • The equipment that will be required
Bike Set-up & Load Carrying	By the end of this session leaders will be able to: • Describe methods of carrying expedition kit using a bike • Discuss the pros and cons of panniers, trailers and rucksacks • Describe variations to bike set-up appropriate to expedition cycling • Describe good practice for packing expedition kit for a journey

Trailside Repairs	By the end of this session leaders will be able to: • Describe additional serious faults which may occur on a bike • List tools and spares that should be considered • Carry out more involved repairs such as replacing a broken spoke, adjusting a bottom bracket, adjusting cones
Planning	By the end of this session leaders will be able to: • Plan a route (route card) for an expedition • Prepare escape plans, late back procedures • Take account of significant hazards on the route • Apply weather forecasts, observations and act appropriately • Deal safely with water hazards • Describe the medical, competency and contact information that should be collected about individuals
Riding the Expedition Bike	By the end of this session leaders will have practised: • Loading and unloading the bike • Negotiating a range of terrain • Techniques to overcome obstacles
Camp-craft	By the end of this session leaders will be able to: • Select a suitable location to camp • Pitch a tent and simulate preparations for an overnight stay • Make appropriate arrangements to ensure good hygiene • Prepare a hot meal and clean cooking equipment etc • Break camp, pack, clean site
Equipment Audit	By the end of this session leaders will have: • Reviewed the equipment they have carried • Considered any additional kit to be carried • Considered anything that could be left
Review	By the end of this session leaders will have: • Evaluated their performance on the course • Received personal feedback • An opportunity to ask any outstanding questions • Completed an evaluation of the course

Expedition Module Assessment Outcomes

Holders of the Expedition Module will be able to lead expeditions with the terrain covered by the remit of their SMBLA award.

Assessment Outcomes	Stage of learning
Bike Set Up	
• Produce a bike in good mechanical order and fitted out for expeditioning	2
• Be able to advise on bikes and fixtures suitable for the task	2
• Demonstrate that equipment will be safely and securely carried in the main on the bike, or on a bike trailer	2
Clothing and Equipment	
• Be suitably dressed and have clothes to hand for all conditions likely to be encountered	3
• Be able to advise on technical clothing and safety equipment (gloves, glasses, helmets)	2
• Carry equipment in such a way that all essential items are in waterproof covers so that they are dry when needed	3
Expedition Trips	
• Demonstrate the additional equipment and planning required to undertake self-supporting expedition trips	2
Techniques	
• Demonstrate the basic skills and techniques associated with riding a loaded mountain bike	2
• Describe the differences between loaded and unloaded bikes	2
Managing a group	
• Demonstrate responsible, effective and safe management of a group, off-road in a remote environment	3
• State how to prepare a group for a mountain bike expedition	3
Trailside Repairs	
• Carry appropriate expedition tools and repair kit, to include such extras as spare tyres, tools to tighten bottom brackets etc.	3
• State how to effect advanced trail side repairs to "get you home" e.g., buckled wheels, broken rear derailleur	3

Assessment Outcomes	Stage of Learning
Camp-craft Show good camp-craft skills including: • Ability to choose a good campsite • Ability to pitch a tent securely and quickly • State considerations of hygiene, and toilet arrangements around the campsite • Describe safety and environmental considerations, especially with regard to cooking around tents • Describe different types of tents, stoves, sleeping bags etc and their advantages and disadvantages	2 2 2 3 2
Navigation • Be able to identify location at all times to within 100 metres, using a map, compass and cycle computer • Demonstrate the use of these common navigational aids in a remote environment • Accurately determine length and trip time for a route or leg and deliver a flowing journey • Demonstrate timing and pacing on foot	3 3 3 3
Planning and Preparation - The perfect mountain bike expedition • Demonstrate the ability to plan and prepare a group for a mountain bike expedition • Demonstrate effective knowledge of weather and its effect on a group • Interpret a variety of weather charts and demonstrate the ability to interpret obvious weather patterns in the field • Provide a copy of "Late Back Procedures" • Demonstrate techniques used to deal with a variety of water hazards • Outline group qualities and competence including:- medical history, parental consent, emergency contact numbers	2 3 3 3 3 2
Dealing with Emergencies • Carry out a risk assessment of the planned activity • Demonstrate the techniques used to deal with an emergency in a remote environment • Describe contingency plans and escape routes for when things go wrong • State the uses and limitations of mobile phones and radios on mountain bike expeditions • State an awareness of the shortcomings of the above techniques	3 3 3 2 2

Assessment Outcomes	Stage of Learning
Countryside Awareness • State the current access legislation in Scotland and where to get information both locally and nationally • Describe the Scottish Outdoor Access Code when sharing the countryside with other users • Demonstrate a basic background knowledge of the natural history, history, geology and geography of the area being used, and show evidence of the ability to communicate this to other people • Describe the impact that mountain biking has on the environment	2 2 1 1
Lecture Topic/Planning • Deliver a ten minute talk on a topic allocated by the Tutor • Produce suitable route plans / route cards for the expedition	2 2

Night Riding Module

PLANNING AND PREPARATION

Everyone who attends this module has already been assessed competent to lead groups either as a Trail Cycle Leader or a Mountain Bike Leader. These competencies will be built on during this module. It is likely that candidates attending the first session will be asked to demonstrate some of these competencies by arriving with a current weather forecast for the location being used, a copy of late back procedures, and a copy of information normally given to their home based contact. In addition candidates may be asked to attend with a route which they think would be suitable for riding with a group in darkness. These tasks will allow some initial assessment of the level of experience of the candidate and provide the opportunity to focus on them early in the course. In addition to the information contained in the sections on **Weather**, **Hazards & Risk Management** and **Emergency Planning & Procedures**, the following information will be helpful for night riding.

Weather

Initial sessions will be challenging enough for groups without wet or windy conditions.

It is recognized that cold, clear nights are good for introductory rides as they make it easier to see. Moonless nights are more challenging.

A sharp frost can firm up muddy puddles but can produce big ruts and icy patches.

In wet conditions sandy soils drain best. Pine forests can remain dry even after days of rain.

Risk Assessment

As a leader it is important to know the area and the route well.
Careful selection of location for a first night riding venture is important as contending with darkness alone will be a sufficient challenge for some members of the group.

The technical standard should be low as even familiar terrain can become unfamiliar in darkness and become quite challenging. Ensure the route is at the right level for the group. Even easy trails appear more difficult at night.

Overhanging branches, locked gates, walkers, and dogs etc. are additionally hazardous in the dark.

Consideration should be given to advising the landowner of your intended route as the appearance of unfamiliar strange lights might cause alarm.

Emergency Procedures
Emergency procedures must be robust. The ones used in normal daylight hours should have been tested to ensure they work before relying on them at night. Have good "late back" procedures in place and ensure that your emergency contact information is up to date.

BIKE LIGHTS

Lights
Selecting bike lights that enable a leader to function effectively can be quite crucial, as extended use and greater lighting power than that required for personal use might be necessary. Leaders might have to travel part of the route using their lights as the sole lighting source for a small group. They may have to carry out trailside repairs or deal with an emergency requiring extended use of lights. Given these possibilities the following information should be helpful in the selection of bike lights for use leading groups off road in darkness.

- 15 watts is a recommended output (halogen equivalent)
- Helmet mounted lights are best for cornering, but they obscure drops
- Bar mounted lights give best depth perception, but turns are unlit
- Halogen lamps are relatively cheap and last fairly long but their output is not as good as the new generation of lamps
- Halide lamps are expensive and require careful handling but their output is much higher than halogens. They do not like being switched on and off frequently
- Light Emitting Diodes (LEDs) require very little battery power and are very robust. The only LEDs that produce enough light for night riding are very expensive (usually developed for the car industry)
- Take care to disconnect lights when storing. Bulbs will be very hot during and after use, hot enough to burn flesh and melt or burn clothing
- Manufacturers instructions must be followed at all times

Batteries

- Lead acid batteries are cheap but heavy and require regular charging whether or not the light has been used
- Ni-Cad batteries are lighter than Lead acid but need careful charging to avoid memory effect (where the battery "remembers" where in the charge cycle the recharge began and suffers a drop in voltage when it reaches that point during use). Repeated overcharging can also cause the battery to discharge quickly in use.
- Nickel Metal Hydride (Ni-Mh) are lighter still but quite expensive. They suffer less from memory effect
- Lithium Ion batteries (mobile phone batteries) are the lightest and most powerful but are the most expensive
- Cold conditions will reduce battery life.

Light Choice
Bar mounted lights with a frame pack or bottle battery and an output of 10+10 watts is probably the best choice for most trail riding sessions. It is a simple and effective set-up and is usually adequate for up to 2 hour rides (depending on battery life).

An additional helmet mounted light is recommended for the leader to help with Trailside Repairs, Navigation and Group Management.

A number of head torches are available. The one chosen should have a powerful beam, long battery life and be able to be securely fixed to a bike helmet.

Light Legal
The Highway Code (2007) states:
"At night you must have white front and red rear lights. The bike must also be fitted with a red rear reflector (and amber pedal reflectors if manufactured after 1/10/85)"

"White front reflectors and spoke reflectors will also help you be seen. Flashing lights are permitted but it is recommended that cyclists who are riding in areas without street lighting use a steady front lamp."

Should a route contain some road section then compliance with the Highway Code is required. However, lighting much more powerful than the legal minimum for road use is required to enable the cyclist to see effectively off road in darkness.

There will be occasions (off road) when use of a rear light might dazzle someone cycling behind and it may be safer not to use rear lights in these circumstances.

THE SAFE CYCLE

Securing Lights, Cables and Batteries

It is important that all cables are carefully fastened and lights properly secured as an insecure light or cable could work its way loose in the dark without being noticed. Velcro straps are good for ensuring batteries and cables don't snag or fall off. Cable ties are a cheap but less easily reused alternative.

Gears, brakes and steering should all be tested after fitting lights to ensure they are not affected by lights or cables

Adjusting Bike Lights

The light beam should be positioned about 10 meters in front of the bike. Consideration needs to be given to the sag of suspension when adjusting the light beam.

If a special tool is required to adjust a light it must be in the leader's toolkit.

The Effect of the Lights on the Bike

It should be remembered that lights may make steering a little more awkward.

If the battery is a bottle type the bike will require a second bottle cage where water can be carried (unless it can be carried in a back pack).

The addition of lights to the bars may make the bars very crowded. It is useful to practise locating light switches in darkness to become slick at switching on and off, especially where more that one light is fitted.

Light sets will increase the weight of the bike and can make it more difficult to handle and lift therefore extra care should be taken when transporting a bike fitted with lights.

CLOTHING AND EQUIPMENT

In addition to the points covered in the **Clothing** chapter extra knowledge, particularly on hi-viz clothing, is necessary for night riding.

Clothing

As these sessions will generally take place in darkness during the winter months additional care should be given to ensuring that the layering principle is adhered to.

In addition, warm, full-fingered gloves are essential for everyone in the group.

A hat under a helmet is also good, but a check needs to be made to ensure the helmet still fits well.

Footwear must be strong, warm and dry.

Protective eye wear is essential as overhanging branches are less likely to be spotted on time.

High Visibility Garments

There are 2 European Standards applicable to high visibility garments:

EN471 – aimed at professional users, emergency services, highway maintenance and airside airport staff

EN1150 – for non-professional use, jogging, cycling or other traffic related interaction

All compliant garments must be marked with CE and the relevant standard. Each of the standards effectively indicates the minimum surface areas of both background material and retro-reflective material that is visible for a given persons height. On this basis, the smaller the garment, the more difficult it become to achieve compliance. This is an important point, as non-compliant vests and tabards will invariably be shorter in the body than the compliant versions. It represents an effective cost saving for manufacturers, even though chest sizes can remain the same.

There are a limited number of fully compliant manufacturers of reflective tape. The big three are 3M, Reflexite and Untika. These are the preferred choice of the emergency services, and as such have proven manufacturing and performance criteria. Non compliant garments often use less effective reflective strips / patches to keep costs down.

Other reflective items.

Other items include slap bands, stickers or hangers, and CE marking still has a role to play. Again it is not obligatory, but if items are attached to Road Safety initiatives they should comply:

EN 13356 is the standard applicable to all hi-viz accessories:

Type 1 is for free-hanging reflectors, pram reflectors, garment hangers etc.

Type 2 is for removable items such as slap bands, arm bands etc.

Type 3 is for mounted items like stickers

Again the standards centre on the amount of reflective area available in each case. Thus the larger, the better, and if it's made from one of the previously discussed proprietary reflective tape manufacturers, better still.

The New Highway Code (2007) states
"You should wear light coloured or fluorescent clothing which helps other road users see you in daylight and poor light" and *"reflective clothing and/ or accessories (belt, arm or ankle bands) in the dark"*

When riding off road, reflective strips on outer garments can prove useful for group management and safety. The use of different colours of slap bands can also help. Having sets of varying colours allows pairs of riders to be given the same colour. For example, there can be one pair in red, a pair in green etc. This can help management of paired riding in the dark.

Flashing armbands and other night biking accessories are available from a number of companies now specialising in this area including:
www.reflectives.gbr.cc
www.brightsportz.co.uk
www.rspp.co.uk

Safety Equipment
In addition to carrying a First Aid Kit it is recommended that the following safety equipment is carried :

- An emergency shelter. Emergency situations are likely to take longer to resolve at night and this could prove to be a most valuable part of a Leaders' kit
- Everyone should be encouraged to carry a flask containing hot juice. At the very least one should be carried by the Leader for use by everyone in the group.
- In line with normal practice spare clothing and space for removed clothing should be available
- A whistle should be supplied to each rider which can be used to communicate to find a missing rider
- A mobile phone (fully charged, of course) can be invaluable
- For those who have access to them, 2 way radios may help contact with a back marker
- A spare head torch should be carried for repairs, navigation and as a back-up light, along with spare batteries

TRAILSIDE REPAIRS

This module will include the usual trailside repairs carried out as part of a Trail Cycle Leader course, namely, brake and gear cable adjustments, broken chain and puncture repairs. However, these tasks require to be undertaken in darkness. Care should be taken to ensure that all tools are readily available and easily accessible. Something such as a hi-viz or light coloured rucksack cover should be laid on the ground as a receptacle for parts and tools to ensure that nothing goes missing during the repair.

Without a good head torch carrying out trailside repairs can be difficult. A repair needs to be carried out quickly to avoid the group becoming cold and restless.

GROUP MANAGEMENT

Safe group management Off-road
A thorough briefing is required to include boundaries, conduct and actions in an emergency, including actions in the event of becoming separated from the group. (Riders finding themselves separated from the group should stop and remain where they are.)

It is important that the Leader keeps in regular contact with the back marker if riding at the front of the group. As normal the Leader must carefully select their position in the group and if required vary it.

Head counts must be taken very regularly and certainly at every stop.

For safety reasons, spacing between riders needs to be greater than in daytime. This, however, can lead to the group being stretched (on single track) and the use of a buddy system would be helpful here. (The use of slap bands in colours can be a great help in identifying pairs of riders.)

All riders should be given a whistle and it should only be used to attract attention by someone separated and in need of assistance.

Safe group management On-road
When riding on-road the same briefing regarding boundaries, conduct and actions in an emergency should be given.

All lights must be on, in compliance with the Highway Code.
When riding in a group, dipped lights are better than full beam as full beam can produce glare from the rider in front especially if they are wearing reflective clothing.

The best place for the leader is at the rear and with the group cycling close together.

Care must be taken when turning right across a road. If it is too dangerous, stop at the left side of the road, past the junction, and walk across together under control. When crossing road, the leader must be positioned to give best view of road for the safe crossing of the group.

NAVIGATION

Navigation needs to be of the highest standard. It would be highly unlikely that a Leader would chose to lead a route in darkness which they were unfamiliar with in both daylight and darkness. Navigation needs to be completed to the same standard as TCL assessment.

Computers and maps are difficult to see at night without a head torch and even with one it needs to be adjusted to ensure the beam can be directed towards the computer.

Route cards and preparation are vital as there will be sufficient challenges for the leader without navigation being one of them.

DEALING WITH EMERGENCIES

Emergency procedures must be robust, as the ones used in normal daylight hours might not be available at night.

A few likely emergency scenarios should be considered and a strategy worked out for dealing with them prepared in advance. These might include:

- Someone requiring medical assistance being brought to them
- Dealing with an injury which you are able to tend to and self rescue
- Managing the group safely if the groups lights start failing
- Dealing with someone becoming very cold

Have good "late back" procedures in place and ensure that your emergency contact information is up to date and working at night.

Night Riding Module Learning Outcomes

Session	Learning Outcomes
Planning and Preparation	*By the end of this session leaders will be able to:* • Obtain a weather forecast and explain the effect it will have on a night ride, its participants and the environment • Select a route appropriate to the ability of the riders, battery life and weather conditions • State the importance of route/area familiarity
Bike Lights	*By the end of this session leaders will be able to:* • Describe the different kinds of front and rear lights available • Describe the different kinds of batteries available • State the best light set-up for your needs and those of the groups • State the current legal lighting requirements for cycling on public highways
The Safe Cycle	*By the end of this session leaders will be able to:* • Demonstrate secure lights, batteries and cables • Adjust the bike lights to the correct position • Describe the effect that lights, cables and battery will have on the function of the bike
Clothing and Equipment	*By the end of this session leaders will be able to:* • Dress and be equipped, appropriate to the conditions, to lead a Night Ride • List appropriate safety equipment for a night ride • Describe other visible aids
Practical Journey	*By the end of this session leaders will be able to apply some of the outcomes for sessions 1, 2, 3 and 4, including:* • State the importance of route familiarity and when this might not be necessary • State the best lighting set up for your needs • Adjust the bike lights to correct position • Describe the effect that lights, cables and battery will have on the function of the bike • List appropriate safety equipment for a night ride • Demonstrate a puncture repair

Trailside Repairs	*By the end of this session leaders will be able to demonstrate the following in darkness and outside:* • Puncture repair (within 10 minutes) • Mend a broken chain (within 10 minutes) • Adjust brakes • Adjust gears
Group Management	*By the end of this session leaders will be able to:* • Demonstrate safe group management off road and on road • Give an appropriate and thorough briefing on safe protocol for a night ride • Demonstrate a head count at regular intervals • Demonstrate optimum position for leading with a group at night
Navigation	*By the end of this session, in darkness, leaders will be able to:* • State their location to within 100 metres using map, compass and cycle computer • Calculate the length of, and time for, a route or leg of a journey • Demonstrate the use of common navigational aids • Demonstrate their ability to lead a flowing journey which they have planned using a pre-prepared route card
Dealing with Emergencies	*By the end of this session leaders will be able to:* • Describe the additional risks of riding at night (scenarios) • State the techniques to be used to deal with an emergency during a night ride • List emergency procedures for area of night ride
Practical Journey	*By the end of this session leaders will be able to:* • Apply some of the session outcomes for sessions 6, 7, 8 and 9 • Describe what you require to do before attending for assessment

Night Riding Module Assessment Outcomes

Holders of the Night Riding Module will be able to operate in conditions outside the '**daytime only**' remit of their award.

Assessment Outcomes	Learning Stage
Planning and Preparation	
• Report a current weather forecast and state the effect of different weather conditions on the trip	3
• Explain late back procedures	3
• State emergency contact / consent information if appropriate	3
• State appropriate medical information	3
Bike Lights	
• Describe the different kinds of lights available	2
• Describe the different kinds of batteries available	2
• State the best set-up for your needs	2
The Safe Cycle	
• Demonstrate how to secure lights, battery and cables to a bike.	2
• Demonstrate adjustment of bike lights to correct position.	2
• Describe the effect that lights, cables and battery will have on the function of the bike	2
Clothing and Equipment	
• Describe appropriate clothing for a Night Ride	2
• List appropriate safety equipment for a Night Ride	2
Managing a Group	
• Demonstrate safe group management off-road in darkness.	3
• Demonstrate safe group management on-road in darkness	3
Trailside Repairs	
• Demonstrate the following in darkness:	
– Puncture repair	3
– Mend a broken chain	3
– Adjust brakes	2
– Adjust gears	2

Assessment Outcomes	Learning Stage
Navigation • State location to within 100 metres using map, compass and cycle computer • Calculate and state the distance and riding time for a route or leg • Demonstrate the use of common navigational aids • Demonstrate ability to lead a flowing journey which has been planned	3 3 3 2
Dealing with Emergencies • Assess and state the additional risks of riding at night • State the techniques to be used to deal with an emergency during a Night Ride	3 3

Winter Conditions Module

INTRODUCTION

The Winter Conditions Module is an additional qualification enabling Trail Cycle Leaders and Mountain Bike Leaders to work outside the **'summer conditions only'** remit of the TCL and MBL qualifications. It consists of a 2 day training module and a 1 day assessment. The module enables leaders to work in defined **'intermediate'** and **'winter'** conditions **but operate only in TCL terrain regardless of the level of award that they hold.** (Please refer to the manual **SMBLA Awards** section for the definition of TCL terrain).

Training Course

- Day 1 of training is classroom based and can take place at any time
- Day 2 of training is practical and will take place in 'winter' conditions. This may be expected to be at short notice to take advantage of conditions as they occur

Conditions

The conditions covered by the SMBLA awards and the Winter Conditions module are defined as follows:

Summer Conditions

Includes all conditions but those when snow or freezing conditions are either prevalent or forecast

Intermediate Conditions

Intermediate conditions include occasions when some snow (e.g. a light dusting or avoidable patches) or brief freezing conditions (e.g. an overnight frost) are either prevalent or forecast

Winter Conditions

Winter conditions include occasions when a more substantial layer of snow (e.g. to several inches) or longer lying snow, and prolonged freezing conditions are either prevalent or forecast

Please refer to the table in the chapter on **Legal Issues and Liability** for a summary of the SMBLA awards required for AALS defined terrain in both summer and winter conditions.

WINTER RIDING

Clothing & Footwear

In addition to the points covered in the **Clothing** chapter the following are specific to winter cycling:

Headwear: A great deal of heat can be lost through the head so an insulating layer such as a balaclava, buff, beanie hat or bandana should be considered.

Helmet covers also help to retain heat as well as offering protection from rain and snow. These can be obtained in breathable materials.

Eye protection: It is conceivable that, in bright sunny conditions, protection from reflected light from lying snow could be required. Even clear protective shields could offer some protection. Failure to take adequate precautions could lead to snow blindness.

Gloves: Personal experience is valuable in ascertaining your needs in terms of gloves. It is worth considering carrying several options which could include silk inner gloves, cycling specific gloves of varying degrees of insulation through to down-filled mittens for the most extreme conditions. Sealskins™ provide reasonable insulation and waterproof qualities but can become damp inside after prolonged use. Experience shows that there will always be someone in your group who is inadequately gloved so it is always worth carrying an additional pair.

Footwear: (see also section on **Bike Set-up** for winter use of clipless pedals) If you are using a clipless system in cold conditions the cleat, when connected to the pedal, acts as a heat sink and accelerates heat loss through the sole of the foot. To counteract this effect a larger size of shoe will allow space for thicker socks and an insulated insole. (heat reflective on one side and insulated on the other) Winter specific footwear is available from at least two manufacturers and provides a waterproof and insulated solution to cold feet.

Sealskin™ socks can help delay the onset of cold feet. Being completely waterproof they may get damp inside and eventually become cold as well. Woollen socks used in conjunction with Goretex™ socks are another warm and waterproof option.

Ensuring that the lower legs are well insulated helps keep the feet warm. If flat pedals or toeclips are used, light hill walking boots can be effective. Snow gaiters are a useful addition to any kind of boot in snowy conditions.

Keeping your feet warm is very much linked to an individual's physiology so experiment with different combinations. In extreme conditions experience shows that at best you will delay the onset of cold feet rather than prevent them.

BIKE SET-UP

Most mountain bikes equipped for trail riding should cope to some degree with winter conditions. Tyres, handlebars and pedals are worthy of some discussion though:

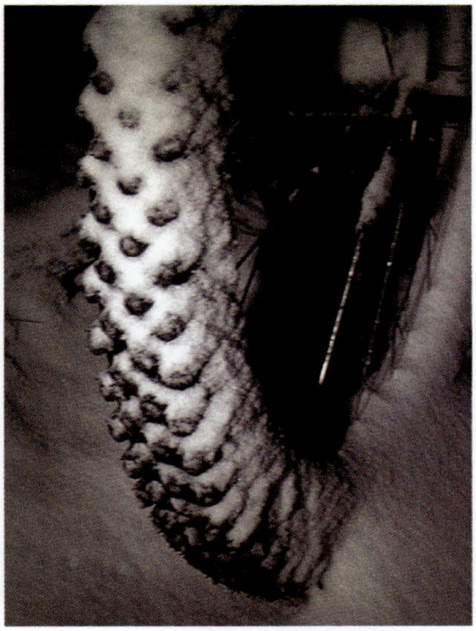

Tyres: An open, knobbly tread pattern should cope best with UK snow and mud conditions. This type of tread pattern allows the snow and mud to clear from the tyre. Snow is very variable however and you may find that an alternative tread pattern is more appropriate. Given that very few riders will change the tyre from one excursion to another a good compromise has to be found. In countries where a permanent winter snow cover is established a studded winter tyre works well.

Pedals: Cleated pedals work well in most conditions. Where there is snow cover the cleats tend to block up with snow and with foot pressure on the ground this turns to ice and prevents correct engagement of the cleat with the pedal. If you ride clipless it is useful to have a small sharp implement handy to clear the cleat of ice.

Flat (BMX) type pedals or toe-clip pedals allow more flexibility with footwear choice and avoid the problems encountered with clipless systems in snowy conditions.

Handlebars: Because bulkier gloves are frequently worn in the winter it is worth considering the layout of brake levers and gear shifters on the handlebars. By moving them slightly inboard you will allow more space for a comfortable grip.

Winter related bike issues

In extreme cold conditions it is not uncommon for the freewheel to freeze. Solutions could include urinating over the sprockets or if a flask is carried, pouring a little hot water, tea etc over the sprockets.

Build-up of snow on transmission can make it very difficult to change gear. Since the time spent sorting bikes needs to be minimised, particularly with groups, it is suggested that the front gear changer is used and a low to medium gear is selected at the rear. In this situation it is better to progress with two or three operational gears than to have frequent stops.

GROUND CONDITIONS

Whilst under-wheel conditions can vary a great deal from day to day at any time of year, in winter, especially in snow, conditions can vary dramatically from hour to hour. Maintaining a good event horizon (forward vision) is of particular importance in winter conditions. Typically in summer biking, the climbing element of the ride is rewarded by a flowing descent. In winter, ice or frozen rutted snow may render the descent as long and arduous as the ascent.

Frost: Frost can often work to your benefit making easily passable trails that were previously bogged down in mud. Equally, trails that would be damaged by the passage of mountain bikes can be negotiated without leaving a trace. Tyre adhesion can be improved, particularly on gravel covered trails. Care should be taken when there are dips which might now contain ice rather than puddles and when riding over smooth areas of trail or rock which might now be ice clad.

The exhilaration of riding on crisp winter mornings needs to be accompanied by excellent observation, anticipation and caution. A feeling for the amount of grip available develops with experience.

Ice: Avoid or walk is the best advice here. Take care when there is unfrozen surface water and temperatures are low. The road or trail surface underneath may be frozen and a fall into water at these temperatures is to be avoided at all costs.

Snow: In the UK consistent snow cover is virtually unknown. Constantly variable snow conditions are the norm.

Riding in snow deeper than 15cm (6inches) is rarely practicable and even below this depth is tiring and a skilled operation. Consequently taking any but the most mature and experienced groups into conditions where deep snow riding is likely is best avoided.

One of the key points to bear in mind is that trail hazards such as rocks and roots are hidden but are no less hazardous than when visible.

Snowfalls of a few centimetres when settled and frosted can offer an excellent riding surface. Often the cover will have sufficient strength to support rider and bike and will offer excellent grip.

Riding in powder snow may lead to a rapid build-up of ice on the bike's transmission resulting in a temporary gear shift malfunction. Since this affects the rear more than the front mechanism it may be best to select a rear sprocket that will function well with all chain rings. This will provide at least three operational gears.

Refrozen snow: Snow that has been previously ridden, walked or skied and then has become frozen provides a very uncomfortable riding surface. If a well established groove has been ridden it may be possible to stay within this. Frequently the bike will slew wildly but with a little practice balance can be maintained and forward progress continued. Scan ahead to select the best route. Choose a gear that balances forward progress against energy output and traction.

Slush: Slush is as likely to be encountered in the UK as is snow. If snow is lying on higher ground then slush is likely to be encountered at the start and finish of any excursion. Although the main danger lies in its unpredictability, in many instances tyres will press through the slush and provide grip against the underlying surface. Riding at slow speed will prevent a soaking ride in cold conditions. Moderate speeds, good observation and anticipation should allow a safe passage in these conditions.

RIDING TECHNIQUE

The key difference in winter is the variety of conditions that occur over short periods of time or short distances on the trail. The key to success is in adapting the riding style and riding position to obtain the best compromise for the conditions.

When riding over snow cover you can never be certain of the underlying profile and sudden decelerations can occur when the front wheel enters a dip hidden by fallen snow. In addition the front wheel will have a tendency to plough into the snow. For both these reasons it is often more successful to have the balance of weight to the rear of the bike. When riding snow that has been previously ridden dramatic slewing of both front and rear wheels will occur. With a little practice it is surprising how many of these situations can be ridden without putting a foot down. Riding through snow, even of modest depth is tiring. A low gear is to be preferred but this has to be balanced against traction requirements.

Steering has to be light and gently progressive. Your attitude on the bike should be light and nimble, relaxed but ready to respond instantly to a skid or change in under-wheel conditions.

WEATHER

In addition to the chapter on **Weather** considerable care should be taken when planning winter excursions, particularly with young clients. The shortness of the day, combined with modest altitude, and locations where the sun does not penetrate to any extent in winter means that low temperatures can easily persist throughout the day. When this is combined with high levels of energy output and high transpiration of body fluids, hypothermia becomes a very real issue. It is suggested that a number of forecasts are consulted prior to undertaking any excursion including avalanche forecasts where applicable.

EMERGENCY SHELTERS

In the same way that sudden snowfalls can benight motorists, it is easily conceivable that snowfall, terrain, mechanical, medical or other issues could combine to require the group to remain where it is. It is recommended that leaders familiarise themselves with some of the many winter survival techniques. In ordinary situations it can be expected that late back procedures will be triggered.

Here are a few suggestions:

- Make a positive decision based on conditions. Do not wait until the group is cold, uncertain and losing confidence
- Control communication. If you can contact base with your decision do so immediately. Calling 112 will utilise any mobile network provider and increase the chance of successful communication
- Look around you and decide where the best shelter can be found. A group shelter is an excellent starting point
- Consider how best you can shelter from the wind and how you can insulate from ground chill
- Be reasonably near water but not in danger from it or unable to hear rescuers because of the sound of it
- Ensure that rescuers will be able to find the spot
- Get everyone involved in making the shelter or collecting materials to do so

If a group shelter is available, use it in conjunction with some of the following, if not, make a rapid appraisal of your surroundings. Pine forest offers excellent shelter from the wind and temperatures under the foliage canopy will be higher. There is likely to be good ground insulation from fallen needles. Create a shelter for the group by harvesting small, well covered branches and piling them against a supporting framework. It may be possible to use the group's bikes as a framework. Speed and involvement of everyone are important.

In more open terrain, look for hollows, fallen trees, snow banks, drystane dykes, deep vegetation etc as the starting point for your shelter.

Whatever shelter you use, ensure everyone is in bodily contact and that you constantly monitor the group for signs of cold related injuries. Ensure available food and drinks are pooled and rationed.

COLD RELATED INJURIES

Frostnip, evidenced by the exposed flesh looking white may be seen on nose, ears and cheeks. Less visibly fingers and toes can also suffer. The observation of companions is important. Treatment to prevent its escalation to frostbite should be immediate and involve placing the affected area in contact with an unaffected part of your or a companion's anatomy.

Cold feet are a particular concern as the condition will not be seen and even a feeling of warmth after feeling cold could still be evidence of frost-nip. Although it requires overcoming considerable inertia to do so, removal of footwear to thaw the frozen area is vital to prevent more serious injury.

In extreme conditions, where some of the group are at risk of cold related injury, a rapid return to base is the wisest course.

Should frostbite occur, evacuation is the only course and the affected area should be left alone as full recovery is best managed by medical experts.

Winter Conditions Module Learning Outcomes

Session	Learning Outcomes
Introduction	*By the end of this session leaders will be able to:* • Restate the limitations of the module • Describe the type of conditions included in the module • Restate the outcomes of the module • Describe the requirements for assessment
Bikes & Winter Specific Issues	*By the end of this session leaders will be able to:* • Set up a bike for winter use • Discuss and advise on winter specific bike issues • Apply solutions to common winter bike problems • Explain the pros and cons of different types of equipment in a winter context
Clothing & Equipment	*By the end of this session leaders will be able to:* • Advise on foot, hand and head gear • Describe layering of clothing on upper and lower body • State the equipment to be carried for group survival • Employ techniques to carry additional equipment
Fitness, Fuelling and Hydration	*By the end of this session leaders will be able to describe:* • The additional requirements on fuelling and hydration in winter conditions • The effects of cold on physical performance • The additional requirements for leaders in winter
Cold Related Injuries	*By the end of this session leaders will be able to:* • Recognise cold related injuries • Prevent cold related injuries • Treat cold related injuries • Recognise conditions in which sun protection for eyes and exposed skin are required
Weather & Forecasts	*By the end of this session leaders will be able to:* • List relevant weather & avalanche forecasts • Interpret the forecast in the context of mountain biking • Describe situations where there is the potential for avalanches

Winter Riding Techniques	*By the end of this session leaders will be able to:* • Recognise a range of ground conditions • Employ a range of techniques to negotiate varying terrain and ground conditions • Advise clients on skills and techniques
Trailside Repairs	*By the end of this session leaders will be able to:* • Employ techniques to assist repairs in cold conditions • Manage the wellbeing of clients whilst repairs are undertaken
Emergencies	*By the end of this session leaders will be able to:* • Identify and assess the additional risks associated with working in winter conditions • Evaluate an emergency situation and act appropriately • Employ a group shelter for maximum benefit • Maximise use of available natural shelter • Recognise cold related injuries and conditions
Feedback & Review	*By the end of this session leaders will be able to:* • Evaluate their performance on the module • Receive personal feedback • Ask tutor questions where appropriate

Winter Conditions Module Assessment Outcomes

Holders of the Winter Conditions Module will be able to work in defined '**intermediate**' and '**winter**' conditions **but operate only in TCL terrain regardless of the level of the award they hold**.

Assessment Outcomes	Learning Stage
Appropriately Equipped Cycle	
• Attend module with a cycle appropriate to winter conditions	3
• Describe the pros and cons of various types of bike equipment	3
Clothing & Equipment	
• Attend with clothing, foot, hand and headgear appropriate to the conditions	3
• Advise on appropriate clothing for winter cycling	3
• Carry appropriate group survival equipment	3
• List the additional personal and group equipment that will be required and describe techniques to carry this	3
Trailside Repairs	
• Demonstrate common repairs in extreme conditions	3
Fitness, Fuelling and Hydration	
• Demonstrate a suitable level of fitness to lead given the additional rigours of winter conditions	3
• Describe what is meant by adequately fuelled and hydrated	3
• Have sufficient food/fluids to contend with a day's outing in winter conditions	3
Winter Riding Techniques	
• Demonstrate skills and techniques required to negotiate a range of ground conditions including, fresh snow (up to 15cm), frost, refrozen rutted snow, patchy ice	3
• Demonstrate appropriate body position, gearing, braking, climbing and descending skills	3
Winter Specific Bike Issues	
• Describe and prevent or remedy winter specific issues such as icing of gear mechanisms and brakes, freezing of free-hubs and clogging of cleated pedals	3

Assessment Outcomes	Learning Stage
Dealing with emergencies/first aid • Carry out a risk assessment of the planned winter activity • Demonstrate appropriate techniques to deal with emergencies in a winter environment • Demonstrate appropriate skills to prevent, recognise, and treat cold-specific injuries and conditions • Construct an emergency shelter with available resources	3 3 3 3
Leadership • Describe the additional rigours of a winter environment and adapt style to ensure all group members operate well within their, skill, fitness and equipment limits • Describe the of type terrain in which (Winter) Mountain Leader skills would be required and demonstrate understanding that such terrain is outwith the scope of this award • Describe where to access winter weather forecasts and avalanche conditions and attend the assessment with knowledge of current conditions	3 3 3

Mountain Biking in Scotland

Whether you want technical singletrack, relaxed scenic routes, North Shore style constructions or a wilderness expedition you will find it all in Scotland. The International Mountain Bicycling Association (IMBA) has rated Scotland as one of the top five destinations in the world for mountain biking, and the best outside North America. Scotland was also voted number one in the world for mountain biking under the 'People's Choice" category in an on-line poll.

As well as a growing number of purpose-built and regularly maintained trails, many of which have on-site facilities such as cafés, bike washes and showers, there are also miles and miles of natural trails which were used by cyclists long before mountain biking became a sport. Scotland has a long history of off-road cycling and the bicycle has always been a popular way for walkers and climbers to reach more remote areas. Many long distance walks such as the Great Glen Way can be biked and there are a couple of Scottish off-road coast to coast routes too.

The trails which are now being developed across the country mean that mountain biking is becoming more accessible, with way-marked and graded all-weather trails offering something for everyone from the complete novice to expert riders. The Forestry Commission has been instrumental in developing many of these trails, including the hugely successful 7 Stanes, which includes Glentress, Scotland's biggest mountain bike centre, and the new trails at Laggan Wolftrax, near Spean Bridge in the Highlands. The Forestry Commission is currently working in conjunction with other organisations to create a consistent trail grading system throughout the country.

There are downhill courses at Innerleithen, Ae and Fort William, all of which offer transport to the top. The Nevis Range's Aonach Mor and Leanachan Forest, Fort William, have hosted rounds of the UCI Mountain Bike World Cup since 2002. In 2007 Fort William played host to the UCI Mountain Bike and Trials World Championships, by far the biggest mountain bike event ever to be staged in Britain and which brought a week-long festival of mountain biking to the UK's Outdoor Capital. The World Championship downhill and cross country (Witch's Trail) courses are open to ride and form just part of a network of trails in the Lochaber area.

In recent years new trails have been developed at Lochgilphead (Fire Tower Trail), Drumlanrig, Carron Valley, Pollock Park, Black Isle, and Fochabers (Moray Monster Trails) in Morayshire.

As a side attraction, Drumlanrig Castle has a Cycle Museum containing a replica of the "velocipede", the first pedal cycle invented by local blacksmith, Kirkpatrick Macmillan in 1840.

Scottish Local Authorities are currently identifying "Core Path Networks", and all have appointed Access Officers with this responsibility. Core Paths are local paths which form a network of local access for multiple user categories, including cycling. As paths are formally identified, issues of signage and maintenance will be addressed, so improving information and access to many existing paths for cyclists. See the **Access** section for related information.

Further information on many of the places mentioned above can be found under "Places to ride" in the **Useful Contacts** section. Visit Scotland produces annually a very handy Scottish Mountain Biking Guide covering all the main mountain biking centres in Scotland. Leaflets are available for Forestry Commission routes, and there are various books and maps available from book shops and bike shops. Local bike shops are often the best source of information on where to ride, and the majority of them are happy to help.

Leaving the way-marked purpose-built trails and dedicated mountain bike centres behind, Scotland has just as much to offer "off-piste", from suburban woods, hills and shorelines to remote wilderness areas where all the skills of navigation and route-planning are called upon.

Local knowledge, maps, publications and websites are valuable resources to help you plan an off-road journey on non-waymarked routes. There are some classic multi-day rides on coast-coast routes such as Highland Cross, from Morvich to Beauly, or long day trips in areas such as Cairngorms and Assynt. Routes may include paths, stalking tracks and single-track roads, and the challenge and freedom comes from linking these up to create a flowing journey.

For sources of information on where to ride see the **Useful Contacts** section.

Mountain Biking as a Sport

INTRODUCTION

Riding bikes off road and away from the inherent risks and conflicts with traffic is an excellent opportunity for a broad cross-section of society to become involved in the sport of cycling, and for people to engage with the outdoors in an exciting and accessible way. It promotes the use of urban as well as remote environments, and allows the benefits of an 'outdoor activity' to transfer into the everyday lives of participants. Mountain biking can be a spiritual and enjoyable experience and it is quick to reward those who desire to improve their skills by regular riding. For many it has become their first-choice sport and a pathway to health, fitness and competition.

Of all the cycle sport disciplines, mountain biking is the most popular in Scotland, with events in the Scottish Race Calendar regularly attracting several hundred riders of all ages and abilities. It is a very spectator-friendly sport and some of the race venues are within areas of high scenic value. Scotland is acknowledged as hosting some of the best mountain bike racing in the UK, with many competitors traveling from south of the Border to access more challenging and technical courses and regularly plays host to major international events,

This section aims to provide an introduction to the sport of mountain biking in its various forms and provide some guidance on how to get involved. The complimentary section, "Mountain Biking in Scotland" gives ideas on where to ride and some of the highlights for mountain biking in Scotland.

SUB-DISCIPLINES OF MOUNTAIN BIKING

Mountain Biking is undoubtedly a sport for everyone, whatever their age or ability. The two main branches of competitive mountain biking are cross-country and downhill, however, there has also been a growth in the area of participation events, which include trailquest (mountain bike orienteering) and single-day and multi-day endurance events.

Downhill

With its thrills and spills, downhill has rapidly become the most popular discipline in the sport of mountain biking. Competitors race on full suspension bikes and wear full-face helmets and body armour to protect against the potential dangers of a high speed crash. Both power and speed are needed to cover the ground as fast as possible, and exceptional bike handling skills honed through hours and hours of practice. At the top level, downhill requires a high level of fitness, but anyone with sufficient experience of mountain biking can have a go and test themselves against the course.

Cross-country
Cross-country racing has more of an endurance element than downhill, but the technical nature of some courses requires a high degree of skill as well. Within cross-country and downhill events there are races for all categories of rider, from Juvenile to Grand Veteran. The Fun category is where many first-time racers start and is the ideal entry-level event.

Cyclo-cross
The sister discipline to cross-country is **cyclo-cross**. Cyclo-cross races take place on a short off-road circuit and generally last about an hour, considerably shorter than the average cross-country race which lasts 2-3 hours. You can use a mountain bike for all cyclo-cross races in Scotland, and for most races in the British Calendar, except Premier races (National Trophy and National Championships).

The dedicated cyclo-cross bike is more like a road bike, but with wider knobbly tires, cantilever or V-brakes and a frame which allows greater mud clearance. It will be lighter than a mountain bike, which makes it easier to carry on sections of the course where it may be faster to dismount and run with your bike. However, because cyclo-cross is a winter sport and ground conditions tend to be muddy, using a mountain bike is often no disadvantage.

Trailquest
The sport of mountain bike orienteering, known as trailquest, is growing in popularity. Trailquest is an activity which requires many of the skills developed by Mountain Bike Leader training: navigation, route choice, core skills, planning and group organisation. A typical trailquest event consists of 20-30 control sites positioned alongside tracks and trails which competitors must identify on pre-printed maps, or by copying from master maps onto their own map or from grid references. Depending on the event, between 2 and 7 hours are allowed to visit as many sites as possible in order to score the highest possible points total. The majority of trailquest events are held south of the Border; for a full list and more details of how to enter visit www.trailquest.co.uk

MTB endurance events
There are several well established endurance or ultra-endurance mountain bike events in the UK and abroad. These events are usually supported by one or more major sponsors and are often more like a mini festival than a one day race. Sleepless in the Saddle, held annually near Stoke-on-Trent is one of the most popular 24 hour endurance events in Britain, attracting several hundred individual and team entries (www.sleeplessinthesaddle.com). If you don't fancy riding all day and night, but still want a challenge you could choose to ride one of the MTB Marathon Series (www.mtb-marathon.co.uk) organised in various locations around the country.

For anyone who considers themselves a strong endurance rider, the TransAlp is the ultimate test (www.bike-transalp.de). Ridden over eight days, three countries, 600km and 19,500m of climbing, the TransAlp is not for the faint hearted, but to sweeten the bitter pill of pain there is the pleasure of being in some of the most spectacular mountain terrain in Europe. The Grand Raid Cristalp is a similarly tough Alpine marathon, held in the Swiss Alps (www.grand-raid-cristalp.ch). These events attract both pros and serious amateurs, numbering several thousand in total, and are truly international in their membership.

HOW TO GET INVOLVED IN RACING
In Scotland mountain bike races are organised by the Scottish Cross-country Association (SXC), the Scottish Downhill Association (SDA), and the Scottish Cross Association (SCA) on behalf of Scottish Cycling. The British Cross-country and Downhill series are organised by British Cycling (www.britishcycling.org.uk). The Scottish Race Calendar consists of a series of between 7 and 10 events in each discipline (cross country, downhill and cyclo-cross), and Scottish Championships in each discipline. Both the series and championship events attract large numbers of people – riders, supporters and spectators, especially in downhill, and make a great day out in the country.

There are no pre-requirements to ride in Scottish Cycling mountain bike or cyclo-cross events, other than a bike and a helmet, but in order to be eligible for the Scottish Championships you must be both a Scottish Cycling member and a member of a Scottish Club. Race details can be obtained from Scottish Cycling and the SXC, SDA and SCA websites:

Scottish Cross-Country Association www.sxc.org.uk
Scottish Downhill Association www.sda-races.com
Scottish Cyclo-Cross Association www.scottishcyclocross.co.uk

Joining a club which caters for mountain biking or a dedicated mountain bike club is a good way to access mountain bike sport and meet other riders whom you can learn from, ride with and share transport to events. There are details of Scottish cycling clubs on the Scottish Cycling website (www.scottishcycling.com).

Bibliography

The texts below are additional reading matter which the mountain biker and mountain bike leader may find useful to increase their knowledge of the topics covered in this manual and to have as guides and reference books.

ACCESS RIGHTS & RESPONSIBILITIES

The Scottish Glens, P.D. Koch-Osborne Cicerone Press 1. The Cairngorm Glens 2. The Atholl Glens 3. The Glens of Rannoch 4. The Trossachs Glens 5. Argyll Glens 6. The Great Glen 7. The Angus Glens 8. Knoydart to Morvern 9. The Glens of Ross-shire
A series of guides for mountain bikers and walkers, with hand drawn maps giving a good deal of detail

Exploring Scottish Hill Tracks: For Walkers and Mountain Bikers, Ralph Storer, 1994, David & Charles, ISBN 0715302574.
Describes a selection of routes in the Scottish Highlands and Islands

Scottish Hill Tracks, Moir, Bennet & Stone 1999, Scottish Rights of Way and Access Society, ISBN 0950281182.
A great aid to route planning where the requirement is to link a series of routes cross-country, covering roads, tracks and paths, some of them remote. Accompanied by a useful (removable) map

Scottish Outdoor Access Code, Scottish Natural Heritage 2005, ISBN 1-85397-422-6
The definitive guide to public access in Scotland's outdoors, detailing your rights and responsibilities. Available to download from www.snh.org.uk/pubs

SKILLS & TECHNIQUES

Mastering Mountain Bike Skills, Brian Lopes & Lee McCormack, Human Kinetics 2005, ISBN 0736056246

Mountain Bike Like a Champion: Master the Techniques to Tackle the Toughest Terrain, Ned Overend & Ed Pavelka, 1999, Rodale Press, ISBN 1579540813
Top tips from mountain bike ace, Ned Overend whose experience and skill drills inspire and explain how to become a better rider

Mountain Bike!: A Manual of Beginning to Advanced Technique, William Nealy, 1992, Menasha Ridge Press, ISBN: 0897321146

Mountain Biking Skills, Strickland et al, 1996, Rodale Press ISBN 0875963005
A book aimed at the "improver", full of tips, humour and inspiration

Ultimate Guide to Mountain Biking, Steve Geal & Ronbin Kitchin, 2001, Harper Collins Willow, ISBN: 0007110871
With authoritative content, this book is for all mountain bikers, from the relative beginner to the experienced practitioner, offering practical advice and tips on how to improve your skills

FUEL & HYDRATION

Sport Nutrition, Jeukendrup, A.E. & Gleson, M., 2004, Human Kinetics Europe Ltd, ISBN 0736034048

LEADERSHIP & TEACHING

Leading & Managing Groups in the Outdoors, K. Ogilvie, 1993, NAOI Publications, ISBN: 1898555001

Teaching Physical Education, M. Mosston & S. Ashworth, 2002, Allyn & Bacon, ISBN 0205340938
"Offers teachers/leaders a foundation for understanding the decision-making structures that exist in all teaching/learning environments, and for recognising the variables that increase effectiveness while teaching physical education."

LEGAL ISSUES

Equity in your Coaching, Simon Kirkland, 2007, sports coach UK (available from www.1st4sport.com)

Safety, Risk and Adventure in Outdoor Activities, Bob Barton, Paul Chapman Education Publishing 2007, ISBN 1-4129-2077-9
This practical guide shows how adventurous outdoor activities can be provided to acceptable standards of safety, essential reading for anyone involved in providing adventurous outdoor activities

MOUNTAIN BIKING IN SCOTLAND

Bike Scotland Trails Guide: 40 of the Best Mountain Bike Routes in Scotland, Richard Moore & Andy McCandlish, Pocket Mountains Ltd (2nd Edition) 2007, ISBN 0955454808

Mountain Bike Guide: Inverness, the Great Glen and the Cairngorms, Timothy King and Derek Purdy, 2004, The Ernest Press, ISBN 0948153733
One of a series of 17 route guides covering much of the UK (this is currently the only Scottish title)

Mountain Bike Scotland: The Highlands v. 1, Kenny Wilson, Ernest Press 2006, ISBN 0948153814

Scottish Mountain Bike Guide, (published annually), www.visitscotland.com
Excellent guide to Scottish MTB centres with travel information, maps, bike shops and useful websites listed for each area

Southern Scotland and the 7 Stanes: Bikefax—Selected Mountain Bike Rides, Sue Savage, Alistair Chant & Iain Withers, Bikefax Ltd, 2006, ISBN 0954976282

NAVIGATION
Advanced Mountain Biking, Derek Purdy, 1995 ppb., A & C Black, ISBN 185688046X
Includes sections on bike choice and preparation, map reading, weather forecasting and mountain rescue

Mountaincraft and Leadership, Eric Langmuir, 1995, Scottish Sports Council – sportscotland, ISBN 1850602956

Land Navigation, Wally Keay, 1994, Ordnance Survey, ISBN 0319008452
Explains the basics of navigation from grid references to complex navigation in remote highland/mountain areas

Map and Compass: The Art of Navigation, Peter Hawkins, 2004, Cicerone Press, ISBN 1852843942
Using plenty of diagrams, OS and Harvey Maps to illustrate points in the text, this book takes you logically through the various stages of learning map and compass skills. Includes a look at GPS and mapping software

TRAILSIDE REPAIRS
Big Blue Book of Bicycle Repair, C. Calvin Jones, Park Tool Company 2005, ISBN 0-9765530-0-7
Not strictly a trailside repair book, but quite simply the best, most comprehensive and easy to use bike repair manual

The Bike Book, Fred Milson (ed.), 2003, Haynes Group, ISBN 1844250008
Well illustrated "how-to" guide, covering the most popular range of bikes and components in detail

Mountain Bike Owners Manual, Lennard Zinn, 1998, VeloPress, ISBN 1884737471
A clear and fun maintenance manual, explaining the workings of parts as well as how to effect repairs

Mountain Bike Performance Handbook, Lennard Zinn, 1998, Bicycle Books Inc., ISBN 0933201958

Zinn and the Art of Mountain Bike Maintenance, Lennard Zinn, 2001, VeloPress, ISBN 1884737994
Useful guide to mountain bike maintenance, illustrating tools, components and a wide range of repairs

Mountain Bike Maintenance: The Illustrated Manual, Melanie Allwood, 2004, Firefly Books Ltd, ISBN 155297734X
A very practical guide to mountain bike maintenance

WEATHER
Mountain Weather: A Practical Guide for Hillwalkers and Climbers in the British Isles, David Pedgley 2004, Cicerone Press, ISBN 1852842563

The Weather Handbook, Alan Watts, 2004, Adlard Coles Nautical, ISBN 0713669381
This book explains how to combine information given in weather forecasts with the reader's own observations to arrive at a correct assessment of what the coming weather is likely to be.

EXPEDITION MODULE

The Backpacker's Cookbook, David Coustic, 1996, Neil Wilson Publishing Ltd, ISBN 1897784384
An inspired guide to camp cooking, describing a range of simple but tasty one-pot meals made from real food, with tips on stoves and cooking equipment

Expedition Guide, Wally Keay, 1995, Duke of Edinburgh Award Scheme, ISBN 0905425146

How to Shit in the Woods: An Environmentally Sound Approach to a Lost Art, Kathleen Meyer, 1994, Ten Speed Press, ISBN 0898156270
A frank and practical guide to a vital part of expeditioning

WINTER MODULE

A Chance in a Million? Scottish Avalanches (2nd Edition), Bob Barton and Blyth Wright, Scottish Mountaineering Trust 2000, ISBN 0907521592
The definitive text on Scottish avalanches. Essential reading for anyone who ventures out on in the hills when there is snow on the ground

Winter Skills: Essential Walking and Climbing Techniques (The Official Handbook of the Mountaineering Instructor Certificate and Winter Mountain Leader Scheme), Andy Cunningham and Allen Fyffe, UK Mountain Leader Training Board 2007, ISBN 0954151135
Written mainly from a walking and climbing perspective but with valuable information on winter clothing and equipment, weather, navigation, snow and avalanche, shelters and cold injuries

GENERAL

Hostile Habitats—Scotland's Mountain Environment, A Hillwalkers' Guide to Wildlife and the Lanscape, Mark Wrightham & Nick Kempe (Eds.), Scottish Mountaineering Trust 2006, ISBN 0907521932
Offers detailed introduction to the outdoor environment of Scotland. Covers geology, climate, flora, fauna, land use and a thought provoking chapter on the future of our mountains. Seen as essential reading for all aspiring mountain leaders, and endorsed by the Mountain Leader Training Board

Mountain Bike Fitness Training, John Metcalfe, 2004, Mainstream Publishing, ISBN 1840188588
Includes detailed descriptions of do-it-yourself fitness tests, skill drills and training exercises designed to improve off-road fitness. Although focused on cross-country and downhill racing, other chapters deal with expeditions and endurance mountain biking

Hill Walking: The Official Handbook of the Mountain Leader and Walking Group Leader Schemes, Steve Long, 2003, The Mountain Training Trust, ISBN 0954151100
Valuable reference book covering navigation, weather and related topics from a hill walking leadership perspective

NOLS Wilderness Medicine, Tod Schimelpfenig & Joan Safford, 2006 (4th Ed.), Stackpole Books, ISBN 978-0811733069

Useful Contacts

GENERAL

Adventure Activities Licensing Authority
44 Lambourne Crescent
Cardiff Business Park
Llanishen
Cardiff, CF14 5GF
Tel. 029 2075 5715
www.aala.org.uk

British Cycling
National Cycling Centre
Stuart Street
Manchester
M11 4DQ
Tel. 0161 274 2010
www.britishcycling.org.uk

Child Protection in Sport
CHILDREN 1ST
Sussex House
61 Sussex Street
Kinning Park
Glasgow, G41 1DY
Tel. 0141 418 5674
www.children1st.org.uk

CTC (Cyclists Touring Club)
Railton Road, Guilford
Surrey, GU2 GJX
Tel. 0870 873 0060
www.ctc.org.uk

CTC Scotland
www.ctcscotland.org.uk

CTC Cymru
www.ctc-wales.org.uk

Cycling Scotland
The Pentagon Suite
Washington Street
Glasgow
www.cyclingscotland.org

Disclosure Scotland
PO Box 250
Glasgow
G51 1YU
Tel. 0870 609 6006
www.disclosurescotland.co.uk

Fort William World Cup
Rare Management
17 Calton Road
Edinburgh
EH8 8DL
Tel. 0131 557 3012
www.fortwilliamworldcup.co.uk

Glenmore Lodge
Aviemore
Inverness-shire
PH22 1QU
Tel. 01479 861 256
www.glenmorelodge.org.uk

International Mountain Bicycling Association UK (IMBA-UK)
www.imba.org.uk

Institute for Outdoor Learning
The Barn, Plumpton Old Hall
Plumpton
Penrith
CA11 9NP
01768 885800
www.outdoor-learning.org

Mountain Bothies Association
www.mountainbothies.org.uk

Mountain Leader Training – Scotland
Glenmore
Aviemore
PH22 1QU
Tel. 01479 861 248
www.mltuk.org

Mountain Leader Training – England
MLTE Registered Office
Development Officer
177-179 Burton Road
Manchester
M20 2BB
Tel. 08700 104878
www.mlte.org

Mountain Leader Training – Northern Ireland
Tollymore M.C.
Bryansford
Newcastle
BT 2BB
Tel. 02843 722 158
admin@tollymoremc.com

Mountain Leader Training – Wales
Capel Curig
Conway
LL24 0ET
Tel. 01690 720248
www.mltw.org

The Mountaineering Council of Scotland
The Old Granary
West Mill Street
Perth
PH1 5QP
Tel. 01738 638227
www.mountaineering-scotland.org.uk

NSPCC Child Protection Training
NSPCC National Training Centre
3 Gilmour Close
Beaumont Leys
Leicester
LE4 1EZ
Tel. 0116 234 7225
www.nspcc.org.uk/inform/training

Park Tool
www.parktool.com

Paths for All Partnership
Inglewood House
Tullibody Road
ALLOA FK10 2HU
Tel. 01259 218888
www.pathsforall.org.uk

Professional Cycle Mechanics
(provide cycle maintenance courses to the public)
www.pjcsonline.co.uk

Ruff Stuff Fellowship
www.rsf.org.uk

Singletrack magazine
www.singletrackworld.com

Scottish Advisory Panel for Outdoor Education (SAPOE)
www.sapoe.ik.org

Scottish Cross-Country Association (SXC)
www.sxc.org.uk

Scottish Downhill Association
www.sda-races.com

Scottish Executive
www.scotland.gov.uk

Scottish Independent Hostels
PO Box 7024
Fort William
PH33 6YX
www.hostel-scotland.co.uk

Scottish Natural Heritage
www.snh.org.uk

Scotways
24 Annandale Street
Edinburgh, EH7 4AN
Tel. 0131 558 1222
www.scotways.com

Scottish Youth Hostel Association
SYHA National Office
7 Glebe Crescent
Stirling, FK8 2JA
Tel. 08701 553255
www.syha.org.uk

sportscotland
Caledonia House
South Gyle
Edinburgh
EH12 9DQ
Tel. 0131 317 7200
www.sportscotland.org.uk

Sustrans
National Cycle Network Centre
2 Cathedral Square
College Green
Bristol, BS1 5DD
Tel: 0117 926 8893
www.sustrans.org.uk

Visit Scotland
(Tourist information)
www.visitscotland.com

PLACES TO RIDE

Forestry Commission
(MTB centres and trails throughout the UK)
www.forestry.gov.uk

The Hub (Café, Bike Hire & Shop)
Glentress Forest
near Peebles
EH45 8NB
Tel. 01721 721736
www.thehubintheforest.co.uk

Laggan Wolftrax
BaseCamp MTB
Strathmashie Forest
Laggan
Newtonmore
Tel. 01528 544 780 / 786
www.laggan.com

7 Stanes Project
Forestry Commission Scotland
55/57 Moffat Road
Dumfries
DG1 1NP
Tel. 01387 272 440
www.7stanes.gov.uk

Drumlanrig Castle
(Country Park and Cycle Museum)
Ranger Service
Drumlanrig Castle
Thornhill
Dumfriesshire
DG3 4AQ
Tel. 01848 331 555
www.drumlanrig.com

Mountain Biking Wales
www.mtb-wales.com

FIRST AID COURSE PROVIDERS

For an up to date list of first aid providers see Scottish Cycling website www.scottishcycling.com

Appendix

On the following pages is a selection of forms. Some of them are required for training/assessment, some will be more useful once you have passed your assessment and are working as a Leader.

- SMBLA Logbook
- Route Card
- Accident Report Form
- Emergency Contact List
- Bike Safety Check
- Risk Assessment Form
- Child Protection Checklist
- Parental Consent Form

SMBLA Logbook

To be completed by the **Candidate** prior to training and sent to the Course Tutor. Logbook evidence should consist of at least 20 mountain bike rides of 1.5h duration in a variety of weather conditions. Longer rides of 2-3 hrs duration, with at least one of 6h, and 2-3 detailed route cards should also be included. **The terrain covered should be appropriate to the level of award sought**. Rides may be undertaken in the UK or abroad any time within the last 12 months.

Candidate Name: | **SMBLA Reg. no.** | **Contact Tel.**

Please enter below brief details of your recent mountain bike experience

Ride	**Date**	**Venue** (e.g. Glentress Forest)	**Duration** (hrs)	**Terrain** (e.g. singletrack)	**Weather**
1					
2					
3					
4					
5					
6					
7					
8					
9					
10					
11					
12					

Ride	Date	Venue	Duration (hrs)	Terrain	Weather
13					
14					
15					
16					
17					
18					
19					
20					

Please give any other relevant experience e.g. outdoor qualifications

Please give the name and contact details of someone willing to act as a referee for your mountain bike experience

Name	Position
Address	E-mail
	Tel.

SMBLA

Scottish Cycling, The Velodrome, London Road, Edinburgh, EH7 6AD
Tel 0131 652 0187 smbla@scottishcycling.com www.scottishcycling.com

Route Card

Cumulative Distance (km)	O.S. Map(s):		Intermediate Distance (km)
	Grid ref.	Navigational Feature or Point of Interest	
Start			
End			

Escape / Alternative Route(s):

1.

2.

3.

Date:	Start time:	Expected finishing time:
Base / venue:	**Group Leader:**	**Phone / Mobile no.**

Additional Comments (transport details, parking facilities, river crossings, viewpoints, food stops, other useful info)

ACCIDENT REPORT FORM

1. GROUP DETAILS

CALLERS NAME .... **TEL NO.** ....
(This information is to be given to the emergency services by the *person who has gone for help so the emergency services can contact them)*

2. TIME OF ACCIDENT .... **DATE** ....

3. LOCATION: GRID REF ....

DETAILS OF LOCATION, IDENTIFICATION MARKERS ETC... ....

....

4. WHAT HAPPENED? ....

....

5. WHO IS INJURED?

NAME ....

AGE .... **SEX** ....

6. WHAT IS THE INJURY? ....

....

WHAT TREATMENT HAS BEEN CARRIED OUT? ....

....

7. HOW MANY ARE IN THE REMAINING PARTY AND WHAT IS THEIR CONDITION?

....

HOW ARE THEY EQUIPPED? ....

8. WEATHER & TERRAIN DETAILS AT SITE if relevant: ....

....

9. ANY OTHER INFORMATION: ....

....

10. YOUR BASE EMERGENCY TEL NO. ....
Complete before departure on your expedition!

EMERGENCY CONTACT LIST

NAME of GROUP MEMBER	NAME of EMERGENCY CONTACT	RELATIONSHIP	TELEPHONE NUMBER(S)
Date(s) of Trip		Base contact	
Leader		Base tel. nos.	
Comments			

BIKE SAFETY CHECK LIST

BIKE FEATURE	CONDITION / WHAT TO CHECK FOR	PASS	FAIL	COMMENTS
Front tyre	Good tread; no splits; cracks or holes; properly inflated; inner tube valve straight			
Front wheel	True; no broken/missing spokes; rim free of dents, not excessively worn			
Front hub	No wobble/play; turns smoothly; wheel securely fixed (bolts/quick release)			
Front brake	Firmly fixed; correctly adjusted			
Front brake pads	Correctly fitted and aligned; not excessively worn			
Front brake lever	Correctly positioned; firmly fixed; no excessive travel; cable not frayed			
Headset/steering	No wobble/play; correctly adjusted			
Handlebars	Not bent/dented; ends protected			
Forks	Appear true and undamaged; suspension forks functioning; no leaks			
Frame	Appears true and undamaged, no visible cracks			
Rear brake lever	Correctly positioned; firmly fixed; no excessive travel; cable not frayed			
Rear Brake	Firmly fixed; correctly adjusted			
Rear brake pads	Correctly fitted and aligned; not excessively worn			
Rear tyre	Good tread; no splits; cracks or holes; properly inflated; inner tube valve straight			
Rear wheel	True; no broken/missing spokes; rim free of dents, not excessively worn			
Rear hub	No wobble/play; turns smoothly; wheel securely fixed			
Bottom bracket	No wobble; turns smoothly; lock rings tight;			
Chainset	Straight; firmly fixed; chain ring teeth not bent or excessively worn			
Pedals	Complete; turning freely; not bent; firmly fixed			
Cassette	Firmly fixed; cog teeth not excessively worn			
Chain	Not excessively worn; not slack; not rusty; not dirt-encrusted, lubricated well			
Gears	Properly adjusted; lubricated sufficiently; cables not frayed			
Saddle	Firmly fixed; correctly positioned (height and setback)			
Lights (if necessary)	Red rear, white front and suitable for purpose; firmly fixed; working!			
Mudguards and any other attachments	Securely fixed, no sharp edges or loose straps			

SAMPLE RISK ASSESSMENT FORM					
Date____________ Reassessment date_____		Leader____________ Signature____________		Start location / venue____________	
Hazards		Risk Evaluation		Controlling measures	
Location / Map ref.	Description of Hazard	Potential risk & who might be affected	Risk Rating High//Medium/Low	Control measures to reduce the risk	Assessment of effectiveness or proposed amendment

CHILD PROTECTION CHECKLIST

Information source	Be familiar with and keep a copy of:	
Child Protection Policy	√	
Code of Conduct	√	
Parental Consent Form	√	
	Name	**Tel. Nos.**
Main Contact Person		
Child Protection Officer / Co-ordinator		
Other Contacts		
Local Social Work Department		
Police Family Protection Unit		
Children 1st		

PARENTAL CONSENT FORM (Sample)	
PARTICIPANT DETAILS	
Name	**Date of Birth**
Address	
Home Tel. No.	
Emergency Contact Tel. No(s).	
Name of Doctor	**Surgery Tel. No.**

I agree to my son/daughter / the above named child in my care taking part in the activities outlined below. I understand that he/she takes part at his/her own risk, and accept that no responsibility for accidents or injury or loss or damage to personal property rests with the supervisory staff, unless proven to be caused by their negligence. I declare that to the best of my knowledge my child is competent and medically fit to participate in the activities as part of a group. I agree that medical treatment will be given if necessary and in case of emergency.

Signature of Parent or Guardian..

Date..

Date(s) of activities	
Start time	**End time**
Meeting / Pick-up point	
Activity venue	
Name of Leader	

NATURE OF ACTIVITIES

Summary risk assessment for these activities attached ☐